"I know Arthur Manuel as a strong and wise leader, seasoned in the long battle that has been his life. To read this book, his detailed and very personal history of the long struggle of Indigenous people in Canada, is to go through an emotional rollercoaster of disillusionment, despair, flinty resolve, and, finally, growing hope, building to a present in which the struggle for their rights continues. This is not history buried in the past, it is going on right now and as Canadians we are all a part of it."

—James Cameron, filmmaker

"I cannot recommend this book too highly: it weaves together a compelling life history, an account of the last nearly fifty years of Indigenous activism, and a relentless and compelling criticism of the doctrine of discovery that continues to underlie Canadian claims to Indigenous land. Everyone in Canada should read this book; if they did we might become a better country!"

—peter kulchyski, Department of Native Studies, University of Manitoba

"Art Manuel is like a tall cedar, watching the landscape of Canadian Indian policies through time and offering sturdy and dependable resistance. In *Unsettling Canada* his account of our recent history is dense with compelling personal stories, behind-the-scenes political anecdotes, an honest account of the dynamics of Indigenous activism, and revealing insights about the continuity of colonialism. In the often difficult conversation about Indigenous politics in Canada, Manuel offers us shade to reflect on our past and consider the future. This is a rigorous but very accessible and vitally important book."

—Hayden King, Anishinaabe writer, educator, and activist

"*Unsettling Canada* should be truly unsettling to many Canadians. Canada's treatment of Aboriginal people and their struggle to have a chair at the country's political table reveals an almost Machiavellian sense of politics. No wonder the life expectancy of Native people is substantially lower than non-Natives. It's the sense of heart-rending frustration and the collective banging of heads against the wall that probably kills us."

— Drew Hayden Taylor, author of *Me Funny* and *Me Sexy*

"Arthur Manuel passionately builds a detailed historical analysis of creative and determined Indigenous movement-building, grounded in the day-to-day harsh reality most Indigenous peoples continue to live. It is an engaging and vivid memoir that demonstrates how critical legal victories are embedded in and reliant on grassroots political movements that have a global reach. Offering many organizing lessons, this book is a frank and inspiring call to action in support of Indigenous sovereignty, including building alliances with and involvement of non-Indigenous people, whose future is inseparable from Indigenous struggles for the realization of inherent rights to self-determination."

— Sheila Wilmot, PhD, author of *Taking Responsibility, Taking Direction: White Anti-Racism in Canada*

"Based on his experience as a leader and activist, Arthur Manuel recounts key moments in the struggles of Canada's Aboriginal population over the past fifty years. Part memoir, part political statement, *Unsettling Canada* is an insightful and articulate account of the challenges governments and Aboriginal people face in resolving disputes between them."

— William Wicken, Professor of History, York University

"For those of us with enough winters to remember George Manuel in life, reading his son's *Unsettling Canada* can be an almost eerie experience. No book of which I'm aware has ever conveyed with such clarity the continuities of voice and principle across generations in the Fourth World struggle for self-determination. Even we who might question whether liberation can be achieved non-violently, as Manuel believes, have much to gain from his consistency and strategic vision."

— Ward Churchill, author of *Struggle for the Land*

# UNSETTLING CANADA

# Unsettling Canada
## A National Wake-up Call

by Arthur Manuel
and Grand Chief Ronald M. Derrickson

with a Foreword by Naomi Klein

Between the Lines
Toronto

First published in 2015 by
Between the Lines
401 Richmond Street West
Studio 277
Toronto, Ontario M5V 3A8
Canada
1-800-718-7201
www.btlbooks.com

**Library and Archives Canada Cataloguing in Publication**

Manuel, Arthur, author
Unsettling Canada : a national wake-up call / by Arthur Manuel and
Grand Chief Ronald M. Derrickson ; with a foreword by Naomi Klein.

Includes index.
Issued in print and electronic formats.

ISBN 978-1-77113-176-6 (pbk.). — ISBN 978-1-77113-177-3 (epub). — ISBN 978-1-77113-178-0 (pdf)

1. Native peoples—Canada—Economic conditions.
2. Native peoples—Canada—Social conditions.
3. Native peoples—Canada—Government relations.
4. Native peoples—Legal status, laws, etc.—Canada.
I. Derrickson, Ronald M., author
II. Title.

E78.C2M3369 2015      971.004'97      C2014-906715-1
C2014-906716-x

Cover art by Tania Willard, Red Willow Designs
Printed in Canada
Third Printing October 2015

RECYCLED
Paper made from
recycled material
FSC
www.fsc.org    FSC® C103567

GCC/IBT

Between the Lines gratefully acknowledges assistance for its publishing activities from
the Canada Council for the Arts, the Ontario Arts Council, the Government of Ontario
through the Ontario Book Publishers Tax Credit program and through the Ontario
Book Initiative, and the Government of Canada through the Canada Book Fund.

Canada Council
for the Arts
Conseil des Arts
du Canada

Canada

ONTARIO ARTS COUNCIL
CONSEIL DES ARTS DE L'ONTARIO
an Ontario government agency
un organisme du gouvernement de l'Ontario

To all of the volunteer Indigenous activists
and to my grandchildren

— ARTHUR MANUEL


To my Elders, now passed on, who taught me
to love and respect my people and to fight for their rights:
Millie Jack, Margaret Derrickson (my mother),
Elizabeth Lindley (wife of Westbank's first chief),
and Mary Anne Eli

— GRAND CHIEF RONALD M. DERRICKSON

# CONTENTS

# FOREWORD

## Naomi Klein

**U**NSETTLING CANADA is a book that was a long time in coming, and yet it arrives at the perfect time. It comes at a moment when a great many non-Indigenous Canadians are deeply unsettled by the direction the country is going and are searching for new and bold paths forward.

The current government seems to have one idea about how to build an economy. Dig lots of holes, lay lots of pipe. Stick the stuff from the pipes onto ships—or trucks, or railway cars—and take it to places where it will be refined and burned. Repeat, but more and faster. It's an approach to the world based on taking and taking without giving back. Taking as if there are no limits to what can be taken—no limits to what bodies can take, no limits to what a functioning society can take, no limits to what the earth can take.

Never mind the impacts on water. On wildlife. On forests. On the stability of the climate itself. Anyone who stands in their way, who points out inconvenient truths about health, human rights, or climate change, is treated as an enemy and various attempts are made to silence them—be they activists, First Nations communities, or the government's own scientists. The opposition parties offer meek objections and little by way of alternative.

It is in this context that a great many Canadians are discovering that First Nations land rights and title—if robustly defended—represent the most powerful barrier to this destructive, extractivist mindset. And so, unprecedented coalitions are emerging to fight tar sands pipelines in British Columbia, fracking in New Brunswick, and clear-cut logging in Ontario. In these battles we are beginning to see the outlines of a new kind of relationship, based on nation-to-nation respect, not assimilation or merger.

This wise, enlightening, and tremendously readable book will both strengthen and deepen these relationships. Interweaving policy and history with the personal stories of a remarkable family packed with leaders and healers, Manuel offers a unique education in the painful history that brought us to this juncture. He also provides a crash course in the legal concepts and humane principles that will help us all move forward.

With confidence and care, Manuel guides readers through the many clever disguises the Canadian government has used to rob First Nations of their land rights and title, unmasking each attempt at "extinguishment" in turn. This is a heart-wrenching story of how might triumphed over rights. Yet simultaneously, and with a palpable sense of momentum, Manuel takes us through the various legal victories that steadily strengthened the movement's hand, bringing us to the current turning point. This is the back story of both grassroots and backroom struggles that created the context in which we find ourselves today, one in which a new generation of First Nations leaders is demanding sovereignty and self-determination, and more and more non-Indigenous Canadians finally understand that huge swaths of this country we call Canada is not ours— or our government's—to sell.

Even those who are sure they know this material already will be taken aback by the originality of the legal and financial strategies described in these pages, and inspired by the hope they represent. This is a transformative journey of a truly visionary thinker, leading us all to a wide open door.

*March 2015*

# ACKNOWLEDGEMENTS

**W**HEN I FIRST SAT DOWN to write the acknowledgements for this book, I was a bit overwhelmed. There are so many people to thank for helping in so many different ways. There are those who encouraged me and assisted me directly in the writing process. There are those who have fought alongside me and who have made important individual contributions to our common struggle. And there are those who are part of organizations that have believed enough in my work to help me along the way. Unfortunately I do not have nearly the space I would need to thank all of the people in these three groups, but I would like to mention at least a few of them here.

Those most directly involved in getting the book project launched were Grand Chief Ron Derrickson and Naomi Klein. It was Naomi who first suggested, even gently insisted, that I pull together the ideas I had been promoting in British Columbia, in Canada, and internationally in book form. And she was duly punished for this by having to write the Foreword, which she has done, as she does everything, with great generosity and wit.

Grand Chief Derrickson had echoed Naomi's call for a book and offered to participate in the project as an adviser. He contributed greatly to this book in every way, including by writing the Afterword. In fact, Grand Chief Derrickson has been part of the formulation of the ideas in this book from the time we led the B.C. Interior peoples into the forest in the Indian logging initiative in 1999. At the time I was the chief of Neskonlith, chair of the Shuswap Nation Tribal Council, and spokesperson of the Interior Alliance of B.C. It was in the aftermath of that action that I developed the Indigenous Network on Economies and Trade, and Grand Chief Derrickson has continued to offer his leadership, support, and unique insights along the way.

I began work on the book almost three years ago, and I have been given invaluable assistance in shaping the manuscript by Peter McFarlane, a writer and friend.

Nicole Schabus provided crucial input during the editorial process; with her contribution, as with so much else, she is in a class by herself. My life partner, Nicole was also a leading contributor, through her legal training and brilliant insights, in the formulation of many of these ideas, and as you see in the book, she has been at my side throughout the international struggle with NAFTA and the WTO.

I would be remiss not to acknowledge how both my parents imprinted on me a deep belief in the nationhood of our people. My late father, Grand Chief George Manuel, taught me about politics but would also call on me as a young person to speak at every meeting, appreciating the energy of our youth. My mother, Marceline, carried the heavy burden of supporting our family through the movement and stood on the front lines. My siblings share in much of the same burden and carry the same strength, from my late brother Robert and sister Vera, to Emaline, Richard, and Doreen to the youngest Martha, George, Ida, and Ara, who are following in the footsteps of our parents.

I also want to mention important contributors to our struggle whom we have lost: I still hear the booming voice of Irene Billy (1928–2011) ringing in my ears, reminding us not to sleep on our rights. I remember the knowledge shared by Dr. Mary Thomas and Coleen McCrory. I miss my friend Qwatsinas (Ed Moody). Nuxalk Strong! Nuxalk Forever! And I think about young leaders we lost far too early: Ethan Baptiste and my dear son Neskie Manuel.

Another person in a class by himself is my Mohawk friend, Russell Diabo, who has never wavered in his commitment to Indigenous rights and Indigenous nationhood. It has been a pleasure to work with him over the years and virtually all of the ideas discussed here were also discussed with him or published in his *Strategic Bulletin*. Between me and Russell and our friend David Nahwegahbow, LL.B., an Anishinabek from Whitefish River, we have spent decades fighting to change the federal Comprehensive Claims policy, with the important contributions of Algonquin Chief Harry St. Denis of Wolf Lake and former Chief Jean Maurice (Poncho) Matchewan from Barriere Lake. I would also like to thank Chief Donny Morris and Sam McKay from Kitchenuhmaykoosib Inninuwug, who have also inspired us all.

I want to mention some of my partners and friends from my early political life who remain friends to date: Beverly Manuel, Stó:lō activist Eddy Gardner, the late Stan (Butch) Plante of the Metis Nation, Tantoo Cardinal, Ken and Dana Williams, Pottawatomis from Moose Deer Point, Dave Monture, a Six Nations Mohawk, and Maya Lix Lopez.

At the community level, I have worked closely with my own chief, Judy Wilson, and with Secwepemc activists Dr. Janice Billy, Dawn Morrison, and Garry Gottfriedson and Elders Sarah Deneault (91) and William Ignace (82). I believe that it is important for Elders to speak out on political issues, to teach younger generations how to protect our land and build upon our values. We need them to take their place in every part of our lives and to speak out and give guidance in the political sphere.

I have also been honoured to work with community activists like Bertha Williams from Tsawwassen, Judy DaSilva of the Asubpeeschoseewagong Anishinabek (Grassy Narrows First Nation), Rosalin Sam and Hubert (Hubie) Jim, the lone fighter from Sutikalh and fishers June, Fred, and Rick Quipp of Cheam.

I would also like to thank Tsilhqot'in chiefs, Chief Roger William from Xeni Gwet'in, Tribal Chairman Chief Joe Alphonse of Tl'etinqox, Chief Francis Laceese from Toosey Indian Band, and Chief Russell Ross Myers from Yunesit'in Government. I would also like to thank Tsilhqot'in leaders like Stanley Stump, Danny Case, and David Quilt.

There are also many young Indigenous activists like lawyer June McCue, my IGov master's student Ryan Day, and young Indigenous leaders from across Canada all the way home to my own children who give me new hope every day in our struggle for self-determination. As do all of the members of the Defenders of the Land and Idle No More, with a special thanks to the four women founders of Idle No More—Jessica Gordon, Sylvia McAdam, Nina Wilson, and Sheelah McLean—to whom we all owe a debt of gratitude for inspiring a new activism among our peoples.

I would also like to acknowledge the work of a small team of very talented volunteers who have worked with INET: Dr. Shiri Pasternak,

Emma Feltes, Corvin Russell, and Pam Baley as well as activists like Harsha Walia and Brigette DePape who have understood the importance of our struggle and the broader struggle for Indigenous self-determination. A special thanks goes to Judy Rebick, one of the great progressive thinkers and journalists of our generation whose support is always much appreciated.

There are so many others and I am afraid it would take another book-length manuscript to mention them all. But I must make room to mention Ed Bianchi from KAIROS, an organization that has always stood by us. As have Ramsey Hart from Mining Watch, Maude Barlow from the Council of Canadians, Tara Scurr from Amnesty International, Dave Bleakney, the national union representative from CUPW, and those like Dr. Peter Schwarzbauer, Michaela Mayer, Gawan Maringer, and Evelyn Schiemer from Arbeitskreis Indianer Nordamerikas (AKIN) from Vienna, Austria. Vivian Gonik and Olivier de Marcellus from Geneva and Helen Nyberg from Incomindios in Zurich, Switzerland, and Ludwig and Monika Seiller from the Aktionsgruppe Indianer & Menschenrechte e. V. from Munich, Germany, who defend us in the solidarity network in Europe, as well as my friend Kenichi Matsui from Japan. I would also like to thank Nicole's parents, Eric and Traude Schabus, for their hospitality while we are in Austria. Closer to home I would like to thank singer/songwriter Kelly Derrickson and the ongoing support of the RMD team (Cathy, Kim, and Julia).

I would also like to thank leading academics like Professor Kent McNeil, Professor Brian Noble, Professor Michael Asch, and Professor Constance McIntosh, who have helped me develop my thinking in clarifying our Indigenous territorial authority. Along with Terry Tobias, traditional land map maker, and Herb Hammond, an ecosystem-based conservationist, who have helped me in resource-based planning.

I would like to offer a special thanks to my colleagues on the board of the Seventh Generation Fund: Vice-chair Tupac Enrique Acosta, Dr. Luis Macas, Dr. Henrietta Mann, Oren Lyons, Chris Peters, and Deborah Sanchez, and the executive director, Tia Peters. All of us were deeply saddened by the recent death of our chairperson, Tonya Gonnella Frichner, a woman who inspired us all.

I would also like to thank the North American Indigenous Peoples Caucus (NAIPC) and the present two Co-chairs Dr. Debra Harry,

Northern Paiute from Pyramid Lake, Nevada, and Janice Makokis LL.B. from the Cree Nation of Saddle Lake, Alberta.

Finally, my biggest thank you goes to my children, Mandy, Niki, Ska7cis, and Anita-Rosie, and my inspiring and energetic grandchildren— Aaron, Mahegan, Tuwiwt, Suli, P'exmes, Anaoni, Ske7cissiselt, and Mali Nali—who give me reason to continue the struggle that I inherited from my mother and my father, my grandparents and great-grandparents, for justice for our peoples. I love you and I am proud of you.

*Arthur Manuel*
*March 2015*

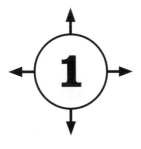

# The Lay of the Land

**T**HERE IS NO DENYING the beauty of the land. From the hills above Neskonlith—the community where I was born and grew up and where I served as band chief from 1995 to 2003— you can see the blue waters of the Shuswap lakes, the dry scrubland of the valley, and the cooler hills shaded by stands of ponderosa pines. Below, the South Thompson River empties from the lake and winds westward through the valley toward Kamloops, where it joins the North Thompson and flows to the Fraser and down to the sea.

This is British Columbia's Interior Plateau. The land my people have shared for thousands of years, and still share with our ancient neighbours. Our Secwepemc territory spreads north to the Dakelh lands, south to the Syilx (Okanagan) lands, west to the Nlaka'pamux, St'at'imc, and Tsilhqot'in lands, and to the east by the Ktunaxa territory, where the Rocky Mountains rise to the sky, marking the boundary between the Interior tribes and the Nakota and Cree peoples on the Great Plains.

The village itself is moulded around a wide bend in the river. From the hills above, you see a handful of houses and the band office, and on the west side of the river, the gas station and store. Along the riverbank are small gardens, and now, after many decades of grasslands, the hayfields have been replanted with the help of the new sprinkler irrigation system.

Further upstream, where Little Shuswap Lake empties into the river, is the town of Chase. It began to form around the lumber mill built just before the First World War. We have generally had peaceable relations with the people of the town, with only occasional flashes of open conflict.

As co-chair of the Global Indigenous Peoples Caucus, reading the statement on the colonial doctrine of discovery at the UN Permanent Forum on Indigenous Issues, New York City, May 7, 2012

But even when it is peaceful, there has been a steady note of racism from across the river. Our parents and grandparents faced open Jim Crow and were forbidden access to most services in the white world. The only restaurants that would serve us were the Chinese restaurants; for the rest, Indians would be stopped at the door or, even more humiliating, left to sit unserved until they slunk away. My generation felt the sting of blatant racism in a less formal way, but it was still shocking to be confronted by it. A generation later, as chief, I was still dealing with racist acts against our children.

There are, of course, many decent people in Chase, as there are anywhere, but the underlying noise is there. And even the well-meaning people of the town have a difficult time understanding us. To a large extent, we live in separate worlds. They live in Chase, British Columbia, Canada. We live in Neskonlith, Secwepemc territory.

I drove up to the hills above Neskonlith on an afternoon in June 2012. I was just back from New York, where I was serving as the co-chair to the

Global Indigenous Peoples Caucus at the United Nations' Permanent Forum on Indigenous Issues (UNPFII), and I was looking for a quiet place to think things over.

Somehow we had gotten our message through the clamour of states that make up the United Nations. We had condemned, as Indigenous peoples, the innocent-sounding doctrine of discovery, which was the tool—the legal fiction—Europeans used to claim our lands for themselves. Even that claim rested on obvious mistruths. The Americas were first portrayed as *terra nullius* on European maps. But in almost all cases, Europeans were met, at times within minutes of their arrival, by Indigenous peoples. There was an attempt to get around this inconvenient fact by declaring us non-human, but this was difficult even for Europeans to sustain over time. The doctrine of discovery remained because it was a legal fig leaf they could use to cover naked thievery.

In New York, the United Nations report had called this doctrine frankly racist and described it as no more legitimate than the slavery laws of the same era. Most important, the Permanent Forum on Indigenous Issues' committee report attacked the ongoing efforts to extinguish our title to the land through force or one-sided negotiations as a continuing violation of international law.[1]

I would like to think that we live in a world where enlightenment—like the Permanent Forum statement on the doctrine of discovery—is a warm breeze spreading across the planet, and that with patience and good faith we will finally be warmed by the justice we have been so long denied. But I know that is not the case. At an earlier session of the UN, Canada, the United States, Australia, and New Zealand fought bitterly against the whole world to try to block the Declaration on the Rights of Indigenous Peoples (UNDRIP), which eventually passed in 2007 by a vote of 144 to 4, with Canada leading the charge of the rights deniers.[2]

Nothing we have ever gained has been given to us or surrendered without a fight. When circumstances forced the Europeans to make concessions, as was the case with the parts of the Royal Proclamation of 1763 that recognized Indigenous sovereignty, the next generation would take advantage of a resurgence in its strength to reverse the concessions and try to push us even further into poverty and dependence.

Still, we have not given up and, as my father, Grand Chief George Manuel, often pointed out, the most important gift we have received from our parents, grandparents, and great-grandparents is the legacy of struggle. They have opened the trail we now pass along and, in a very real way, set the destination for our journey.

Before we look at where we are today and where we are heading, it is important that we first look at how we arrived at this place. I will briefly describe the process for my Secwepemc people. Among the other Indigenous peoples in Canada and throughout the Americas, there are many variations, but there is one constant: the land was stolen from underneath us.

Europeans made their initial land claim on our Secwepemc lands in 1778 when Captain Cook sailed along the British Columbia coast, more than four hundred kilometres away from our territory. According to the tenets of the doctrine of discovery, all that Europeans had to do to expropriate the lands in a region was to sail past a river mouth and make a claim to all of the lands in its watershed. Our lands, given to us by our Creator and inhabited by us for thousands of years, were transformed into a British "possession," not only without our consent and without our knowledge, but also without a single European setting foot on our territory.

In the early 1800s, European traders and advance men like Simon Fraser did begin to show up on our rivers. For the first fifty years, they were seen and treated as guests on our lands. We had more or less friendly relations. We traded with them, we shared food with them, and we often helped them on their journeys through our territory. On a personal level, we tolerated their eccentricities and they tolerated ours.

But gradually, the numbers of these uninvited guests began to increase, and they began to act less and less like guests and more and more as lords. It was a process that Indigenous peoples around the world have experienced. The strangers arrive and offer trade and friendship. The Indigenous population responds in kind. Gradually the strangers begin to take up more and more space and make more and more requests from their hosts, until finally they are not requesting at all. They are demanding. And they are backing their demands with garrisoned outposts.

In the case of the people of the Interior Plateau, we are fortunate to have a document from our ancestors that describes the precise pattern of usurpation. This declaration, which is known as the Laurier Memorial, was presented to Prime Minister Wilfrid Laurier on August 25, 1910, by the Interior chiefs when the prime minister was visiting Kamloops on an election campaign stop.[3]

It was prepared in the months before in mass meetings by our chiefs and people, who wanted to ensure that Canadians knew that we clearly remembered the betrayals of the previous century and that we demand redress in the current one. We called it a *memorial* because it represented, in a very precise way, our collective memories of our history with the settlers.

Europeans first came to the Interior Plateau looking for things they could pick up and cart away, as they did around the world. In this case, it was precious metals. The following are excerpts of what our chiefs told Laurier about their initial experience with Europeans:

> At first they looked only for gold. We knew the latter was our property, but as we did not use it much nor need it to live by we did not object to their searching for it. They told us, "Your country is rich and you will be made wealthy by our coming. We wish just to pass over your lands in quest of gold."
>
> Soon they saw the country was good and some of them made up their minds, to settle it. They commenced to take up pieces of land here and there. They told us they wanted only the use of these pieces of land for a few years, and then would hand them back to us in an improved condition; meanwhile they would give us some of the products they raised for the loan of our land.
>
> Thus they commenced to enter our "houses," or live on our "ranches." With us when a person enters our house he becomes our guest, and we must treat him hospitably as long as he shows no hostile intentions. At the same time we expect him to return to us equal treatment for what he receives.

It soon became apparent that the settlers were not offering equal treatment, and they were not planning to leave. On the contrary, their numbers were increasing. This led to growing unrest in the 1860s at a time when the route to the newly discovered Cariboo gold fields passed along the Fraser River to the Thompson and North Thompson rivers, directly through Secwepemc territory. The trickle of prospectors grew into a full-blown gold rush. With the unrest putting this new mining wealth at risk, James Douglas, the governor of the small colony on the coast, sent an emissary to meet with Chief Neskonlith to try to defuse the situation.

Chief Neskonlith, who was known as a tough and uncompromising leader, had been chosen to speak for the four bands around the Shuswap lakes. At the time, our people were under great stress because European diseases were sweeping through our country. First smallpox, then waves of measles, influenza, and tuberculosis. But even with our people in a weakened state, Neskonlith was forceful with the colonial representative. He told him that the encroachments on our land had reached an intolerable level and we would not accept any more European settlement. The emissary understood that this was not a bluff. But he had no financial or other resources that he could offer a deal with. So he simply asked Chief Neskonlith what the necessary lands were for his people and the other three Secwepemc bands.

Neskonlith showed the essential area on the emissary's map. Together they marked out the territory for exclusive Secwepemc use; today, this area is known as the Neskonlith Douglas Reserve 1862. On this map, our land area totals almost a million acres; the emissary agreed this territory was for the exclusive use of our people. Chief Neskonlith then went out and staked the land where non-Secwepemc settlement was to be forbidden.

But as Indigenous peoples around the world have discovered, a deal is not a deal when it comes to settler governments. No restraint was placed on settlers moving onto our lands. In fact, colonial powers began to give away 160 acres of our land, free of charge, to each settler who applied. At the same time, in an astounding act of racism, the authorities allocated only 20 acres for Indian families. Our forests were then handed over to the control of the lumber companies. Our million acres was gradually, without our consent or even notification, whittled down to barely seven thousand acres scattered in small strips across our territory. The Interior chiefs told Laurier in 1910 that they had been betrayed by the government.

[The settlers] have knocked down . . . the posts of all the Indian tribes. They say there are no lines, except what they make. They have taken possession of all the Indian country and claim it as their own. . . . They have stolen our lands and everything on them. . . .

After a time when they saw that our patience might get exhausted and that we might cause trouble if we thought all the land was to be occupied by whites they set aside many small reservations for us here and there over the country. This was their proposal not ours, and we never accepted these reservations as settlement for anything, nor did we sign any papers or make any treaties. . . . They thought we would be satisfied with this, but we never have been satisfied and never will be until we get our rights.

Bitter insult, the Interior chiefs told Laurier, was added to injury when the settlers not only invaded our territory, but also began to treat us as trespassers and bar us from the lands that had been ours since time immemorial.

> Gradually as the whites . . . became more and more powerful, and we less and less powerful, they little by little changed their policy towards us, and commenced to put restrictions on us. . . . They treat us as subjects without any agreement to that effect, and force their laws on us without our consent and irrespective of whether they are good for us or not. . . .
>
> In many places we are debarred from camping, traveling, gathering roots and obtaining wood and water as heretofore. Our people are fined and imprisoned for breaking the game and fish laws and using the same game and fish which we were told would always be ours for food. Gradually we are becoming regarded as trespassers over a large portion of this our country.

Indigenous peoples from around the world recognize this process of slow, lawless confiscation of their lands, with promises made and laws of protection enacted, then quickly broken as soon as the coalescence of forces again favours the settlers.

Non-Indigenous readers may be thinking—yes, terrible things went on in those days, but really, it's all ancient history. To you, I want to stress that this is not at all ancient history. The meeting with Laurier occurred in my own grandfather's time. When I was young, I hunted on Secwepemc lands with my father, and I remember being surprised to see how nervous he was that he would get caught by the authorities. In recent years, my daughters have been arrested and sent to jail for protesting a new encroachment on Secwepemc lands. My people have been beaten, jailed, and shot at by the authorities simply for occupying our own lands.

And it is the loss of our land that has been the precise cause of our impoverishment. Indigenous lands today account for only 0.36 per cent of British Columbian territory. The settler share is the remaining 99.64

per cent. In Canada overall the percentage is even worse, with Indigenous peoples controlling only 0.2 per cent of the land and the settlers 99.8 per cent. With this distribution of the land, you don't have to have a doctorate in economics to understand who will be poor and who will be rich. And our poverty is crushing. Along with suffering all of the calamities of life that hit the poor with greater impact, our lives are seven years shorter than the lives of non-Indigenous Canadians. Our unemployment rates are four times higher. The resources to educate our children are only a third of what is spent on non-Indigenous Canadian children. Our youth commit suicide at a rate more than five times higher. We are living the effects of this dispossession every day of our lives, and we have been living this misery in Canada for almost 150 years.

What has been the response of the Canadian government when we protest the illegal seizure of our lands and the intentional impoverishment of our people? Generally, it has been to simply turn away. Until our voices become too loud to ignore; then false promises or outright repression come into play. This was the response after our chiefs made their determined plea to Laurier. First, silence from Canada. Then, after the First World War, when Indigenous veterans returned to their communities and began to insist on action on the land and on rights issues, the Dominion government responded with unprecedented repression.

The returning First World War veterans, like my father's uncles, François and William Pierrish, were radicalized by the war. François had been band chief before he went overseas, and he returned to his post at war's end with a new determination to hold the government to account for its broken promises to our people. François had the toughness of old Chief Neskonlith, and he began to resist the government at every turn. But the stress of the war and the fight against the government took its toll on him; while still a young man in the 1920s, he died of a heart attack in his hayfield. His brother, William, who had lost an arm in the nightmarish battles in the trenches in France, took over as chief and as leader in our resistance. In 1926, William Pierrish and two other B.C. chiefs travelled to London, England, to present a petition to the Privy Council to demand action on the land question. Their petition stated:

> We Indians want our native titles to our native lands, and all our land contains as we are the original people of Canada. We Indians want our consent before laws are made upon our possessions.[4]

The Privy Council refused to get involved in a fight with the Dominion government and pointed the chiefs back to Ottawa. Ottawa responded to the threat posed by this new Indian activism by passing draconian Indian Act amendments in 1927 that tightened the control over our daily lives and that made Indian organizing, for all intents and purposes, illegal. The government tried to separate activist veterans like Chief William Pierrish from the people by offering them citizenship—with the basic human rights afforded other Canadians—but only if they surrendered their Indian status. Virtually none of the veterans accepted this poison pill. Chief Pierrish summed it up when he said, "We do not want enfranchisement, we want to be Indians to the end of the time."[5]

The purpose of these measures was made clear by the Indian super-intendent in the 1920s, Duncan Campbell Scott. Speaking with uncharacteristic frankness, he called our people "a weird and waning race" and said: "I want to get rid of the Indian problem. Our object is to continue until there is not a single Indian in Canada that has not been absorbed."[6]

The 1927 Indian Act amendments, which were in force until 1951, brought about a shameful period in Canada's history. Our people were, by Canadian law, virtually forbidden to leave our reserves without permission from the Indian agent, who now controlled almost every aspect of our lives, and the courts were effectively cut off to us as an avenue for addressing a land claim against the government. Our reserves began to resemble the internment camps that were set up during the world wars for enemy aliens.

But this repression did not extinguish resistance. It merely drove it underground. Communities met at night with travelling activists like Andrew Paull, who kept the fight for Aboriginal title alive. Paull, a Skwxwú7mesh (Squamish) political organizer, had attended law school, and he was able to travel the country as the manager of an Indian lacrosse team. He founded the Allied Tribes of British Columbia in the 1920s and later founded a loose coalition he somewhat grandly called the North American Indian Brotherhood. Because of the restrictions of the day, both organizations existed mainly in his briefcase, but Paull, tirelessly criss-crossing the country to preach resistance, provided the light in this period of darkness.

It was at these travelling meetings, where Andrew Paull called for justice on the land question, that my father and many others of his generation headed down the path of national and international struggle. In the 1950s, when some of the more oppressive laws against our people were finally lifted, my father's generation began to build the national organization— the National Indian Brotherhood (NIB), forerunner of the Assembly of First Nations (AFN)—to take their fight to Ottawa and to Canadians. But first they had to find each other again. Organizing meant taking a collection at a local meeting, travelling long distances, and sleeping in their cars. As we will see in the following chapters, these men and women—for women were extraordinarily present in these battles—led us back out of political wilderness and fought for our rights in the national and provincial capitals, in the courts, and when necessary, by demonstrating in the streets. The struggles of my parents' generation are part of this book not only because it is important that we honour them, but also because we can learn from their successes and their failures.

Along the way, we will examine their civil rights battle in the 1960s, the critical battle against the 1969 White Paper, court victories like the 1973 *Calder* decision, and the direct action of the 1980s that won recognition of Aboriginal rights in the Canadian Constitution. We will also look at how their ongoing fight for justice on the international stage transformed our struggle from a group of isolated activists fighting for survival to a movement of more than 350 million Indigenous peoples from around the world working together to regain our land and dignity.

The book then focuses on how my generation has been able to build on the successes of our parents' generation, but we will also look at some of our missed chances and wrong turns. This history is still being written with our deeds; the story includes some tensions and conflicts within our movement. As we search for the path through the chaotic and often bruising world we all inhabit, we should not be afraid to disagree among ourselves.

This is a fault that sometimes appears in our movement. It is a fundamental tenet of Indigenous peoples that everyone is allowed to speak their mind. That is the only way we can move forward as a people. It shows no lack of respect to point out that someone may be leading us down the wrong path or that another path may take us more quickly to our goal.

Finally, before we embark on this journey, it is important to note that when we speak of rebuilding Indigenous societies and Indigenous economies, we are not seeking to join the multinationals on Wall Street or Bay

Street as junior partners, but to win back the tools to build our own societies that are consistent with our culture and values. Our goal is not simply to replace Settlers Resource Inc. with Indigenous Resource Inc. Instead we are interested in building true Indigenous economies that begin and end with our unique relationship to the land. This is essential so we can be true not only to ourselves, but also to a future we share with all of the peoples of the world.

Our Indigenous view—which includes air, water, land, animals, and people in a continually sustaining circle—is increasingly seen by both scientists and citizens as the only way to a sustainable future. As Indigenous peoples, we must always keep in mind that taking care of Mother Earth is the most important contribution we can make. This is how we can support a new international economy that is not based on the outdated and environmentally unsound laissez-faire concepts of economics. In this endeavour, we can be an important ally of those growing forces—in Canadian society and internationally—that understand that for our collective survival on the planet, fundamental changes must be made. Mother Earth cannot simply be reduced to the industrial binary of profit and garbage.

We welcome the new alliances. And when we speak about reclaiming a measure of control over our lands, we obviously do not mean throwing Canadians off it and sending them back to the countries they came from—that is the kind of *reductio ad absurdum* that some of those who refuse to acknowledge our title try to use against us. We know that for centuries Canadians have been here building their society, which, despite its failings, has become the envy of many in the world. All Canadians have acquired a basic human right to be here. We also know that Canada does not have the astronomical amount of money it would cost to pay us for the centuries of use of our lands. We are certainly asking for compensation for the illegal seizures, but those amounts we can discuss. And we can begin these more precise discussions with Grand Chief Ron Derrickson's Afterword to this book. At present, we are asking for the right to protect our Aboriginal title land, to have a say on any development on our lands, and when we find the land can be safely and sustainably developed, to be compensated for the wealth it generates.

That is the thought I had in the hills above Neskonlith that warm June afternoon, when I returned from the UN meeting. The land retains its power and its beauty. All we have to do is rethink our place on it. Simply by removing the shadow of the doctrine of discovery, you find a rich tapestry of peoples who need to sit down to speak to each other as equals and build a new mechanism to co-operate with each other, to satisfy each other's needs and aspirations in the modern world.

There is room on this land for all of us and there must also be, after centuries of struggle, room for justice for Indigenous peoples. That is all that we ask. And we will settle for nothing less.

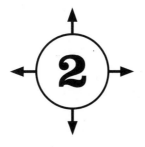

# Institutionalizing a People

## Indian School, Indian Jail

**M**Y OWN HISTORY of challenging the unacceptable treatment of my people had modest beginnings. I was still a teenager at St. Mary's residential school in Mission, British Columbia, and I was just back from summer vacation. Seated in the noisy dining hall, I was eating another mushy macaroni dinner when I realized that the food they were serving us was worse than the food they serve in jail. That moment led to my first political act—a strike over the food in residential school, where meat and fresh vegetables were almost unknown.

I knew the school was below the standards of jail food because I had spent most of my summer holiday housed at the Spy Hill Gaol in Calgary. That adventure began in July when I decided to hitchhike to nowhere, heading east and meeting up with others on similar journeys. Canadian highways were full of wandering young people then. Immersed in the youth culture of the 1960s, we all wore our hair long after the fashion of the day.

When I reached Golden, an old logging town and railway junction just west of the Rockies, thirty young people were lined up for rides. The group I was with went to the back of the line at the foot of Ten Mile Hill. I thought it would be days before we'd get a ride out. But late in the afternoon, we noticed a freight train, made up of a long line of empty boxcars, chugging up the hill parallel to the highway.

"I know how to jump freights," one of the older guys said, and he began to run across the scrubby field to the tracks. We followed. The train car doors were open. We ran alongside the slow-moving train, then slung ourselves on board by grabbing the door handle, feeling a kind of youthful euphoria as we stood in the open doorway watching the valley disappear below.

The sun was setting as the train levelled off at the five-thousand-foot-high Kicking Horse Pass. By the time we reached the foothills in the east, moonlight filled the doorway. It was the type of adventure that you dream about when you are trapped in the airless dormitories of residential school.

But my journey to nowhere ended abruptly in Calgary. When the train halted along a side track in the Calgary yard, we stayed quiet in the corner of the box car while a flashlight swept by the open door. We expected that at some point the train would move east again, so we waited wordlessly. But half an hour later the flashlight returned, this time with Canadian Pacific Railway police and a barking German shepherd. They hauled us out of the freight car, and it seemed that they were about to let us go when the CPR police sergeant came by, looked us over, and made some remark like, "Call the police and send these girls to jail." *Girls* no doubt referred to our long hair.

We spent the night in the city jail and were led into court the next morning. The charge was trespassing, and we were given thirty days in jail or a twenty-five-dollar fine. The two older boys paid their fines on the spot. The other young guy was from Ontario. He called his parents, who actually drove non-stop from that province to get him out. I did not have anything near twenty-five dollars in my pocket or anyone who would send me the money. And that, finally, was the "crime" I was jailed for.

I was only sixteen years old and I knew that I wasn't supposed to be held in an adult jail like Spy Hill. Whoever processed me must have known this, too, but they went ahead and locked me up anyway. I didn't protest because even more than jail I feared being turned over to child protection. As Indian kids, we all knew that that was the worst that could happen to you. Any of our friends who were taken away had disappeared into the system only to be thrown out a few years later as emotional wrecks.

It was something we talked about as kids. Until I was eighteen, when anyone asked my age, I would lie and say I was older. It was safer that way.

Still, for a sixteen-year-old, Spy Hill was a fearful place. The building was made of cement and iron and, at first sight, the men there also seemed to be made of cement and iron. I kept very quiet and tried hard not to attract attention to myself.

But I soon realized that, with the regimen and boredom and the dorm-style sleeping, it was not so different from residential school. Most of the men were there on drunk and disorderly charges. Virtually all of them were Native, and the main pastime was playing cribbage. I still remember the relentless sound of it. The shuffling of the cards and the snap of the deck: *fifteen two, fifteen four, a pair is six* . . . All day long. With breaks only for meals or to take their turns at the other jail pastime, cutting the expansive jail lawn with rattling, old gas-powered mowers.

It was a familiar routine for these men, as they passed in and out of the jail's revolving door. Quite a few were released and returned to jail even in the short time I was there. In Canada then, as today, it is not uncommon among Indigenous peoples to have family members go to jail. It is part of the system that we live with, in which a young Indian man still has a greater chance of going to jail than he does of finishing high school.

It is another a sad commentary on our place in the world that what struck me most about Spy Hill was how superior the food was to what they served us at residential school. Instead of the school's pasta mush, we were served meat and potatoes, pork chops, broiled chicken, and sometimes even steak. Breakfast, I was especially impressed to discover, included sausages.

Like most teenagers, I was not given to thinking too deeply about things. When I started agitating for a food strike at the school that fall, I was inspired most, I think, by the sausages. But even then, I understood instinctively that this simple injustice, of feeding Indian kids food below the standards that you feed jail inmates, was a symbol of—and very much part of—the vast system that placed my people at the bottom of the heap in Canadian society. I began urging my classmates to join me in a strike, and I found a number of willing comrades. But we were still a minority. I decided we needed outside support.

I wrote to an organization, Native Alliance for Red Power (NARP), that I'd read about in *The Star Weekly* magazine. It was portrayed as a radical Indian organization that was ready to take direct action against any act of racism against Indian people. I wrote the letter in secret, all in red ink, and sent it to their address in Vancouver, asking for help in fighting the poor food at residential schools.

For a long while, I heard nothing. I was beginning to think that the organization was just some white journalist's invention when NARP, quite literally, appeared before me.

It began as a bit of a mystery. I was told by another student that I was to show up at the school clinic for an eye exam. I knew the examiner was at the school, because some of the students had been called to go for an examination, generally on the recommendation of one of the teachers who had noticed them straining to read. But my eyesight was excellent. I couldn't imagine why the eye examiner would insist on seeing me.

When I arrived at the clinic, the Stó:lō Indian eye technician, whom I came to know as Wayne Bobb, held the sides of my head, looked into my eyes, and said quietly, "Don't say anything, just listen. I'm from NARP. We received your letter. We support you."

I couldn't believe my eyes and ears. The travelling Indian eye technician was a NARP agent. Bobb, who would later become chief of his Seabird Island Band, explained, "We didn't want to risk sending a letter because the school would intercept it. But we will support the strike."

He then slipped me a pack of papers, which he said were for my eyes only. Later, when I opened them, I was deeply impressed to find not only the NARP newspaper but also radical writings of Malcolm X and the Black Panthers. I was amazed and thrilled by the cache and by NARP's clandestine wiles. Looking back now, I understand that Bobb risked losing his job in this act of solidarity.

I hid the papers in the locker beside my bed, which was protected by a combination lock. I eventually showed this material to some of my closest friends, but I kept it well hidden from most. I knew that the majority of my fellow students, especially those who had been in residential school since they were five or six years old, were frightened at even the thought of breaking the rules or challenging the authority of the priests. But word travels fast in institutions. My strike plans and my contact with NARP were quickly transmitted to the teachers, and I was summoned to the principal's office.

When I entered, I was surprised to see a stocky figure in a brush cut sitting with the principal. It was my father. He was the last person I expected to see there. We were not close in those years, and I had built up a certain amount of resentment toward him. I blamed him for the family breakup. I blamed him for my being forced into residential school. I blamed him for leaving me in jail in Calgary for almost a month because I couldn't pay a twenty-five-dollar fine.

At the time, I was aware that he was working as a community development officer in Cowichan on Vancouver Island. I wondered how he had gotten here and how he even knew about my troubles. It turned out he had been almost 750 kilometres away at a meeting in Prince George when the call came from the school. He had immediately flown down to Vancouver and rented a car, the first time in his life that he had ever done so, and driven to St. Mary's. The principal outlined my acts of insurrection. My father listened quietly. Then he asked if he could take me out for a while.

We drove to Sumas, about a half an hour away, just across the American border, for lunch. To my surprise, my father showed both concern and understanding. "I know what these places are like," he said. "But if you keep pushing the food strike, you are responsible for all of the kids you lead out. You have to think on how you will feed them. Really, if you are going to lead people, you are responsible for your actions, not only for yourself, but for the people who follow you. And if you can't feed them, you'll find yourself with both sides mad at you."

Then he surprised me again by adding, "But I'll support whatever decision you make."

It was the beginning of our reconciliation. From that moment, I began to know my father not as a dark force driving the family apart, as he had seemed in my childhood, but as the man I would soon come to know: a fighter, yes, but also a man of rare intelligence and a profound understanding of people.

My father, George Manuel, would go on to become national chief of the National Indian Brotherhood and founder of the World Council of Indigenous Peoples (WCIP). In many ways, I was both lucky and unlucky to grow up in a family that was devoted to the struggle of our people. Lucky in the sense that I often had a front-row seat in the political theatre of my father's generation, and witnessed their often single-minded determination to advance the cause of our Aboriginal title and treaty rights. Throughout my childhood, I felt their unshakeable commitment, something that I came to understand through living my own life.

At one time, I was very upset with my father and mother as parents, but I now know that they did their best under some extremely difficult circumstances.

I will not go into a great deal of detail about my childhood; this is not that kind of book. But to understand the struggle of my parents' generation, you have to understand how exceptionally difficult their day-to-day lives were. They lived in a hostile world. They weren't welcome in the town and, in their youth, had been explicitly excluded from the life there. Their economic prospects were slim to non-existent. It was a daily struggle simply to survive.

In my parents' case, these challenges were compounded by the fact that they were both physically disabled at a time when disabled people were routinely mocked and ridiculed. My father had osseous tuberculosis as a child, which left him with a twisted hip bone and a profound limp. My mother, Marceline, suffered throughout her life from painful arthritis that left her, in many periods, unable to walk; she was also hospitalized for long periods as a child. That is what life dealt them.

But their circumstances left no time for self-pity. Both of them had to work hard physically to ensure the survival of the family. My father, despite his bad leg, became a boom man on the South Thompson River. It is dangerous, exhausting work, requiring exceptional balance. The boom man leaps from log to log, corralling and keeping the booms together and moving them to the conveyor belt that feeds the sawmill. He was the only Indian working for the lumber company, and to do his job while physically handicapped took amazing athletic ability and an iron will. To make extra money, he also worked as a Secwepemc language interpreter for a very understanding local lawyer, Henry Castillou, who defended our people in court. My father was a man determined to find a place in the world for himself and for his people.

My mother was a Ktunaxa (Kootenay) from the St. Mary's Indian Band near Cranbrook, British Columbia. She was also a very hard-working woman. She was skilful at beadwork, and she would make tanned hides from the deer and other animals. She came from a long line of strong women. Her mother, Mary Paul, known by her Indian name of Kupe, had always expressed pride that the whites had not undermined her Ktunaxa language, which she passed on to my mother. In fact, she had taken the school bell from the school in her community as a kind of trophy for her victory against the nuns there, and passed it down to my mother.

I kept it to remind my own children and grandchildren that we can and must outlive our oppressors.

On summer weekends, we all pitched in to take in the hay from our fields. Even when I was seven or eight years old, I would work dawn to dusk haying with the family. When haying was done, we repaired fences or hauled wood. In the late fall and early winter, we would go into the bush and cut Christmas trees. We did this after school, so it was always in the dark. My mother used to cut the trees and my older brother, Bobby, and I would haul them out to the logging road where my father was waiting with the car—with the seats stripped out to make room for the trees—and take them down to the valley where they were sold. I remember those cold, dark nights and my mother—despite her physical disabilities—bent over in the snow cutting the spruce trees with her double-bladed saw by the light of the first winter moon.

For several summers, my mother took us down to Washington State to pick strawberries for industrial producers. She had done this since she was very young. The farmers used to send battered old school buses up into British Columbia to pick up Indians to work in their fields because we could cross the border to work without a permit. For many years, it was an important source of income for our people. But then Mexican workers began being brought in for the first time and Indian berry pickers were pushed aside—housed in the worst camps and sent to the lower-yield fields where it was difficult to make any money. After a few seasons, my mother realized that we were no longer wanted as farm labour, either, and we never went back.

Despite their unrelenting toil, both of my parents understood that you had to give back to your community. In my mother's case, it was as an active member of the homemakers' club. The club raised money through raffles and sales for community projects or for emergency help for those who needed it most. In later years, she also became an alcohol and drug counsellor, and she was recognized in the community as a medicine woman.

My father's personal work was Indian politics. It took up increasing amounts of his time and energy, as well as family money. He had grown up with his grandparents, who had reached adulthood before the intense invasion of our territory and the founding of the town of Chase. Through his grandparents, he understood what had been lost and what that loss had done to us. In the early 1960s, he had inherited the leadership of Andrew Paull's North American Indian Brotherhood, a role that kept him on the road most weekends. Few Indian people had telephones, and writing letters was the only way Indigenous activists could communicate with each other between meetings. When he was home, I remember him working long into the night, pecking away at an old Underwood typewriter with his fingers smudged from the carbon paper, working long after I fell asleep, and then up and already working at his daily chores when I awakened in the morning.

As I grew older, he was more often on the road, travelling as cheaply as possible, sleeping in his car or in the homes of political supporters, but still having to spend his hard-earned money on gas and food that my mother knew was needed for the family. It is not that she didn't support the struggle, but she became increasingly frustrated at her children having to do without while meagre family funds subsidized my father's political work. I remember my mother and father getting into arguments about this, which I think were made a little more fierce because each knew in their hearts that the other had a valid point and that really there was no resolution. My father was a determined, independent man who saw the struggle as the only avenue to make life more livable for his children; my mother was an equally determined and independent woman who knew that the cause, however noble, was hurting the family. Tensions grew until they pushed my parents completely apart and we found ourselves boarding the train with our mother for Chilliwack, leaving my father behind.

I remember the five of us standing on the platform. I was about thirteen years old at the time. My sister Vera was fifteen, Arlene was nine, Richard was seven, and Doreen was only five years old. My older brother, Bobby, was not with us. He was seventeen and he had run off a few months before. By coincidence, he was getting off the train, returning for a visit to Neskonlith, just as we were leaving. He had picked up some mill work while he was away and he had money in his pocket. There were lots of jobs in those days, to the point that you could arrive in most Western towns in the evening and by the next morning be working as some kind of labourer. Bobby was happy to see us at the station—thinking that somehow we had known he was coming and gone out to meet him.

My mother explained that she was leaving our father, and Bobby said he understood. She asked him not to tell our father that he had seen us. Bobby said don't worry, he didn't even plan on speaking to him. That's how things were between Bobby and my father in those days, and they would remain like that for some time. My father, for all his accomplishments, was not a great success at fatherhood in those early years. He later recognized this and made efforts to make amends.

My brother Bobby stayed on the platform, and we headed south to Chilliwack. Looking back to our time there, it seems like a strange sort of exile. My mother rented a house in the rundown part of town. My brothers and sisters were upset with the sudden breakup of the family, and my mother was forced to work hard as a domestic and at local farm work to support us. We did not realize that the family crisis had only started.

The new ordeal began while we were in the fields picking strawberries for a local producer in Yarrow, British Columbia. While we were working, the owner came out to speak to my mother. He pointed at a government man waiting for her in the shade at the end of the field.

My mother limped over to speak to him. A few minutes later she returned and called us around. She said the man was from Indian health services. He had told her that if she agreed to go into the Coqualeetza Indian Hospital in Sardis right away, she would be eligible for a long-awaited hip replacement operation that could relieve the daily pain from the arthritis and ensure her continued mobility. If she didn't accept the immediate operation, he told her that her name would be put at the bottom of the list and it could be many years, if ever, before she would be eligible for treatment again. The operation would involve months of convalescence in the hospital, which meant she would not be able to take care of us for a long time. It was her only chance if she hoped to remain mobile.

My father drove from Neskonlith to pick us up a few days later. We went back with him to our house on the river, but even this would be temporary. At the end of the summer, he would leave for a community development course at Laval University in Quebec City. It was the 1960s and a faint breeze of reform was passing through the Indian Affairs Department. There was a program to select the most active and effective local leaders and train them in skills that they could apply at the community level. My father was one of those selected. It was supposed be an independent initiative, but the design of the program still had the Department's fingerprints on it. The Indian community development workers were to be paired with white workers, who were paid far more and given leadership roles. Indian community workers described this as working Lone Ranger style, with themselves inevitably given the role of Tonto.

But the course would get my father off the river and position him to work full-time for our people. He had to go, and Indian Affairs made it clear that he would not be able to bring his children with him. For the family, my father's imminent departure presented a painful choice. We were faced with going either into foster care or to residential school.

School, we hoped, was a way that at least some of us could stay together. My father, like most kids of his generation, had spent much of his youth in institutions, first in the Kamloops Indian Residential School and then, when he was sick with tuberculosis, several years recuperating at the Indian hospital. He knew residential school could be tough and he warned us about it. He told us that, at the school, what they teach you is to follow a set of institutional rules and minute-by-minute instructions. So all they really teach you is how to follow orders from the authorities. We would sleep in large dorms, he told us, and we would have to line up for everything.

That summer my father continued to work as a boom man on the river and at his political work. Bobby returned to his mill job and my oldest sister, Vera, who was now sixteen, had elected to stay in Chilliwack. So I was the oldest one at home, in charge of the cooking and taking care of the younger ones. When the summer ended, it was finally decided that my youngest sister, Doreen, would stay with a family on the reserve and the three of us—Arlene, Richard, and I—would go to the Kamloops Indian Residential School.

I remember feeling profoundly sad when my father drove us up to the school. As I sat in the waiting room with my sister and brother, that sadness was overtaken by fear. The principal, Father Noonan, came into the room, introduced himself, and told us we would be divided up. My sister would go to the girls' dorm. My brother Richard would be a junior boy and I would be a senior boy. We were split up after all and although we would remain close for most of our lives, we never did live as a family again. In fact, it would be a couple of years before I even saw my mother. But when I did, she always made me understand that we were a family and that I had to help my sisters and brothers. That feeling has remained with me all of my life. My mother was a very strong spiritual leader whose medicine I learned to trust.

During these years, I went to three different residential schools (Kamloops Indian Residential School, St. Mary's in Mission, and St. Eugene's Residential School in Cranbrook, British Columbia). I did not suffer any extreme abuse, nothing like the terrible legacy of physical and, as we have all heard, sexual abuse that was suffered by many. But even without this extreme abuse, I remember the residential school experience as a time of great loneliness and alienation. The schools are cold places to spend your youth, and the staff worked diligently to reinforce in us a sense that in Canadian society, we were the bottom of the heap and were powerless to resist. They demanded, and rewarded, obedience. Nothing else.

After my lunch in Sumas with my father, I went back to the school and dropped the planned food strike. But not the ideas behind it. I understood from my father that simply lashing out against injustice is rarely productive. You have to think things through; you have to work with people first and develop clear objectives and then be ready to act. You are responsible for those you lead.

At that moment, my father and his generation were ready to act. They were aided in an unexpected way by rise of the civil rights movement in the United States. Canadian journalists suddenly began to compare the treatment of Indians in Canada to that of blacks in the United States, and Canadian politicians began to look at program solutions they could borrow from the Americans. There were, in fact, important similarities in the situations of American blacks and of Indians in Canada. Both peoples had been subjected to prolonged institutional and informal discrimination that had left them in abject poverty on the fringes of society. But there was an important distinction as well. Indigenous peoples had not been stolen into slavery and brought to a foreign land, but had had their land stolen out from underneath them.

The first basic human rights opening had come after the Second World War. In the 1951 amendments to the Indian Act, the explicit barriers to Indian organizing that had been put into place in 1927, and a few of the more ridiculous laws such as barring Indians from pool halls, were repealed. But the heart of the Act was left intact—with final decisional power over every aspect of our lives under the control of the Indian Affairs minister, and, more precisely, Indian Affairs bureaucrats. The amended Act even presented a new danger by opening the door to provincial powers invading reserves in areas like child welfare, but at least it decriminalized our struggle and allowed our leaders to emerge from the shadows.

Then, in 1960, the Diefenbaker government extended the federal vote to Indians. It was a controversial move for my people. Admittedly, it was clearly an improvement on the earlier policy that allowed certain Indians to "enfranchise," that is, to become full Canadian citizens instead of "wards of the state," but at the price of losing their Indian status. This right had been offered to the thousands of Indians—like my great-uncles François and William Pierrish—who fought in the First and Second World Wars, but only a tiny handful of veterans accepted it. Enfranchisement was also required for Indian people to be accepted into certain professions, like medicine and law. It was because of his refusal to give up his Indian status that Andrew Paull had pulled out of law school before receiving his diploma.

The 1960 change was a significant departure because the clearly racist part of enfranchisement—demanding Indians give up their heritage in order to vote—was dropped. At the same time, many Indian individuals and communities resisted the right to vote. They did not see themselves as Canadians but as members of sovereign nations trapped inside a country they had never sought to be part of.

My father accepted the vote, preferring to see it as a tool we could use to further our cause. Indians became, at least for that brief period during election campaigns, important to whites. As soon as we got the vote, Co-operative Commonwealth Federation (CCF) candidates came to the reserve and witnessed the crushing weight of our poverty. They began to raise issues like our terrible housing, the low levels of assistance given to Indians compared to whites, and the racism we lived with on a daily basis—including the racist drinking laws and the restaurants that refused to serve us. My father fought on this civil rights basis in the 1960s because it was a way to build support for the larger battle to come.

When he finished his course in Laval, my father went to work as a community development worker in Cowichan on Vancouver Island, where he deepened his lifelong respect for the coastal peoples, their spiritualism, their fabulous art, and their rich cultural heritage. It is also where, finding himself parachuted into a community not his own, he learned how essential it is in any social movement to begin by listening to the people—their hopes and dreams, sorrows and fears—before prescribing remedies.

At first, he tried to call the people to action on a range of issues that he thought needed to be addressed. He was met with politeness but no sense of commitment to an outsider's agenda. He called meetings but no one came. Finally he understood that he had gotten it backwards. First listen, then call a meeting on what the people are interested in.

So he visited every household in the community to sit with the people at their kitchen tables and listen to what they had to say. In an overwhelming number of cases, the issue that arose was the crowded and unsanitary housing conditions. When my father finally called a meeting on housing, the community hall was packed. He picked out some natural activists and brought them in to help develop a strategy on fighting the government for improvements. At one point, he led a group of local activists to Victoria and physically walked them through the provincial government departments so they would have a sense of who the people were they were fighting. Finally, they decided that the only thing the government reacted to was embarrassment, and they called in the media to see the terrible conditions the people were living in. As we have seen so often, this strategy can get results, although generally only in the short term. In my father's community development work, however, it lit a flame of resistance in the community, and some of the activists there continued fighting at his side for the rest of his life. I understood the impression he made when, almost fifty years later, I was embraced by the community because of my father's work.

The lesson he took from his experience in Cowichan, which he hung onto throughout the rest of his time in politics, was simply that you have to begin by listening. Programs and organizations that don't serve the people's most basic needs are less than useless—they are hindrances to development.

While he was working in Cowichan, my father was still active in the provincial and national political struggle. He was invited to sit on the National Indian Advisory Board the Liberal government had set up to shape what they promised would be a new approach to Indian Affairs in Canada, and he was elected co-chair of the board.

As a community development worker in Cowichan, he was nominally an employee of Indian Affairs. In 1968, he moved to Edmonton to work at the Indian Association of Alberta (IAA) with the dynamic young Cree leader Harold Cardinal. In Alberta, and across the country by this time, there was a perceived need to build a truly national Indian organization that could take the fundamental issues of the Indigenous struggle to the power centres in Ottawa. Not as advisers to the government, but as representatives of the people. Harold developed a great respect for my father during this period, seeing in him someone who combined a fine strategic instinct with a talent for delivering a stump speech and a boom man's way of attacking problems head-on. My father, for his part, admired

With my father, Grand Chief George Manuel, Edmonton, Alberta, 1969

Harold's quick intelligence and considerable courage in challenging the government from his Alberta base, rare qualities in those days. He was also impressed that while Harold had been well educated in white schools, he still spoke his Cree language and was profoundly rooted in his culture.

Shortly after my father moved to Alberta, Harold suggested he consider running for the presidency of the newly formed National Indian Brotherhood. But at the time, my father wasn't ready. He was planning to return to British Columbia and he was already working with other leaders at founding the Union of B.C. Indian Chiefs (UBCIC). The Union would make a concerted push on the B.C. land question, to have our legal claim to our lands recognized by the government.

There was also, in these initial months, a sense that the National Indian Brotherhood lacked clear focus. It was designed to represent the ten provincial and two territorial Indian organizations, and this made it a grab bag of some six hundred communities, sixty nations, and treaty and non-treaty peoples who were only indirectly represented through their provincial bodies. It was uncertain how anyone could bring such a loose coalition together.

Ironically, the impetus for unity, and what finally put my father into the leadership of the National Indian Brotherhood, was provided by the Trudeau government's Indian Affairs minister, Jean Chrétien. In June 1969, Chrétien unveiled a legislative time bomb that was designed not only to destroy any hope of recognition of Aboriginal title and rights in Canada, but also to terminate Canada's treaties with Indian nations. It was the now infamous White Paper (Statement of the Government of Canada on Indian Policy, 1969).

This statement sparked an epic battle that did not end in 1970 when the Indian Association of Alberta presented its counterproposal in the Red Paper. In many important ways, it was the opening shot in the current battle for our land and our historic rights against a policy designed to terminate our title to our Indigenous territories and our rights as Indigenous peoples. The White Paper of 1969 is where our modern struggle begins.

# White Paper
# to Red Paper
## Drawing the Battle Lines

I**T COULD HAVE BEEN** a scene from a movie. More than two hundred chiefs from across Canada packed the parliamentary visitors' gallery to hear the announcement of the government's long-awaited new Indian policy. It had been preceded by years of consultations with Indian leaders throughout Canada, including with National Indian Advisory Board that my father co-chaired. When the Indian Affairs minister of the day, Jean Chrétien, stood to deliver his White Paper in the House of Commons, the leaders waited with great anticipation that, finally, a government was preparing to move on their demands.

In the movie version, the young Québécois Indian Affairs minister would have announced a new era in Canadian-Indigenous relations based on historic rights and international justice for all nations. That is what the leaders in the gallery were hoping to hear. But instead, they received the shock of their lives.

After beginning with oddly empty phrases like "to be an Indian is to be a man, with all a man's needs and abilities," the 1969 White Paper proposed abolishing the Indian Act and at the same time sweeping aside Indian status and Indian lands and turning First Nations people into ethnic groups—like Italian-Canadians or Irish-Canadians—to be gradually absorbed into the melting pot. Any further services to Indigenous peoples would be turned over to the provinces, and existing treaties would be wound down. This policy would, in the cheerful words of the White Paper, "enable the Indian people to be free—free to develop Indian cultures in an environment of legal, social and economic equality with other Canadians."7

To understand the full depth of the anger and sense of betrayal felt by my people, you only have to imagine what would have followed if the federal government announced in Parliament that it was stripping Quebecers of all of their constitutional protections, including their political institutions like the National Assembly and all control over the territory of Quebec, under the noble goal of ensuring they were completely absorbed into the English-Canadian mainstream. Outrage is not a strong enough word to describe the reaction of the Québécois in that situation, and outrage is not strong enough to describe the reaction of my people.

The White Paper's attack on our lands and on our very essence as Indigenous peoples galvanized the newly formed National Indian Brotherhood. For my father, it became the battle of the decade. He and his fellow leaders organized mass meetings across the country to send Ottawa the message that the White Paper would never be accepted. Its mission, after all, was the same as Duncan Campbell Scott's stated goal in the 1920s: solving the Indian problem by ensuring that every individual in that "weird and waning race" would disappear into the Canadian body politic. Unfortunately, these goals and most of the specific policies of the White Paper have remained constant in Canadian Indian policy ever since.

Concerning our constitutional rights, the White Paper pointed out that "under the authority of Head 24, Section 91 of the British North America [BNA] Act, the Parliament of Canada has enacted the Indian Act. Various federal-provincial agreements and some other statutes also affect Indian policies." To address this fact, the White Paper argued, "the removal of the reference in the constitution would be necessary to end the legal distinction between Indians and other Canadians." In other words, we were to be ejected from the Constitution and not recognized at all in Canada.

To drive this point home, the White Paper went after our lands. Again, it began with the banal. "The result of Crown ownership and the Indian Act has been to tie the Indian people to a land system that lacks flexibility and inhibits development. Indian people do not have control of their lands except as the Government allows and this is no longer acceptable to them."

They proposed that our land, after some "intermediate states," be reduced to "fee simple" ownership. That is to say, to turn our homelands into real estate that is bought and sold on the open market with property taxes collected by the provinces, as with all other mortgage lots. Aboriginal title lands would be struck out of existence and reserve lands would cease to exist under the fee simple arrangement. As the White Paper put it:

> The Government believes that full ownership implies many things. It carries with it the free choice of use, of retention or of disposition. In our society it also carries with it an obligation to pay for certain services. The Government recognizes that it may not be acceptable to put all lands into the provincial systems immediately and make them subject to taxes. When the Indian people see that the only way they can own and fully control land is to accept taxation the way other Canadians do, they will make that decision.

This last point is crucial in our struggle today. A small number of Indian people are working with the government and conservative think tanks like the Fraser Institute in support of the fee simple trap, which is still very much part of the government strategy for getting rid of our collective land base. We will look at the return of this idea, which has risen from the grave like the undead in a zombie tale, in more detail in chapter 15.

The fact that these measures would not only contravene but also render inoperative the treaties was immediately recognized by the chiefs. Their protests were met with an astounding response by Prime Minister Pierre Trudeau.

"It is inconceivable," he said, "that in a given society, one section of the society have a treaty with the other section of the society. We must be all equal under the laws and we must not sign treaties amongst ourselves." Furthermore, "we can't recognize aboriginal rights because no society can be built on historical *might have beens*."[8]

To finalize the evisceration of Indian status in Canada, and for the federal government to wash its hands of its obligation to Indigenous nations, all federal programs for Indians would be terminated and our people's

welfare turned over to the provinces. This is clearly stated in the White
Paper.

> The Government further proposes that federal disbursements for
> Indian programs in each province be transferred to that province.
> Subject to negotiations with the provinces, such provisions would
> as a matter of principle eventually decline, the provinces ultimately
> assuming the same responsibility for services to Indian residents as
> they do for services to others.

The destruction of our nations and the final theft of our lands was to
occur over a very short period. As the White Paper blandly described the
timetable:

> The Government hopes to have the bulk of the policy in effect within
> five years and believes that the necessary financial and other arrange-
> ments can be concluded so that Indians will have full access to provin-
> cial services within that time.

Among the Indian leaders in Ottawa for the White Paper announcement was Walter Dieter, the provisional president of the newly formed
National Indian Brotherhood. He issued a press release describing the
White Paper as "the destruction of a nation of people by legislation and
cultural genocide." The popular resistance that followed caught the government by surprise; it caught many Indian leaders by surprise as well, as
people at the community level rose against the government's termination
policy. The government, true to form, found a small number of leaders
willing to work against their own people and sent them and Indian Affairs
across the country to try to convince them to drink Chrétien's Kool-Aid.
One of the few who accepted the contract to sell the White Paper in the
communities was William Wuttunee, an Indian lawyer who at the time
had close ties to the Liberal government. Time and again he found himself ejected from or refused entry to reserves.

As Harold Cardinal saw it: "In spite of all government attempts to
convince Indians to accept the White Paper, their efforts will fail, because
Indians understand that the path outlined by the Department of Indian
Affairs through its mouthpiece, the Honourable Mr. Chrétien, leads
directly to cultural genocide. We will not walk this path." In Alberta,

Harold asked his people "forcibly if necessary to eject federal officials from Indian lands."[9]

In the House of Commons, the government tried to use the affable and well-respected Len Marchand, an Okanagan Indian who had been elected as a Liberal in the Interior of British Columbia in the 1968 election, as a shield. Marchand stood up in the House several times to try to defend the White Paper, but after catching heat from his own community, he dampened his praise considerably. He was finally reduced in the House to pleading with his own minister to "look at this matter very carefully and clarify it so it will be clearly understood."[10]

In British Columbia, and elsewhere, the mass movements against the White Paper continued to grow. In the fall of 1969, Philip Paul and my father organized a meeting in Kamloops to formally launch the Union of B.C. Indian Chiefs with a specific mandate to fight the White Paper by any means. Philip Paul, from the Tsartlip band on Vancouver Island, had been a young protege of Andrew Paull; he had roomed in Paull's house in Vancouver when he was in town for Buckskin Gloves tournaments. A talented boxer in his youth, he went on to become a respected educator and director of Camosun College, a Victoria, British Columbia, college that supports Indigenous students. My father had been working with him in the National Indian Advisory Board since the early 1960s and Philip Paul, a fighter in and out of the ring, quickly became one of the driving forces in the development of the Union of B.C. Indian Chiefs.

It was around this time that Harold Cardinal engineered my father's election as leader of the National Indian Brotherhood. In the serious situation following the White Paper, Harold once again urged him to take over the leadership of the organization. My father, Harold later said, reluctantly agreed to have his name put forward, but not to campaign for the job. Harold told him, "Don't worry, I'll do the campaigning. You go take a vacation and I'll do the campaigning."[11]

My father withdrew for a tactical break and Harold kept his promise. By the time he returned, Walter Dieter had been manoeuvred out of the leadership at a special executive meeting in Winnipeg, and my father was offered the presidency of the NIB. He was also given the daunting mandate of battling the White Paper at the same time as he needed to set up and staff an office in Ottawa.

In discussions within the NIB, it was decided that it wasn't enough to merely block the White Paper; they had to counter it with an Indian agenda. Several agendas were produced by different provincial associations. Among them were the Brown Paper in British Columbia and the Red Paper in Alberta. The Red Paper demanded, first, the obvious: that no changes be made to Indian status without the consent of the Indian people. It stated that "only Aboriginals and Aboriginal organizations should be given the resources and responsibility to determine their own priorities and future development."[12]

It then addressed the title and treaty rights threatened under the Chrétien proposal and summed up the overall effect: "We would be left with no land and consequently the future generation would be condemned to the despair and ugly spectre of urban poverty in ghettos."

The White Paper was not only frighteningly bad policy, the Red Paper continued, it was a profound insult to all of the Indian people who took part in the consultations that preceded it. "Even if we just talked about the weather the Minister would turn around and tell Parliament and the Canadian public that we accepted the White Paper."

On the land question, the Red Paper flatly rejected the fee simple arrangement.

The government wrongly thinks that the Crown owns reserve lands. The Crown merely "holds" such lands, they belong to Aboriginals. The government also thinks that Aboriginals only can own land in the Old World, European sense of land ownership. Aboriginal peoples should be allowed to control land in a way that respects both their historical and legal rights.

The Red Paper is now best known for the way it was delivered to the prime minister and the full cabinet in 1970, at the same time that the White Paper was formally rejected and returned to its author, Jean Chrétien. The ceremony was accompanied by Indian drumming and singing, something new in Ottawa in those days, and it apparently had an impact on the prime minister.

"You say that the government doesn't understand, that it is dumb, that it is stupid or arrogant," Trudeau said. "Perhaps all of these things are true, at least in part, but don't say we're dishonest and that we're trying to mislead you because we're not. We're trying to find a solution to a very difficult problem that has been created for one or two hundred years."[13]

It was an interesting response, but the real problem hadn't been that the government was being dishonest. It was that they were moving ahead, quite openly in fact, to rob our peoples of our homelands and our heritage. The dishonesty came later. While the government officially buried the White Paper, Chrétien told my father unofficially, in private, that they "were withdrawing the White Paper but they would hold it aside for the generation of leaders who will accept it."

In fact, it has continued to be the federal policy under many different shapes and sizes, in pieces and fragments that successive Canadian governments have unrelentingly tried to get my people to accept. The White Paper lives on in the termination treaty process of the past twenty years. It is in the push for taxing reserves. It is in Tom Flanagan and Manny Jules's recent policy book *Beyond the Indian Act: Restoring Aboriginal Property Rights* that the Fraser Institute is promoting to turn our national lands into fee simple real estate, and in Stephen Harper's "results based" negotiation strategy announced at the end of 2012. All contain essential ingredients of the White Paper: extinguishing our title to our lands, rendering our treaties obsolete, and ending our existence as sovereign peoples.

It is up to our generation to not only continue to refuse to accept our own termination but to also move forward beyond this battle. Fortunately, we increasingly have the means to do so. The effective blocking action against immediate White Paper implementation that our fathers and mothers' generation undertook at the beginning of the 1970s kept the wolf from the door. Over the following ten years, they would win a crucial court battle on Aboriginal title and rights and launch a massive campaign to ensure our rights were enshrined in the Canadian Constitution. This battle would provide us with a constitutional tool for our nation-building efforts.

But part of the strength of the NIB during the 1970s—and in another sense its greatest weakness—was the government core funding that it was awarded. The government funding was necessary to give our people the chance to reply to the White Paper with their own vision. But to continue accepting core funding from the government for our political organizations for decades on end has been a mistake. Slowly but surely, our leadership was drawn into quasi-governmental organizations that reflected the old adage that whoever pays the piper calls the tune. We began seeing the results of this approach in the 1990s, and it is clear to almost all of today's activists—except those who are getting paid, often handsomely, to do those jobs—that these neo-colonial structures have seriously weakened our movement.

This did not happen by accident. Walter Rudnicki, the Department of Indian Affairs insider who switched sides and worked closely (without pay) with my father, charted the DIA plan to create these Indian bureaucracies in ways that made them completely dependent on the non-Indigenous bureaucracy of the Department of Indian Affairs. In band council offices today, you find the same lethargy that you find at DIA headquarters, as the Indian bureaucrats administer the same programs by the same DIA guidelines as the non-Indigenous officials once did. And at 5 p.m., the offices empty. Our band council offices have become perfect little Department of Indian Affairs branch offices and our leadership, too often, serve as junior government officials.

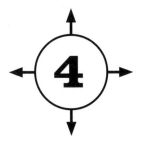

# Occupy Indian Affairs
## Native Youth in Action

HILE MY FATHER and his generation were working with the National Indian Brotherhood, my generation was pursuing the struggle in our own way. Many of us were steeped in the radicalism of the day; the writings of anti-colonial activists from around the world drew us in with their calls for an end to world domination by the white race. Native youth of my generation were also profoundly affected by the rise of the American Indian Movement in the United States. AIM provided a kind of romantic outlaw image that was irresistible to younger people. At one point, I went down to visit AIM headquarters in Minnesota with Tantoo Cardinal and Lawrence Courtoreille—not as any sort of official delegation, but more as a group of wide-eyed admirers.

At the time, Lawrence Courtoreille was on the Indian Association of Alberta staff but I was working with Tantoo, then an aspiring actress and always a dedicated activist, at the provincial Native Youth Society, which we rechristened the Native Alliance for Liberation. We had a small amount of funding from the IAA and, for some reason, some support from B'nai Brith. We were all living on a shoestring; the amount of money we were paid barely covered our rooming house rents. Still, we opened up an office and drop-in centre for Native youth in Edmonton's downtown core where we held meetings and political workshops. We also made prison visits to meet with Native inmates, to give them practical help and as much radical politics as they would accept. In Edmonton at the time, there were many young people brought from local reserves or flown in from far-flung communities to attend schools, and we would go to the students' events at the YMCA to try to politicize them.

We also supported the battle over Indian control of Indian education that erupted in Alberta in the summer of 1970. It began with the occupation of the Blue Quills residential school at Saddle Lake, Alberta, by community members to run it as an on-reserve school, after the Department of Indian Affairs had announced it was closing the school and busing the kids off reserve. When a new federal policy was announced to close all on-reserve schools and bus Native children to provincial schools, the Dene of Cold Lake in Northern Alberta joined the strike by pulling their children from school. Once again, the Department's aim was to accelerate the assimilation of Indian children into the Canadian mainstream. Protesters, beginning with Indian parents, demanded to have Indian-run schools on every reserve. The Cold Lake band went as far as organizing a sit-in of the regional Indian Affairs offices on the 27th floor of the CN tower in Edmonton, which our youth group immediately joined.

The school strike lasted until the spring of 1972, and it was strongly supported by Harold Cardinal and the Indian Association of Alberta. The Trudeau government's response was predictable. Indian Affairs Minister Jean Chrétien did not try to address the issue, but he had his department issue a barrage of propaganda accusing Harold Cardinal and the IAA of mismanagement of funds. It is the same approach the government has taken countless times since, even up to 2013, when the Harper government tried to besmirch the name of Chief Theresa Spence during her hunger strike in Ottawa. The falsity of the claim of mismanagement against Harold Cardinal was soon proven in an audit, and it was underscored a few years later when the Department of Indian Affairs actually offered him the job of regional director of Indian Affairs in Alberta. Still, the trumped up charges were enough to justify the complete cut-off of funds to the IAA, and they created enough of a smokescreen to give Chrétien time to begin part two of the classic strategy—making deals with individual chiefs.

Harold Cardinal was forced to resign from the IAA because of Chrétien's allegations but he was easily re-elected a few months later. I remember he was philosophical about this, comparing the Jean Chrétien of the Red Paper presentation to a "wounded grizzly bear" whom we had failed to finish off, so he had come after us "madder and wiser."[14]

Even though the strike collapsed, the government was forced to drop the most damaging part of its plan: busing all students to off-reserve schools. It was a small victory but an important one. Since then, other gains have been made that have helped some communities regain at least partial control of their children's education. But it is important to note that the Department of Indian Affairs has ensured that in its transfer of funds for our schools, Indian children receive a little more than a third of the funding provided to non-Indian children. It is yet another way that our children begin their life in a disadvantaged position compared to non-Indigenous Canadians. Another way that we are still kept at the bottom of the heap.

Not that much has changed in the more than forty years since the strike. The Department of Indian Affairs has gone through several renamings (although I will use the old version for consistency) but it remains firmly tied to its nineteenth-century ideals and strategies.

After the school strike of the 1970s was broken in Alberta and the IAA was temporarily crippled by the Chrétien funding cut, I went to visit my father in Ottawa. It was there that I heard about the national Native Youth Association. It was receiving project funding from the Secretary of State, enough at least to hold an annual meeting of Indian youth from across the country. At the time, it was based mainly among Indian youth in post-secondary education institutions and was headed by Blair Stonechild, who has since gone on to become a noted academic.

The annual meeting that year was on the Red Pheasant reserve in Saskatchewan, and I went as an interested member. It was an exciting event. I met up with many of the people I knew from British Columbia and people I had worked with in Alberta. We camped out in a tent city on the reserve, where the air was alive with the energy that only young people en masse can generate. But it was also a time for serious politicking. We held several large assemblies and numerous strategy sessions. The Youth Association board had many young leaders, like Bill Erasmus, who went on to become important figures in the movement. They were not a timid group. The major point of discussion at that meeting was the idea of organizing a twenty-four-hour takeover of the Department of Indian Affairs building in Ottawa.

During the meeting, I was not shy in speaking out and, somehow, when the election for a new Youth Association president was called, I ended up elected to the post. I think the group wanted to shed its university student image and engage more at the street level, like we had done in Alberta. In the board meeting afterward, we discussed the planned Indian Affairs takeover. After having experienced the rapid funding cut-off of the IAA in Alberta when the association had stood up to the government, I warned the board that if we took over the Department of Indian Affairs, this organization was probably finished because the government project funding we were receiving would disappear.

The board was undeterred by this, and so was I. When you find yourself clinging to an organization just to continue it in an ineffective way, you have to seriously ask yourself why. Our role was to confront unjust government policies toward our peoples, and it is impossible to do that in a way that will please government funders. This is a reality that too many of the current generation of leaders have yet to face.

The twenty-four-hour takeover was planned for mid-August 1973. A few days before the target date, we amassed 350 activists on St. Regis Island on the Akwesasne reserve, which straddles the Canada-U.S. border near Cornwall, Ontario. At the time, we were still discussing whether we should actually go through with it, and we made it clear to all that it could be the end of our organization if we did. Some were still arguing that we should try to work with the government from the inside, but when the great majority of members rejected that idea, everyone agreed to carry out the action as planned. Late that night before heading to Ottawa, I found a pay phone and, as a courtesy, called my father, then head of the National Indian Brotherhood, to let him know what was happening. He said little, just thanked me for letting me know.

He was, of course, already well aware of what was going on. The day before, my Uncle Joe, then Neskonlith band chief, had arrived on the island after driving with some Neskonlith youth right across the country. Others have since told me that my father had asked Uncle Joe to join us and to keep an eye on things.

We crossed the river in barges before dawn and made the hour-and-a-half drive to Ottawa in a cavalcade of cars, vans, and motorcycles. We arrived at the deserted street in front of the Indian Affairs building on Laurier Avenue at sunrise, feeling the power of our numbers and our cause as we began to stream into the building. The security guard met us in the lobby, but seeing hundreds of young Indians, many carrying sleeping bags and blankets, filling the building, he took a tactful approach. He asked us politely what we were up to. We explained that we would be there for twenty-four hours and we would remain peaceful. He seemed satisfied, handed us the keys to the door, and left.

The occupation was a political act, but it also had a more practical objective. Indian Affairs was where the minutiae of our lives were controlled and where the strategies like the White Paper were hatched. Among us were some activists who well understood the importance of those files to our people, and they went to work rifling through the filing cabinets looking for specific pieces of information.

They found much of what they were looking for in the office of the assistant deputy minister, John Ciaccia, a Quebec Liberal who many believed was sent to Chrétien's Department of Indian Affairs for schooling on how to deal with Indians before taking over the file in Quebec.

On a personal level, Ciaccia had made an impression. In contrast to their attitude toward most DIA bureaucrats, people actually liked Ciaccia as a person. Even the radical elements around my father liked him. He had set up a few progressive youth-oriented programs around the country, and at the time, my brother Bobby was working on contract on one of them. It was based in Alberta, but Bobby was in Ottawa that week and he heard about the Indian Youth Association takeover on the radio while driving to work that morning. The radio announced that the Indian Affairs building was shut down and the downtown core was cordoned off, with the building surrounded by the RCMP. With a smile on his face, Bobby turned his car around and headed back home.

Inside, the burst of busyness continued. Our people found a number of locked filing cabinets inside Ciaccia's office. They hauled them up to the roof and began using fire axes to break off the locks.

The initial buoyant atmosphere began to recede as dozens, then hundreds, of RCMP riot squad officers amassed in front of the building with their menacing-looking helmets, shields, and clubs. Since Indian Affairs was a federal department, Minister Chrétien had been made aware of our presence as soon as we arrived, and he had immediately called in the RCMP riot squad. Inside, Dutch Lerat, our security chief, and some of our more resourceful colleagues had liberated buckets of industrial soap from the janitorial supplies. If the RCMP charged in, they said we should retreat to the second floor, block the elevators, and dump the liquid soap on the stairs to slow the police assault.

When the RCMP began to beat their shields with their clubs in that universal riot squad intimidation tactic, some of our biggest guys stood in front of the lobby to signal that we were not going to give up without a fight. It was a serious group, and we were prepared for serious consequences.

A short time later, an Ottawa police officer came to the door and yelled, "Who's in charge? We want to talk."

At first I was reluctant to go outside, thinking that perhaps it was a trick and I would be arrested and prevented from coming back in. I was so suspicious and, in retrospect, naive, that it took some coaxing for the police to get me to step out to meet with them.

I was surprised when the Ottawa police chief, in his brocaded jacket, came up to speak to me. He was forthright. "You are just here for twenty-four hours, right?"

"Yes," I said.

He nodded. "To tell you the truth, I have no problem with you being here for twenty-four hours, as long as you don't damage property or harm anyone."

I told him that we would be peaceful if we weren't attacked.

"Okay," he said. "If that's your promise, you can stay. I'll tell the Mounties to go home."

Apparently there was some kind of jurisdictional issue. Chrétien had called in the RCMP to protect federal property. But it turned out that the DIA office was not a government building but private property under lease to the government. The Ottawa police chief, who was not at all happy about the RCMP's planned rumble with hundreds of Indian kids in downtown Ottawa, told the RCMP they had no jurisdiction and forced them to move away from the building. We watched with some relief as the RCMP riot squad was moved further back and replaced by Ottawa police.

A few minutes later, we were interrupted by some kind of commotion on the upper floors of the building. An early bird Indian Affairs employee who had apparently been in the building when we arrived was waving and holding a sign that read: COME AND GET ME.

We sent someone up to tell the gentleman that he was free to leave. The police escorted the early bird away but remained on the sidewalk with their cruisers parked all along the street. Later we also saw that they had taken up positions on the surrounding rooftops, which caused another problem when the sharpshooters reported that some kids were up on the roof smashing government filing cabinets with fire axes.

The Ottawa police were at the front door again.

"You gave us your word," they said to me, "that you would not do any damage to property. But there are kids on the roof damaging property."

I apologized and promised we would put an end to that. Word went up to our team to get off the roof and finish whatever they had to do inside the building.

In early evening, I went back out to the police to tell them that some of our younger protesters wanted to go home and ask if they could be let through the police lines. The police agreed, and the young protesters walked through the lines with the files we had collected wrapped up in their sleeping bags. These files eventually made it, through a circuitous route, to the National Indian Brotherhood, where they provided valuable insight into past and current Indian Affairs activities.

The rest of us marched out the next day, as planned, and returned in caravan back to Akwesasne on the American side. Then we had one more protest to make, this one against the Canadian-American border that cut through our lands. When we left Akwesasne, we didn't bother stopping at the Canadian immigration and customs booth. A posse of Canadian border police pulled in behind us and brought us to a stop a few kilometres inside the country. But when we left our cars to meet them, the lead officer, seeing our number and our determination, barked that we were to get back into our vehicles and get out of there.

I drove to Ottawa to meet with my father, proud of the courage and discipline we had displayed. I still see many of these former Youth Association people today, as they have gone on to become leaders of their nations. Although some of them, sad to say, left their sense of defiance in their youth.

As expected, the action against Indian Affairs caused the Secretary of State funding for the Youth Association to immediately dry up. We had run a youth drop-in centre in Ottawa, and we had to close it down and lay off our handful of staff. Soon our organization existed only in newspapers, where stories began to appear, no doubt placed by the Department of Indian Affairs, about visits by some of our members to places like Communist East Germany. The Department was engaged in its own little Cold War against us, one that continues today long after the wall has come down in Germany.

That same year, 1973, a much more enduring event propelled our legal struggle into the modern era: the Supreme Court decision on the *Calder* case. At the core of the *Calder* decision was the recognition by half of the judges of the Supreme Court (it was a 3–3 decision, with one judge deciding not to rule on a technicality) that Aboriginal title—or, as they called it, "Indian title"—was a property right of Indigenous peoples that could continue, despite the assertion of sovereignty by the Crown.

The split nature of the decision caused some momentary confusion at the National Indian Brotherhood. With very little discussion before the press conference, the NIB lawyer, Douglas Sanders, was going to go to the microphone to admit defeat in having "Indian title" confirmed. But my father was a little more far-seeing than his lawyer. He slipped in front of Doug to claim the decision as a major victory, because it was the first time that anyone on the Supreme Court of Canada had recognized "Indian title" in law in this country.

In fact, the decision clearly showed that Indigenous peoples in Canada were far from the quirky ethnic groups that the Trudeau government had portrayed them as only a few years before in the White Paper. Never again could governments claim that all that was needed to extinguish Aboriginal title was a simple claim of sovereignty by the Crown. Rather, they would have to deal with us within the legal parameters set out in the Royal Proclamation of 1763, the imperial law that put forth the rules that Canada could be settled under.

While the Court had ruled that the B.C. Indigenous peoples were outside of the direct reach of the Royal Proclamation of 1763, because their territory did not fall under British sovereignty until the Treaty of Oregon in 1846, that ruling showed that the precepts of the Royal Proclamation were still in force across the country.

Issued by King George III just after the British conquest of New France, the Royal Proclamation defined Indian lands as virtually all of Canadian territory, with the exception of the strip of land along the St. Lawrence River that made up New France, and a crescent of land around Hudson and James bays that had been ceded to the Hudson's Bay Company.

The Proclamation stated that the Indians living on these territories "should not be molested or disturbed" on their lands. Until a lawful purchase had been made by the Crown, the Crown held those lands in trust for the self-governing nations of Indigenous peoples. It is this point that our own chiefs had insisted on in the Laurier Memorial in 1910, and it was this message that William Pierrish had brought to London in his plea to the Privy Council in 1926. It was still part of the basic message of Andrew Paull and my father's generation.

Our whole movement had up to that point been based on having the colonial government, and later the Dominion and Canadian government, respect our rights as sovereign peoples as set out in the Royal Proclamation. It was unequivocal. Settlers who had already strayed onto our lands were ordered by the king to "forthwith to remove themselves from such Settlements." The only exception was colonial peace officers, who were allowed to cross into our lands in hot pursuit of criminals who attempted "to fly from justice and take refuge in the said territory." But even they were not allowed to interfere with us in any way, only to seize the offender and take them "under a proper guard to the Colony where the crime was committed."

The colonial part of the Royal Proclamation, the part where the doctrine of discovery still lurked, was that it gave the Crown the right to extinguish our rights through treaties. It would be another twenty-four years after the *Calder* decision before a Supreme Court ruling would open the way to an alternative to this extinguishment process. But with the *Calder* decision, the Crown's contention that it held "perfect title" over the non-treaty areas of Canada was debunked.

When it became clear that the evenly split *Calder* decision had effectively recognized Indian title, the reaction—especially in British Columbia, where few treaties had been signed—was electric. The fight for Aboriginal title and rights had been, for the previous century, a lonely crusade for our people. Now, for the first time, we had an important ally in half of the judges on the Supreme Court of Canada.

Among the Indigenous peoples who had signed historic treaties, the response was more muted. Most insist that in the peace treaties they signed, they never gave up their underlying title. And they certainly have a compelling case that the treaties, especially in the nineteenth and early twentieth centuries, were legally abusive and signed under duress. In many cases among the nations of the Great Plains, for example, the people were literally starving to death after the wholesale slaughter of the buffalo, and treaties were forced on them in exchange for rations they needed to keep their children from dying. In almost all cases, the verbal agreements that surrounded the peace treaties were far different from the cession, release, or surrender of land that was put down in writing—a key point when you consider that none of the chiefs who signed the treaties could actually read the text. The struggle of the treaty people for justice remains central to the Indian movement today. But the main impact of *Calder* would be in the remaining areas of the country that were not covered by treaty, which still included the majority of Canadian territory.

The federal government response to the decision was initially tepid. "Maybe you have more rights than we thought," Prime Minister Trudeau said. This bland response was not as uncalculated as it might seem. It is the government's public relations response to every major victory of our people. They try—at times with a noticeable measure of desperation—to minimize the consequences of our victories, while working to amass a PR and legislative stockpile to push us back. They would use the same tactic in 1997 when the *Delgamuukw* decision confirmed and significantly extended our rights.

In the back rooms of Ottawa, the confirmation of our Aboriginal title and rights in the *Calder* decision gave rise to only one question: How can we extinguish them as quickly and cheaply as possible? The answer was the Comprehensive Claims policy, which was drafted shortly after the *Calder* decision in 1973 and has been revised several times, most notably in 1981 and 1986, without changing its core purpose. This policy was brought into existence with the simple mandate to get the land back under Canadian control in the most cost-effective manner. The National Indian Brotherhood rejected this policy and its mandate to extinguish Aboriginal title, but the Indian Affairs Department, then still headed by Jean Chrétien, would try to take advantage of our poverty by offering cash-for-land-title deals. They found a test case waiting just across the Ottawa River in Quebec, where the James Bay Cree were challenging the province's massive hydroelectric development project in the courts—and winning.

It was only months after the *Calder* decision that John Ciaccia left Chrétien's office in Ottawa and ran under the Liberal banner in the

Quebec election. He was elected to the National Assembly and immediately sworn in as the Indian Affairs minister in the Quebec government, with one enormous item on his agenda. Clear the Crees out of the way for Robert Bourassa's "project of the century," the massive hydroelectric development on Cree territory. His job was to get the Crees to "cede, release, surrender and convey all their Native claims, rights, titles and interests, whatever they may be"[15] to the Canadian Crown, to the Province of Quebec, and by extension, to Hydro-Québec.

The negotiation of the James Bay and Northern Quebec Agreement, coming on the heels of the *Calder* decision, was one of those pivotal points in our history that revealed both our strengths and our weaknesses. It was the *Calder* decision, with its recognition of the existence Aboriginal title, that forced the Quebec government to put the bulldozers into idle and climb down to talk. But it was clear from the outset that they were willing to accept only one outcome: the cession, release, and surrender of Cree lands. In the end, the road to the James Bay and Northern Quebec Agreement would be paved with the government's usual arsenal of intense manipulation, fear-mongering, and slander against individuals and peoples. It its dealings with Indigenous nations we see clearly Canada's bullying nature, when it determines it is in its interest to beat us into submission.

The young Cree negotiator Billy Diamond began by bravely insisting that Cree land was inalienable and that "only beavers have the right to build dams on our territory."[16] But after he broke with his Indian allies inside and outside of Quebec and decided to go it alone, with his legal team headed by Quebec lawyer James O'Reilly, he was seduced into negotiating away his people's most prized possession, their title to their lands that they had been given not by Canadian law, but by the Creator.

In their initial meeting with the Quebec government, Billy Diamond and his team had been offered the same kind of impoverished reserves that had been foisted on the Ontario Cree at the beginning of the twentieth century in Treaty Number 9. This they refused. But in a private meeting with John Ciaccia in May 1974, Diamond gave Ciaccia a number. A billion dollars. That's what Diamond said it would take for his people to sell their birthright. And that was all the government needed to hear. There was a price on Cree lands. All that was left for the government was the haggling.

The Quebec government came back with an offer of $100 million. Diamond and O'Reilly balked. The provincial government then went on a PR offensive. They released their $100 million offer and the Cree billion-dollar demand, and began to portray the Crees and their leadership as extortionists trying to suck the lifeblood out of Quebec by blocking the project of the century. With that signal, the latent racism poured forth in the Quebec media and the demands grew across the province to simply bulldoze the Cree out of the way. On cue, across the river in Ottawa, Chrétien stood up in Parliament and gave the federal government's full support to the Quebec offer.

My father, still head of the National Indian Brotherhood, knew the Crees were in trouble as soon as the $100 million offer was made public and presented as a kind of gift to the unworthy Cree. He took aim at Chrétien's support for the deal. He accused him of "grossly misleading the general public, deceiving the federal Parliament and attempting to manipulate the Indian people by his recent statement in support of the Quebec government's termination policy for the Indians and Inuit people of the James Bay area."[17]

But the Cree felt cornered. Across the province, Quebec opinion leaders were up in arms demanding that the project go ahead. When in November 1974, Quebec came out with an improved offer of $225 million, the badly outmanoeuvred Cree leadership grabbed onto it like a drowning swimmer onto a lifebuoy.

My father and other First Nations leaders did the math. The $225 million deal sounded like an enormous amount of money, but it was spread over twenty years and it was pay for the birthright of the twelve thousand Cree. It works out to $937.50 per person per year, or $18.02 per week. Or, considering the hand-to-mouth existence of most Cree at the time, about $2.50 a day. That was the price that was paid for a vast country that had existed for thousands of years. It was the deal of the century as well as the project of the century. The wealth taken out of Cree lands since then has been in the hundreds of billions of dollars.

This was the type of cash-for-land and extinguishment-of-title agreement that Canadian governments began to push for under the Comprehensive Claims policy. James Bay was one of six negotiations that they undertook to bring the mainly northern land under these so-called modern treaties. And time and again we have seen that these deals do not fundamentally address our poverty. At best, they freeze it at a certain level. At worst, they create a tiny Indian management elite that profits significantly, while our people are left in the same or in a worse state of distress.

The fight against this extinguishment philosophy remains central to our struggle today.

During this period, I had my own personal brush with the James Bay and Northern Quebec Agreement. It illustrated the divide between those who were willing to cede their rights and those who refused.

The official signing ceremony was scheduled to take place in Quebec City, with Premier Robert Bourassa and Billy Diamond putting their signatures to the agreement. I was in Montreal at the time and my friend Eddie Gardner was the editor of the *Laurentian Alliance*, the newspaper of the Métis and non-Status Indians organization. He had been covering the regional meetings on the agreement, and I had accompanied him on some of his travels. When he told me that he was heading to Quebec the next day to cover the final signing ceremony, he invited me to come along. We drove to Quebec City in a rented car and discovered that the conference centre where the signing was to take place was under a security lockdown. We were stopped at the door and refused entry. Eddie fiercely protested. He was a journalist; he had a right to be there.

A CTV reporter, Del Archer, saw Eddie fuming at the door and came over. Eddie told him we were being refused entry, and Archer went to speak to the Cree organizers. He came back and told us that we were being blocked for "security reasons."

We refused to leave and finally, after the security people discussed it further, we were let in. But when we took our seats, we were suddenly flanked by four burly Quebec National Assembly security officers sitting beside and behind us. One of them leaned forward and whispered in my ear, "Please come with us."

We were taken to a small cloakroom, pushed up against the wall, and frisked for weapons. The police demanded to know what I was doing there. I explained that I was with Eddie and he was covering the ceremony for his newspaper.

The security officer said, "You were one of the people who took over John Ciaccia's office."

At first I had no idea of what he was talking about. I certainly knew who Ciaccia was, but I didn't remember ever being in his office. After some back and forth, it became clear they were referring to the takeover of the Department of Indian Affairs in Ottawa two years earlier. When the security people were finally convinced that we had no weapons and no plan to disrupt the signing, they let us return to our seats.

The signing ceremony itself was a dismal event. The stage was dark except for a spotlight on the table with the documents. The only two people who came on stage were Bourassa and Diamond. They spoke barely a word, signed quickly, and disappeared into the darkness. Those in attendance were then invited for cocktails at a hall across the street. There was no joyful drumming or chanting. It was a hurried closing of a forced sale on a shadowy stage.

The Quebec delegation quickly left to go to the cocktail party. The Crees hung around for a while talking among themselves. When they finally began to move toward the reception hall, Eddie and I joined them. But we stopped before we reached the hall. We did not really want to go to the National Assembly celebration. There was nothing to celebrate, and we knew it was likely the Cree who had tipped off the security about who we were. These were not people we wanted to eat and drink with. At least not at that sad moment.

We headed to our car with the idea of finding a restaurant on our own. But as soon as we arrived in the parking lot, we heard sirens. Police poured into the lot and we were ordered to assume the position with our legs apart and our hands on the roof of the car while they searched us and the vehicle. By this time, Eddie and I had had enough. We protested loudly to the police, and they returned our insults. While the swearing match continued, they searched the trunk and, since it was a rental car, found only one of those little whisk brooms that you see in rentals. Finally they told us to get in the car and leave the city immediately. That was one police order we were happy to comply with. We waited until we were well out of Quebec City before stopping for lunch.

In later years, this incident became something of a joke between Eddie and me. But it was clear that this country welcomed only those willing to sign away their future. And that was not a course I or my people would choose. For Indians who refused to cede, release, and surrender their homelands to the Crown—or to energy companies like Hydro-Québec—the gloves would quickly come off. The battle would be hard and long, and that's what Eddie and I talked about as we drove back to Montreal. How we could keep our people, in their often desperate straits, from falling for these shameful $2.50-a-day offers for their countries?

# Aboriginal Title
## No Surrender

HERE ARE SOME who suggest that the Union of B.C. Indian Chiefs' position during the 1970s and the position of all First Nations that refuse to sign termination agreements with the government—which includes the majority of Indigenous peoples in the B.C. Interior—is to reject all development. Nothing could be further from the truth. We simply understand that the cause of our poverty, and of the enormous distress that comes with it, is the usurpation of our land. The only real remedy is for Canada to enter into true negotiations with us about how our two peoples can live together in a harmonious way that respects each other's rights and needs. We are looking for a partnership with Canada, while Canada is trying to hold on to a harmful and outdated colonial relationship.

We well understand that economically and environmentally sustainable development of our lands is essential. As long as development respects the integrity of the land and minimizes its impacts, we must take advantage of opportunities to build diversified economies that also take into account the modern imperative of clean energy—which is required to save our planet.

Soon after the James Bay and Northern Quebec Agreement, I saw how development can be handled in a much different model. In 1976, a year after the Cree signed the James Bay Agreement, Ron Derrickson was elected chief at Westbank, the Okanagan community across the lake from Kelowna. He showed through his deeds that a community could develop its land without selling or ceding it to the Crown—in fact, by making the community's collective ownership of its land an economic asset.

At the time, Chief (now Grand Chief) Derrickson was already a successful businessman, who had built his business the hard way. He was born into his family's small farm on the Westbank reserve, where his father was barely able to eke out a living to keep his family fed. When he was school-aged, Ron and his brother were sent to the white school in Kelowna, but they encountered such racism that they soon transferred to the nearby residential school. There, at least, they would not be hounded by white bullies.

Derrickson left school at a young age and worked in the orchards of Washington State. Eventually he moved to Vancouver, where he learned the welder's trade. Always a hard worker, he lived frugally and saved enough money to return to Westbank to buy a small ranch. Over several years, he purchased small strips of land and built a number of mobile home parks. Later he invested in more capital-intensive developments like marinas, recreational developments, and real estate. Today he is the owner of more than thirty businesses.

When he was elected chief in 1976, Derrickson immediately put his business knowledge and experience into developing the Westbank economy. Over his first five terms as chief, from 1976 to 1986, he brought about a dramatic rise in revenue for the band and in the standard of living of his people. He accomplished both his private business and the later band development by using the existing tools for Indian on-reserve business: Certificates of Possession (CPs).

Most people think that Indian reserves are without private property, but there has been a system in place since the beginning. In our own Secwepemc culture, families had recognized places on the river for their fishing camps, their own traplines, and territories for their mountain base camps and for their wintering houses. These lands were passed on from generation to generation. They were not formally marked off; everyone simply knew exactly what belonged to whom. Today almost half of the Indian bands in Canada continue with this custom allotments system of ownership.

The others operate on Certificates of Possession. CPs have been around since the original Indian Act in 1876, when they were called

Location Tickets. They give individual band members individual lands in a formal way, but still largely based on the original custom allotments. But while a CP gives the holder lawful possession of an individual tract of land, it is fundamentally different from the fee simple title that Canadians use.

For reserve land to be allotted to individuals through Certificates of Possession, it requires first a land survey and a band council resolution. Then it requires the approval of the Department of Indian Affairs. The CP is then sent to the band council, which forwards it to the title holder. With a CP, band members can pass on the land to their children or sell it to another band member. What they can't do is to sell it to non-Indians, and it is protected from forfeiture by any individual or corporate entity, such as a financial institution. So it is not something that can be directly mortgaged in the way that you mortgage fee simple lands. This means it can never be truly alienated from the community.

It does not prevent you from developing the land, though. Instead of mortgaging it, you can lease it long-term. This can be done by either individual or band CP holders, although it requires approval—which generally moves at a bureaucratic crawl—from the Department of Indian Affairs.

It was this leasing system that Chief Ron Derrickson used to develop the Westbank First Nation. He was able to take advantage of the fact that the community was just across the lake from the rapidly growing city of Kelowna. The land's value was increased when the province built the Connector highway, a faster route to Vancouver joining the Okanagan Valley to the Coquihalla Highway, along the southern edge of the reserve. The band began to lease these lands to businesses, and suddenly a new revenue tap was opened up to the people of Westbank. Today, it is one of the most prosperous Indigenous communities in Canada, and this was done without surrendering an inch of land.

While Chief Derrickson was working to build the economic future of his people, my life was one of wandering. I had returned briefly to British Columbia in 1974 to work with Philip Paul at the Union of B.C. Indian Chiefs. My contract was to organize a demonstration to mark the fifth anniversary of the White Paper. By then, it was already clear that while the White Paper had been formally withdrawn, the broad outline of the policy—terminating the legal existence of the First Nations in Canada—

remained the central drive of the Liberal government and the Department of Indian Affairs.

Travelling through the back roads of British Columbia was an important education for me. I drove a beat-up old Chevy on potholed dirt roads to remote communities, and everywhere I was confronted with the systemic poverty of the people. Communities left in Third World conditions with little access to education and health services. Living on a tiny percentage of their lands and surviving on what amounted to a few dollars a day under the Indian welfare system.

But even with all this, it was not a sombre experience. Along with the poverty, I encountered the richness of the cultures, pride, and a sense of resistance to the outside forces. I spoke to dozens, even hundreds, of Elders and youth, and they did not need me to tell them we had to continue to fight government encroachments on our rights. They understood all too well the source of their poverty and the solution to it. It was not a philosophical question, but something that they had in their DNA. The land was theirs, it was given to them by the Creator, and they would do whatever was necessary to get it back.

After my sojourn in British Columbia was over, I went to Quebec as a youth worker, but I can't say that this period was particularly useful for me. I had a contract as a youth coordinator for Chief Andrew Delisle's Indians of Quebec Association (IQA), and I soon found myself in an uneasy situation. It was in the run-up to the Montreal Olympics, and Chief Delisle and the IQA had already accepted to participate in their assigned role of providing local colour to the ceremony. When I met with the youth, I discovered they pretty well detested everything that the IQA—with its conservative and deferential approach to Aboriginal title and rights—stood for. When the youth, with me standing with them, began protesting the preparations for the 1976 Olympics as a way of bringing attention to the land question in Quebec, I was quietly laid off from my job.

I stayed on in Montreal and attended Concordia University without any academic plan, spending most of my free time working with a group that was trying to set up a Native Friendship Centre in Montreal. Eddie Gardner was the head of the founding group, but I was temporarily made president when they needed someone who could do a little fist pounding to get official accreditation from the national organization of Friendship Centres. We succeeded. Eddie took over again, and I continued with my directionless studies.

Montreal, July 1975

My life was changing during this period. Now in my mid-twenties, I was no longer part of the "youth." On my trip back to Neskonlith in 1974, I had met Beverly Dick, a beautiful and intelligent Secwepemc woman, and we soon became a couple. She had been raised in a traditional way by her grandparents and had avoided residential school, so she still spoke our language. She returned to Montreal with me and we were married there. Our twin daughters, Mandy (Kanahus Pa*ki) and Niki (Mayuk), were born in 1976. We would have five children together. Neskie was born in 1980, Ska7cis in 1982, and Anita-Rose (Snutetkwe) in 1986.

The arrival of the twins made me realize that I had to get more serious about my life. I had a family to support. I decided the best way to take care of my family and continue the struggle for my people was to go to law school. I was part of a small wave of young activists of my generation who saw the law as a promising avenue for the struggle to have our rights respected. I think the Supreme Court's *Calder* decision had something to do with that. Trudeau had mused that we had more rights than he thought, and we were determined to see how far we could push that.

I buried myself for several months in LSAT preparations, which require an enormous amount of work. I took the LSAT at McGill University, and applied and was accepted at Osgoode Hall at York University in Toronto. I then took the six-week preparatory course offered through the Native Law Centre at the University of Saskatchewan.

At Osgoode, it was not easy to find anyone with expertise on Aboriginal issues. No one at law school was interested, and I felt isolated there as I constantly tried to find ways to apply what I was learning to the struggle for recognition of Aboriginal title and rights. I did have a genuine respect for the law professors, though. They stressed that we were not there to learn about the law, but about how judges made decisions on the law. An important distinction when you see how interpretations of the same laws evolve through time, especially the laws related to my people.

In a personal sense, I was moving from the streets to a challenging and competitive part of the academic world, and it was a big step. My law school experience afforded me the opportunity to study the huge amount of colonial material you have to understand in order to understand the true plight of Indigenous peoples. It provided me with the legal framework to think through Aboriginal and treaty rights problems and understand them in relation to national and international human rights. It also helped me understand the limitations of seeking justice solely through the courts.

Our legal decisions always have that political element that, if we want to see the legal opinions implemented on the ground, requires us to also get the co-operation of the federal and provincial governments. And for that, we must be able to put political pressure on the governments to force them to act. In the last twenty years, I have been working at this on the economic and international civil rights spheres. It will not be lawyers, Indigenous or otherwise, who will bring the fundamental changes we need. That power, I am more convinced than ever, rests with the people themselves.

In the end, I did not finish law school. I left still needing to complete one field course on family law that I had no interest in. I have no regrets about leaving before completion, because I know that even if I had graduated from law school, I would never have practised law. I would be doing exactly what I am doing now.

My father was also seeing the need for a people's movement to break the deadlock. He left the presidency of the National Indian Brotherhood in 1976 with the idea of trying to build a movement to try to effect fundamental change. By then, he had decided he had gone as far as he could in Ottawa. He had helped build a fairly highly functioning national organization, and he had carved out a place for Indigenous issues on the national agenda—where there had been none. Indians were able to get a hearing, at times at the highest levels, and there were small gains in a number of areas like health and education. But the gains were always small. My father realized that our people could not simply lobby their way into justice.

One of the avenues for fundamental change, he knew, passed through international institutions. And some of his most important activities during this period were devoted to building up the World Council of Indigenous Peoples, which he had established at a mass meeting of Indigenous peoples from around the world that he organized on Vancouver Island in 1975. After he stepped down from the NIB leadership, he undertook extensive travels to solidify the World Council.

At the back of his mind was the idea of returning to British Columbia to try to build a grassroots movement to push the sort of anti-colonial struggle our situation called for, a struggle that would work to decolonize first our minds and then our lands. But when he returned to the province in 1977 to take over the Union of B.C. Indian Chiefs and build the people's movement, he found an organization racked by internal dissent. A number of the key coastal leaders, notably Bill Wilson and George Watts, had left the Union and were openly trying to build a rival organization. I will not go into detail here about that battle, as it has already been chronicled by others. But I did have personal evidence that the break with the Union by the dissident leaders was, if not orchestrated, at least strongly encouraged by the Department of Indian Affairs.

My accidental insight into this situation came while I was a guest in an Indian Affairs car being driven downtown from the Vancouver airport. I was just out of law school, living in Ottawa, and had flown to a meeting in Vancouver with the Anishinabe lawyer David Nahwegahbow. We met Indian Affairs Minister John Munro and his Indian assistants, Raymond Goode and Danny Grant, on the plane. David and I knew Raymond and Danny well, so we struck up a friendly conversation with them. As we neared Vancouver, Raymond said they had a couple of cars coming from Indian Affairs to pick up the minister and his staff and offered us a ride in the staff car. We accepted the offer thinking that, really, things did seem to be changing at Indian Affairs.

But when we got into the car, the driver, an Indian Affairs official, assumed that David and I were also Munroe's Indian assistants. So during the long drive into the city, he cheerfully described a litany of underhanded actions the Vancouver office was taking to undermine and divide the Union, including secretly supporting the dissidents. Danny, who was in the front seat, turned around with an embarrassed smile on his face and Raymond sat with a frozen grin while the white official spilled the Indian

Affairs beans to David, an activist Indian lawyer, and me, the son of the president of the Union. Neither Raymond nor Danny said a word to stop the outpouring from the white guy. I suspect, in their own way, they were pleased to see DIA exposed for what it was.

For me, it was good to be reminded of the type of people, despite their occasional attempts to charm us, we were dealing with at Indian Affairs. As soon as I was out of the car, I called my father with the news. He wasn't shocked by it at all. He'd known all along about the leadership role the Department was playing in splitting up the Union. His response was to go ahead and try to build the people's movement.

Within the Union, they were working first on an Aboriginal Title and Rights Position Paper that listed twenty-four areas where First Nations had to recoup rights and powers that had been usurped by the governments. I will quote sections of the position paper here, because it gives a clear contrast to the position taken by those Indigenous leaders who accepted "cede, release and surrender" as the only option.

In its preamble, the position paper states that it "represents the foundation upon which First Nations in British Columbia are prepared to negotiate a co-existing relationship with Canada." It begins with an invocation of where our rights come from:

> The Sovereignty of our Nations comes from the Great Spirit. It is not granted nor subject to the approval of any other Nation. Our power to govern rests with the people and like our Aboriginal Title and Rights, it comes from within the people and cannot be taken away.
>
> We are the original people of this land and have the right to survive as distinct Peoples into the future;
>
> Each First Nation collectively maintains Title to the lands in its respective Traditional Territory;
>
> Economic Rights including resource development, manufacturing, trade, and commerce and fiscal relations.
>
> National Rights to enjoy our National identity, language and history as citizens of our Nations.
>
> Political Rights to self-determination to form our political institutions, and to exercise our government through these institutions, and to develop our political relations with other First Nations, Canada and other Nations of the World.

Legal Rights to make, change, enforce and interpret our own laws according to our own processes and judicial institutions including our own Constitutions, systems of justice and law enforcement.

Citizenship Rights of each individual to human rights as embodied in the Universal Declaration of Human Rights.

The conclusion of the paper is unequivocal:

Our people have no desire, under any circumstances, to see our Aboriginal Title and Rights extinguished. Our People Consistently state that our Aboriginal Title and Rights cannot be bought, sold, traded, or extinguished by any Government under any circumstances.[18]

This is the bar, set more than thirty-five years ago, below which no negotiation with governments can fall. No nation on earth should be forced to enter a negotiation that is destined to end with its own extinguishment. The demand that we extinguish our Aboriginal title and rights is an attack on the fundamental rights of our people and a contravention of our basic human rights as set out in the United Nations Declaration on the Rights of Indigenous Peoples, which even Canada finally felt compelled to endorse in 2010. The UN has explicitly recognized that in its essence, "extinguishment" contravenes international law and "the absolute prohibition against racial discrimination." As the UN Permanent Forum on Indigenous Peoples observed in 2010: "No other peoples in the world are pressured to have their rights extinguished."

Some might argue that all people have the right to do whatever deal they want, including to extinguish their sovereign rights. The problem is that the birthrights they are selling are not theirs alone, they are those of their children and grandchildren and great-grandchildren. And those we do not have the right to sell.

When these battles were being fought in British Columbia in the late 1970s, the first issue the Union of B.C. Indian Chiefs took up was fisheries. The government had enacted a plethora of regulations against our Aboriginal right to fish and maintain an economy based on fishing. After launching a province-wide campaign with a Fish Forum in Vancouver, and arming itself with legal opinions, the Union supported a series of symbolic "fish-ins" around the province. In Lillooet, this symbolic act resulted in scuffles and fistfights when twenty-four Department of Fisheries officers descended on the protesters and tried to muscle them off the river. As tensions rose, the Union didn't back down. It issued a press release stating that it would "meet violence with violence."

At a 1978 assembly in Penticton, my father said the fishery was just the first battle. "Self determination has to be our goal in our quest to recover the lands, energy, resources and political authority that we have entrusted to the White political institutions. We are saying that for the past hundred years we gave you, the White government, the responsibility to manage our lands, energy, resources and our political authority. You have mismanaged that trust and responsibility. Now we are taking it back into our hands and we will manage our own resources through our Indian political institutions."

The next issue was child welfare. In 1980, the Union led a massive march on Victoria to demand the government stop scooping our children from our reserves and placing them outside of the community. The impetus for this action came from a young Splatsin Chief, Wayne Christian, who had passed a resolution in his community insisting that Indian children would be cared for in the community, except in the most exceptional circumstances. The B.C. Indian Child Caravan moved through the Interior picking up supporters along the way, until more than a thousand people took to the steps of the legislature demanding a meeting with the minister for Child Welfare, Grace McCarthy. Finally, it took the 1981 three-week Women's Occupation of the B.C. Department of Indian Affairs regional office to win full control of Indian communities to care for their children, an occupation my own mother was part of and was arrested for. The Child Caravan was the opening shot in that ultimately successful Union battle.

British Columbia was in ferment, and my father was emerging now as the war chief of the movement. He was not the only member of my family involved. I had just finished law school when my brother Bobby suddenly emerged onto the national scene to run for the position of national chief. He was still in his early thirties, but he had already made a name for himself in B.C. Indian politics, and he became the torchbearer of the people's movement on the national scene.

Like most Native youth, Bobby had spent a few years trying to find his place in the world. He worked at mill jobs to earn a little money and moved around to see a bit of the country. In 1970, he had a driving offence with a $250 fine that he couldn't afford to pay. To escape a jail term, he headed down to Washington State to pick fruit and lay low for a while. But he received the same surprise visit from our father that I had had as a teenager in residential school.

It must have been an interesting meeting. After we had run into him at the Chase train station on our way to Chilliwack with my mother, Bobby had in fact spoken to my father when he saw him in town. He'd told him, "You don't have a family anymore. They all left!" That was a measure of the youthful anger and resentment he held. But when my father travelled down to Washington to meet with Bobby, several years had passed. Bobby was in his early twenties and my father was beginning to recognize the mistakes he had made with his children. He came to make amends. It was during the period that he had taken his strategic vacation to allow Harold Cardinal to do the politics required to get him elected as president of the National Indian Brotherhood, and visiting Bobby was his first stop. He counselled his eldest son to go back to British Columbia and deal with the legal problem, and he suggested he go to see Philip Paul, then the director of Camosun College. When my father returned to Alberta, he sent Bobby a signed copy of Harold Cardinal's newly published book, *The Unjust Society*.

My father's visit set Bobby on his own path of activism. Philip Paul took Bobby under his wing, and Bobby enrolled in a course at Camosun on community development. When he returned home to Neskonlith a couple of years later, he was elected chief. Bobby also became active in the Union of B.C. Indian Chiefs, where he was a member of the executive in 1977 when my father returned to B.C. to head the Union.

As a leader, Bobby had earned his own base of support across the province, where he was seen as a young, soft-spoken activist with an uncompromising conviction on our Aboriginal title and rights. In 1980, in a last-minute campaign, he took that message to the chiefs across the country when he ran for the National Indian Brotherhood presidency. He began as a long-shot candidate, but by the time the votes were counted, he lost by only a single vote to the much less confrontational Del Riley. It was a message to the government that something serious was brewing in Indian country.

An even greater challenge was waiting just around the corner. In the months before Bobby ran for national chief, my father had visited me at law school. The constitutional issue had been on and off the Canadian agenda for the past decade. Prime Minister Trudeau had tried to patriate the BNA Act from Britain in 1971 and failed when Quebec premier Robert Bourassa withdrew his support. By the end of the decade, Trudeau was trying again to get consensus from the provinces and warning that if they refused, he would do it unilaterally.

This issue was in the news in the spring of 1979 when my father visited me in Toronto. That evening, he told me he was trying to understand the full implications of constitutional patriation for Indigenous peoples. His first thought was that maybe we should just stay out of it, that it was a non-issue for us. And wouldn't trying to get recognition of our rights in the Canadian Constitution imply that we were part of the country—and therefore put in question our sovereign rights?

I disagreed. After almost three years in law school, I understood that the Constitution was where all of the rights, including territorial rights, were sorted out. It was the document that the courts looked to hold governments to account. If we were not in there, we were not in the game at all.

In the BNA Act, the British had allocated all of the powers in Section 91, which outlined federal powers, and Section 92, which outlined provincial powers. There was no room at all for Indian power. Our sovereignty was effectively stamped out in Section 91(24), which gave the federal government complete control over "Indians, and Lands reserved for the Indians"—in other words, over our lives. After approving this colonial document, the British sent it across the ocean to their successor state. We had to turn to older British constitutional decisions, like the Royal Proclamation of 1763, to find any Indigenous rights at all. And we had to hold the British government to task for our exclusion from the BNA Act, in what is essentially a white supremacist constitution, and find a way to break the Section 91 and 92 stranglehold on power.

When he left my flat in Toronto, my father still seemed unconvinced. But when, immediately after the failed Quebec referendum on independence in May 1980, Trudeau was ready to move on his threat to go it alone, and include in the repatriated constitution a Canadian charter of rights and freedoms, it raised alarm bells for First Nations across the country. Even after ten years, the White Paper battle was still fresh in our memory. What would happen if the charter of rights and freedoms could be interpreted to remove our Aboriginal status and protection of our lands in the name of "equality" with other Canadians?

The worst was confirmed in June 1980 when the Continuing Committee of Ministers on the Constitution released a twelve-item agenda for the constitution that did not include a word about Aboriginal title or rights. The Union of B.C. Indian Chiefs immediately launched a court action to block patriation without the consent of Aboriginal peoples.

At the end of the summer in 1980, while the Child Caravan was still marching on Victoria, the Union met to review the federal government's repatriation plan and a decision was taken. The chiefs passed a resolution that "the convention gives full mandate to the UBCIC to take the necessary steps to ensure that Indian Governments, Indian Lands, Aboriginal Rights and Treaty Rights are entrenched in the Canadian Constitution."

By November, the Union launched a massive operation to fight any patriation of the constitution without the explicit recognition of Aboriginal title and rights. The Constitution Express was born.

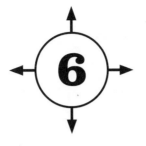

# The Constitution Express

## A Grassroots Movement

THE CONSTITUTION EXPRESS was an expression of a people's movement that changed the country in a fundamental way. Both the issues it addressed and the organization of the protest have important implications for our struggle today.

My own role in the protest was minor, but I was at Ottawa Central Station when the train pulled in on the morning of November 28, 1980. Two trains, with more than a thousand protesters on board, had left Vancouver four days earlier, taking different routes through the Rockies and joining together in Winnipeg, where they stopped for a night of rallies hosted by the Manitoba Indians.

In gathering support for the constitutional battle, the journey had already been a success. In British Columbia, hundreds of Indians had met the trains as they passed through the towns and cities along the route. In Alberta, the crowds reached the thousands. By the time the train left Winnipeg, the whole country was watching. The national news media were filled with speculation of what this Indigenous army would do when it reached the capital. In Ottawa, the RCMP began to fortify Parliament Hill with riot gates, and rumours of violent confrontations began to circulate.

By this time, Canada was in its own turmoil over the constitution. That September, after the failure of a last-ditch federal-provincial constitutional conference that our people were excluded from, the prime minister announced that he was moving ahead as promised to request unilateral

Chief Robert (Bobby) Manuel, Constitution Express, November 1980

patriation from Britain by a simple Act of Parliament. His idea was to move quickly enough that patriation would be a *fait accompli* before the Supreme Court had time to make a ruling on the Indigenous case and another attempt to block patriation filed by eight of the ten provinces. All the British had to do was to take a quick vote to approve the Canadian changes, and the deed would be done. Politically, Trudeau knew it was impossible for the premiers—even those most set against patriation and the charter of rights—to argue that the constitution, once patriated, should be sent back to Britain. Or that a charter of rights, once adopted, would be abrogated.

Prime Minister Trudeau presented his constitutional package for passage by the Canadian Parliament on October 2, 1980. Even though most of the provinces opposed the move, polls showed that he had the support of the majority of Canadian people. He also had the support of the New Democratic Party in the House of Commons.

For Indigenous peoples, it was an example of the often sharp differences between us and non-Indigenous Canadians. For the average Canadian citizen, particularly for English-Canadians, the battle between the premiers and the prime minister was a jurisdictional one between two levels of government. Most wanted a deal to be worked out that provided the benefits of patriation and the charter of rights and preserved the current balance of power, but the worst that could happen is that some power would shift from the provinces to the centre. For us, just as much as in the case of the White Paper, our future as peoples was at stake.

In the "equality" provisions of the charter of rights, the federal government would have the tools to undermine our nations by stripping away Aboriginal rights that were not the same as those as other Canadians enjoyed. At the same time, patriation presented us with an opportunity to correct the exclusion of our rights from the 1867 Constitution, which had given all power over our lives and our lands to the federal government. The protection of our Aboriginal and treaty rights in the new constitution was a question of our very survival.

The thousand grassroots protesters on their way to Ottawa on the Constitution Express were demanding that the recognition of Aboriginal title and treaty rights be explicitly written into the constitution. On the train, the Union of B.C. Indian Chiefs activists, which included my brother Bobby, were running workshops on the constitution and on what it would mean for our rights. They also laid out plans for demonstrations in Ottawa and stressed the need for discipline from all of the participants.

As the Union information package told participants: "Trudeau has challenged the Indian people to prove that we have our own rights and freedoms and these have meaning for us. We must show him in the courts and we must show him to his face. We must take as many Indian people to Ottawa as we possibly can." The Union also stressed the utmost discipline from all participants because "the Government can only hope to make us look bad. We cannot tolerate any alcohol or drugs. This is a very very serious journey that we are undertaking, to defend our existence as Indian people." To ensure discipline, those chosen for the security detail on the trains had been given both physical and spiritual training.

The people on the trains remember the great cultural celebration as they crossed the country, with singing, drumming, and Elders speaking. The protesters drew strength from this celebration with every mile along the track.

They were also made aware of the fears they were generating in official circles. At one point, between giant granite rock cuts in the Northern Ontario bush, the train suddenly screeched to a halt. RCMP officers poured onboard. Bobby asked the RCMP what was happening.

"Bomb threat," they told him. "Everybody off the train. And take your luggage with you."

Bobby looked outside and saw that they were trapped between the granite walls. Not a place you would stop a train if you were worried about a bomb exploding. It soon became obvious, as the thousand protesters opened their luggage for the RCMP search in the wet November snow, that it was not a bomb they were looking for but weapons. That is how edgy many in the country were getting as the train wound its way east through the Laurentian Shield.

Many, but not all. Some Canadians, such as Ottawa mayor Marion Dewar, hoped that the Indians would be able to stop Trudeau's unilateral patriation drive, as the provinces seemed to have failed. While the RCMP were busy fortifying the city, Dewar told the people of Ottawa that the B.C. Indians were on their way and they should open their hearts and their homes to them.

Before the train pulled into the Ottawa station, the Constitution Express had already begun to have a political effect. The House of Commons committee studying Trudeau's legislation had been scheduled to end its hearings that week, but it decided, when the train was just a couple of hundred kilometres from Ottawa, to extend the hearings to give the B.C. Indians an opportunity to have their say.

At the time, I was living in Ottawa doing contract work, sharing an apartment with my friend Dave Monture. For me, the Constitution Express was not only a major political event that shook the city, but also something of a family reunion. My father, who was having health problems at that time, had not taken the train. He had arrived in Ottawa a few days earlier as part of the advance team, and after making a fiery speech at the All Chiefs meeting that was being held in Ottawa to coincide with the Express, he felt ill and was taken to Ottawa General Hospital. It turned out he had had a heart attack, his second. It was a symptom of the slowly progressing heart disease that would continue to weaken his body over the coming years.

My father was forced to follow the Constitution Express from his Ottawa hospital room. But along with Bobby, my wife, Beverly, was on the train with the twins, Mandy and Niki, and our four-month-old son, Neskie.

When I arrived early to meet the train, I was surprised to find a thousand people, many of them Indians from the All Chiefs meeting, already jammed into the station to greet the B.C. protesters. Indian Affairs Minister John Munro was also there, standing with Del Riley, the man who had beaten Bobby for the national chief's job a few months earlier. Del did not look particularly happy. I had heard that at the National Indian Brotherhood, they were peeved that the Manuels were storming into town with the B.C. Indians and stealing their thunder in the anti-patriation fight. These men were, after all, politicians, so we all understood their concerns.

As the train pulled in, the atmosphere was electric. There were drummers and singers gathered to greet the B.C. Indians, and more drummers and singers coming off the train. The station throbbed with Indian music and with the excitement of the arriving protesters. It took me a while to find Beverly and the kids in the crowd. When I finally spotted them, I could see Beverly was exhausted but joyful.

When Bobby got off the train, he was met by a couple of the B.C. Union advance men who told him, shouting in his ear above the noise of the drumming, that Mayor Dewar had installed a set-up for a quick press statement. They led him away, passing close by John Munro and Del Riley, but Bobby didn't glance at them. When he reached the microphone, he didn't mince words.

Bobby denounced the Trudeau constitutional moves as a direct attack on our people. He said they were part of Trudeau's vision to steal Indian people's homelands and leave them to end up in the slums of the cities. He concluded by warning that if the government did not include recognition of Aboriginal title and rights in the constitution, the Constitution Express activists "would not only head to New York to protest at the United Nations, they would begin working toward establishing a seat there."

Then the Constitution Express organizational team went into action, assigning everyone billets and matching them with those who'd offered places to stay. I was enormously impressed by the way people had responded to Mayor Dewar's call. When the advance team had arrived in Ottawa, they had only a few dozen billets. Dewar put her city team behind the search for accommodation, and by the time the train reached the station, there were not enough Indians to go around to meet the offers. We should have a special place of honour to acknowledge those like Mayor Dewar who stand by us in our hour of need.

While the others were heading to their lodgings to rest after the four-day journey, Bobby led a smaller group to Rideau Hall to deliver a petition to the Governor General, as the Queen's representative. It stated: "The Creator has given us the right to govern ourselves and the right to self determination. The rights and responsibilities given us by the Creator cannot be altered or taken away by any other nation."

The petition asked that "Her Majesty refuse the Patriation of the Canadian Constitution until agreement with the Indian Nations is reached." It also asked the Crown to enter into internationally supervised trilateral negotiations to decide the issue and "to separate Indian nations permanently from the jurisdiction and control of the Government of Canada whose intentions are hostile to our people."[19]

There had been a plan for Bobby's delegation to take over Rideau Hall and hold their own constitutional hearings for a couple of days, but at the last minute, Bobby decided against it. He was criticized by some within the movement at the time, but in retrospect, the takeover wasn't really needed.

Over the next several days, our people protested passionately on Parliament Hill. They sang, they chanted, they burned sweetgrass, and they spoke with journalists about the threat that the patriation package presented to our rights as Indigenous peoples. The B.C. Union had done its job well. The protesters were the most eloquent spokespeople imaginable for our cause. They had the grassroots passion and—through the Union workshops before and during the cross-country trip—a deep understanding of how the Trudeau constitutional power play could affect their future.

Their message was getting through to the government and to the Canadian people. In the press, the worried chatter about possible violence in the days before train's arrival was replaced with increasingly positive coverage. More and more voices in Canada were speaking up to support our cause. Finally, a few days after the protesters arrived in the capital, they had their first big victory. Under pressure from his supporters, party leader Ed Broadbent withdrew the New Democratic Party's support for the constitutional deal until Aboriginal people were included. The Trudeau alliance was cracking, and Trudeau knew that the British would be far less likely to agree to unilateral patriation if it was the request of a single party in the Canadian House of Commons.

Jean Chrétien, now minister of justice and Trudeau's point man on the constitution, was sent scrambling to get a deal, of any kind, with the Indians, any Indians. He quickly patched together a couple of clauses that, he said, would ensure that the Indians would not lose anything under the charter of rights and freedoms. Del Riley quickly accepted the offer on behalf of the NIB. But the politics had already moved beyond Riley and the National Indian Brotherhood. My father and the Constitution Express protesters were demanding far more. The constitution could not simply skirt around our rights; it had to recognize and affirm them. The NIB was pushed back onto the sidelines as the Constitution Express continued to dominate Ottawa, and sent a delegation to New York to protest at the United Nations with the support of American Indians.

But the Union continued to direct its main attention to England, where the National Indian Brotherhood had had an active lobby since 1979. Our people understood that ultimately it was a British wrong that had robbed of us our powers in the BNA Act, and it was their responsibility to right it. In Ottawa, the Union sent a message directly to the British:

> We have our own relationship with the British Parliament—a relationship which places a constitutional duty upon the British Parliament to ensure that our rights and interests are protected and that Crown obligations to us continue with the passage of time, until we achieve self determination. The Indian Nations are calling upon the British Parliament to perform their duty to us by refusing to patriate the Canadian constitution until it can be done without prejudice to Crown obligations and until the supervisory jurisdiction presently vested in the British Parliament be vested in the Indian Nations and not in the Federal or Provincial legislatures.[20]

The Union message and the message of the previous NIB lobbying were finally received. While the Constitution Express was still in Ottawa, the British parliamentary committee responsible for passing the patriation legislation fired a warning shot across the Trudeau government's bow. On December 5, the British announced that there would be no quick passage of the bill on their side. They would not move on it until June 1981, at the earliest.

With dwindling support at home and with the British signalling that they would not be rushed into granting the Trudeau government quick passage while the move was so controversial in Canada, the unilateral patriation drive was effectively stalled. Prime Minister Trudeau extended the deadline for the House of Commons Constitutional Committee report. He would have to go back to the provinces and to Aboriginal people to get a deal.

From his hospital bed in Ottawa, my father felt the tide turning. Doctors and nurses and hospital visitors poked their heads into his room to offer encouragement and to let him know they were impressed by the passion and discipline of the protesters on Parliament Hill. Describing his time at the hospital, he told his supporters, "I was treated like a king. That is how much you stimulated Ottawa."[21]

This road would have many twists to come. In February 1981, when the Constitutional Committee presented its report, an affirmation of Aboriginal title and rights was included in Section 35. This set off a new round of the battles between our people, who wanted more, and a group of provincial premiers who wanted Aboriginal rights struck from the deal. The B.C. provincial government delegation took the lead in lobbying for the removal of the clause, and they found support among the other Western premiers.

In September, the Supreme Court blocked Trudeau's patriation drive without "a substantial measure" of provincial government support. The prime minister called a premiers conference, as a last-ditch attempt to strike a constitutional deal, for the first week of November.

The Union decided this time to target British and international opinion directly and make the Indian voice heard with its European Constitution Express. It was planned for the first week of the premiers meeting. The Union delegation left for Europe on November 1, 1981, with an itinerary that included Netherlands, Germany, France, Belgium, and England. The main destination was London, where the delegation would again attempt to convince the British to refuse patriation without a clear recognition of Indigenous nationhood in the constitution.

Once again, it was a grassroots effort. Because of the cost—$2,500 each for transportation and lodging—participants sought support from their bands. To make the maximum impression, they were told to bring their traditional dress and hand drums, and gifts for their hosts (jewellery, carving, beadwork, and so on). They were also told "bring information on [their] own band or area if possible, for example; pictures on conditions of communities and pictures of various traditional activities like pow-wows, hunting with game, fishing, new houses and old houses, mills or plants close to reserves, forests, construction roadways, or logging."

The instructions to participants also detailed personal goods they could bring through customs in Europe; since it was for B.C. Indians, the list included "1 salmon (FRESH OR SMOKED) Per Person or six tins of 4 ounces salmon."[22]

It is important to stress that, just like on the Canadian Constitution Express, the great majority of the people travelling were not leaders or experts but grassroots people. As the Union historian of the period put it:

> The Union, under the leadership of George Manuel sent the Constitutional Express to Europe. The UBCIC brought the voices of the people in the communities throughout the country to the international arena and made it clear that the aboriginal people of Canada would not stand back and allow their rights to be infringed upon.
>
> The excellent organization, forethought and vision of the Constitutional Express not only raised the consciousness of the public but also brought back the pride of the aboriginal peoples and the strength which has always been needed to fight for the recognition, the survival and the promotion of our rights.[23]

While the flights were leaving Vancouver, the premiers were landing in Ottawa to hammer out a constitutional deal. After days of deadlock, nine of the ten premiers reached a backroom deal with Chrétien, in what is widely known as the Night of the Long Knives when Quebec premier René Lévesque was stabbed in the back by the other premiers.

But the knife that night was used first against our people. In his account of the evening, lead B.C. negotiator Mel Smith wrote that some of the other provinces were worried about what effect Aboriginal rights would have on their jurisdiction. Others said it was Smith who expressed "strong reservations because almost none of British Columbia had been ceded by the Indians to the province through treaties. There was an uncertainty about the legal effect of this historical fact; the other provinces reluctantly acquiesced to this argument."[24] So in the middle of night, Aboriginal people were tossed out of constitution, along with Quebec.

In Britain, the presence of the European Express guaranteed extra coverage for the new betrayal of Canada's Indigenous peoples, and once again, British press and parliamentarians began to urge that the Thatcher government refuse patriation under such contested conditions within Canada. When the Trudeau government listened to the Western premiers and presented its final package, without protection for Aboriginal people, it was met with a storm of protest so strong that the premiers themselves were forced to begin a series of conference calls that ended with Section 35 being reinstated.

The result was that Section 91(24) of the BNA Act, which gave the federal government sole responsibility over "Indians, and Lands reserved for the Indians," would now be framed by Section 35(1) of the Constitution Act, 1982: "The existing aboriginal and treaty rights of the aboriginal peoples of Canada are hereby recognized and affirmed."

In the BNA Act, only two entities were recognized in the Constitution—the federal government in the list of Section 91 powers and the provinces in the list of Section 92 powers. These seventeen words in Section 35 announced a new entity in the Canadian power structure: Aboriginal peoples, whose own constitutionally recognized rights would be "recognized and affirmed."

Those who hoped that we had finally reached open water were soon disappointed, however. It is impossible to underestimate the depth and intransigence of the colonial mindset in Canada. While legal recognition of our rights was provided in the fundamental law of the land, political recognition would not be forthcoming.

This political dimension was supposed to be resolved in the series of First Nations/federal and provincial conferences that were mandated in the 1982 Constitution. Meetings to define our self-governing rights were held in 1983, 1984, 1985, and 1987. But each of these constitutional conferences ended in failure. There were some very modest changes to the wording of the subsections of Section 35 but no substantial movement to recognize our new constitutional status at a political level. Despite the promise to "recognize and affirm," it soon became clear that the approach of the federal and many of the provincial governments would be better summed up as to "ignore and deny." It would only be years later, when the courts finally stepped in again, that real weight would be given to Section 35.

The constitutional battle was a roller coaster ride for our people, but it also provided a model for Indigenous struggle. The main reason it was effective in having our rights recognized in the Constitution was that it focused on mass mobilization of the people rather than on leaders pleading their case in committee rooms or behind closed doors with government officials. Throughout this battle, the B.C. Union leadership had numerous invitations to appear before government committees to plead their case, but they refused the offers. They understood that we needed a much wider playing field.

We need to get outside the narrow bounds of parliamentary procedure and official negotiating tables, and demand our rights with a show of strength. Governments are not moved to listen by arguments or pleas for justice from our leadership. These rain on them at all times and governments are oblivious to them. What moved the government and the people of Canada was the passion and power of our people unified at the grassroots level, demanding justice for themselves and their children. The Constitution Express turned the patriation from a serious threat to an important gain for us that we can continue to build on into the future.

This is what our people accomplished by determined action together. And these are the means by which we can make continued advances today.

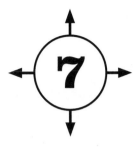

# Don't Let Them Bully You
## A Business Interlude

**O**UR POWER COMES from our people and from their active struggle for their rights. This has been a hard lesson to learn for much of our leadership. The 1980s were largely a lost decade for Indigenous peoples in Canada. One of the main reasons was that, after the victory of the Constitution Express, we left it to our leaders to take care of things behind closed doors or in the staged federal-provincial conferences. We believed again that somehow we could quietly negotiate our way into new breakthroughs for justice for our people. In fact, we could not even get governments in this country to recognize and affirm the rights they had just included in their own Constitution.

Our leadership was lost in this maze. After boycotting the signing ceremony for the Constitution Act in 1982, the National Indian Brotherhood accepted $2.5 million from Ottawa to enter the post-constitutional discussions with the federal government and ten provinces. This was obviously a hopeless task and, at the last minute, before the first federal-provincial conference in 1983, dissension on the issue led to a fracturing of the NIB. The Western organizations pulled out to form the Coalition of First Nations, denouncing the NIB for abandoning the battle for First Nations sovereignty. The NIB's timid position, said the Coalition, meant negotiating at a table with the people who had already indicated— publicly and privately—that they would not take any concrete measures to recognize and affirm our Aboriginal rights and title in legislation.

The great error on our side was to relax the grassroots mobilization within Canada and internationally. Especially when it quickly became apparent how wildly different our people's vision of self-government was from what the provincial and federal governments were peddling. In both of the conferences held under the Trudeau government and, after 1984, those held under Brian Mulroney's Progressive Conservative government, the Canadian state proposed "delegated" self-government, the same sort of municipal-style government that is on the table in today's negotiating tables.

Among the jurisdictional powers the federal government offers are the following:

- administration/enforcement of Aboriginal laws, including the establishment of Aboriginal courts or tribunals of the type normally created by local or regional governments for contravention of their laws and bylaws
- policing
- land management, including zoning, service fees, land tenure and access, and expropriation of Aboriginal land by Aboriginal governments for their own public purposes
- taxation in respect of direct taxes and property taxes of members
- transfer and management of monies and group assets
- management of public works and infrastructure
- housing
- local transportation
- licensing, regulation, and operation of businesses located on Aboriginal lands

Other authorities include limited powers over agriculture, natural resources management, and hunting, fishing, and trapping on Aboriginal lands—all things that any municipality can do within the town limits. And the government made it very clear that when it spoke of "Aboriginal lands," it was referring only to those lands the government recognizes: our Indian reserves, which make up 0.2 per cent of Canadian territory. Even those limited powers would not be granted to us as part of our inherent right to govern ourselves under Section 35 of the Constitution Act, 1982, but would be delegated from federal and provincial powers as set out in Sections 91 and 92 of the BNA Act, as occurs with every hamlet and village in the country.

In effect, the governments were prepared to offer a colonial—or what Mohawk scholar Taiaiake Alfred calls "contemporary colonial"—package. It would freeze our people as virtually landless wards of the state for the foreseeable future, until that state decided we had reached a suitable level of weakness to be simply cut out entirely and reduced to ethnic groups within the Canadian mosaic. It was a continuation of the BNA Act that had left our people powerless and, with the usurpation of our lands, penniless. The Department of Indian Affairs had been created in 1876 to manage our poverty as wards of the state. This is how we were still viewed by Canada's governors.

What the NIB (which reorganized into the Assembly of First Nations in 1985), as well as the non-Status Indian organization and the Métis and Inuit associations, were asking for during the constitutional negotiations amounted to the creation of a third order of government within Canada. An order that would have real constitutional powers and, like the provinces, constitutional protection over its jurisdiction. Our powers would be drawn from Section 35 of the Constitution, with entrenched powers over such matters as self-government, lands, resources, economic and fiscal arrangements, education, preservation and enhancement of language and culture, and equity of access.

Between these two positions—recognition of constitutionally protected self-governing peoples and the colonialist package from the federal and provincial governments—the differences were irreconcilable. The negotiations of the 1980s with the federal and provincial governments inevitably turned into a prolonged *danse macabre* toward a constitutional deadlock that would not be shaken until the Supreme Court intervened with the *Delgamuukw* decision a decade later.

By the end of the negotiations, both camps were infused with anger and bitterness. The government side began to show open contempt for our demands. The federal minister of justice and attorney general, Ray Hnatyshyn, finally rejected even the idea of "self-determination." He said that it was the same as demanding sovereign rights, and sovereignty applied only to Canada as a whole. End of discussion.

On our side, there was a kind of shock that the decolonization process that Section 35 was supposed to begin had been blocked by the Canadian political class. This sense of betrayal was only increased when, after the negotiations collapsed in 1987, the federal government simply dropped the file and moved on to the Quebec issue, leaving our people demobilized and our leadership demoralized.

For the federal and provincial governments, the failure of the negotiations was the intended outcome, the prerequisite for their colonial
business-as-usual approach. And in the Meech Lake accord later that
year, the federal government was careful to open the Constitution only
to Quebec's demands. Our leadership expressed their profound but initially ineffective dissatisfaction. By putting their eggs in the government's
negotiating basket, and distancing themselves from the grassroots and
international lobbying, they had left themselves without any recourse.

Finally, it was only the government's own unwieldy amending formula and a courageous Cree in the Manitoba legislature that put us at
least partly back in the game. The Meech Lake accord required the consent of all of the provincial legislatures. One by one the provinces—with a
greater or lesser degree of reluctance—fell into line, until only Manitoba
and Newfoundland were left. As the ratification date went down to the
wire, the unanimous consent of the Manitoba legislature was necessary
for the accord to pass within the deadline. For days on end, one lonely
voice—Elijah Harper, a northern Manitoba Cree and NDP member of
the legislature—sat clutching an eagle feather for strength. He with-
stood the pressure and impatience of the Mulroneyites, his own party,
and the opinion of most Canadians by refusing the necessary unanimous
consent for the accord. The clock ran out. Meech died in June 1990.

A month later, the Oka Crisis was sparked when a Sûreté du Québec
force attacked a group of Mohawk Warriors who were dug in behind a
barricade to defend a sacred burial place on disputed land on the Kane-
satake Reserve. One police officer died in the raid, and a tense seventy-
eight-day standoff, and Canada's Indian summer, began.

During the period of the drawn-out constitutional negotiations, I returned
to Neskonlith to raise my family and work in my own community. At a
personal level, a kind of exhaustion had set in. I was in my thirties, I had
been involved in the young radical wing of the movement, and now our
leadership was telling us, Okay, we'll talk to the government and take care
of things.

I think that a similar sense of exhaustion among activists across the
country allowed them to cede the terrain to those who believed they could
negotiate our way into freedom. I realize that as I tell this story, I have
been recounting some of the adventures of my earlier days. And it is easier,
as you get older, to romanticize these youthful battles. But it is important

to recall that we often lived without places of our own, sleeping with a blanket on the floor of someone's flat. With not enough to eat. Walking long distances in the cold because there was no money for bus fare. Often facing harassment from the police and in some cases facing arrest for our attempt to protect our land and our rights as members of Indian nations.

I know it is the same for the activists today. I have seen this willingness to sacrifice in my children and their friends and in many young people across the country, and I know what it is like. Their commitment is essential to our struggle. As we have found so many times, when the grassroots are demobilized, for whatever reason, our cause does not move forward. It falls back. I understand their commitment, but I also understand their exhaustion and frustration. In my time, I have felt all of these things. And for a period in the 1980s and into the early 1990s, I took my own sabbatical from our movement.

When Beverly and I returned to Neskonlith in the early 1980s, we did have a plan. Our idea was to try to move our community forward by restarting the community farming that we had engaged in during my parents' and grandparents' time. Over the previous twenty years, the farmlands had gone into disuse and been replaced with wild grasses. What was needed to make them profitable, everyone knew, was a sprinkler irrigation system that could nurse the crops through our long, dry, hot summers. Our band had first water rights at Neskonlith Lake in the hills above the village, but at the time, a neighbouring rancher was using that water. We weren't even exercising our option.

To launch the new community farming endeavour, I wrote up a detailed business plan and called a meeting of the Elders and Certificate of Possession holders. To my surprise, no one showed up. I was upset by this, so a few days later when I saw Clarence, one of the Elders, burning his garbage in a barrel outside his house, I went to see him. I told him about my business plan for the new irrigation system and said I was disappointed that no one came to the meeting.

"You Elders are always telling us to go and get educated, but when we do, you do not even listen to what we have to say." I told him I had put a lot of effort into the plan and I would really appreciate it if he would show up at the meeting.

"Okay," he said. "You call another meeting and I'll be there."

That week I met with all the other Elders and CP holders and told them that Clarence was going to come to the meeting. When I called

it, they all came. It was before computers, so my business plan spread-
sheets were done by a calculator and typed out and the main points were
covered on a flip chart. The Elders and CP holders, I was pleased to see,
listened intently. But when I finished my Neskonlith Irrigation System
presentation, they were silent.

I asked them if they were willing to support it. No one answered;
instead, they retreated into an Elders' scrum at the back of the hall. When
they came back, Susan August had been chosen their spokesperson. "We
cannot support this plan," she said.

I was stunned. I had been working on the plan for months, and I had
expected that I would be rewarded with, if not outright applause, at least
a measure of enthusiasm for what it could do for our community. "Why
not?" I asked.

They looked at each other. Then they went into another scrum
at the back of the room, more excited this time, speaking a rapid mix
of the Secwepemc language and English. When they returned to their
seats, Susan said, "Because you put so much work into this plan, we all
agreed that we should explain why. But first, we noticed that the amount
of money that you have put down for the revenues from irrigated land is
too low." She then listed how much per acre different crops would bring.

I explained that I put the revenues low to show that even if things went
badly, we could still pay for the irrigation system. Susan said, "Okay, we
just wanted to raise that with you, but that is not the reason we made our
decision not to support the plan.

"We know how much farmland Neskonlith can support," she continued, "because we worked the land with our parents and grandparents
when the reserve was under full cultivation. So we know how hard the
work is to farm this land. We would like to see it developed, but we do not
have confidence in our children to be able to do this work, and they will
lose the land if they get into this kind of arrangement."

I did not try to explain how this could be prevented by the lease
arrangement, because it was a basic confidence issue. They did not trust
our generation to put the work into the land. I was enormously disappointed. I had worked for months on this project, and I had planned to
work many months, even years, to get it up and running. But now, the rug
had been pulled out from under me.

After the meeting, I went back to my mother's old trailer across the
road, where Beverly and I and the kids were living at the time. I didn't know

what to do. The trailer was on a hill overlooking the Trans-Canada Highway, and I sat out front watching the stream of cars and trucks passing by on their way east to Chase and the Rockies or west to Kamloops and the coast.

I was struck by the obvious. Why not build a gas station and store on the reserve lands to bring in money from the traffic streaming through our territory on the Trans-Canada? It would at least provide a few jobs and bring some revenue into the community.

I went in and told Beverly about the idea, and I said that I would build it in three to five years. Despite the fact that we didn't have a cent in capital and I had zero experience in business. She was understandably sceptical.

I admit that part of the reason the gas station idea appealed to me was that I wouldn't have to ask anyone's permission to proceed. I was hurt by the rejection of the Elders. On a community level, it would allow me to create some jobs for young people, and on a personal level, it would give me a way to support my children in a way that my father, with his unrelenting commitment to the struggle, hadn't been able to.

It did, finally, take just over three years to build the gas station and convenience store. The first act was a symbolic burning of the old. The best place for the gas station was on the site of the decrepit old family DIA house that we called the "brown house." My father was quite ill by this point and living in a small house in Chase. The family house, like most of the old DIA houses in the community, was beyond repair. To clear the site for the gas station, we arranged for a team to burn it and bulldoze the remains. I called my father the evening before to let him know what we were doing. He came out the next morning to watch it burn but he stayed in his car. Bobby was with me. Neither of us felt any sentimental attachment to the house, but we were both reluctant to do the torching ourselves. One of the construction guys finally took the gas can and doused the house inside and out. A few minutes later, it was engulfed in flames.

It took only minutes to reduce our old home to ashes and a few charred beams. Then the bulldozers moved in to level the standing timbers and push them aside. Within hours it was as if the house had never existed. For me, the fire cleansed some of the unhappier memories of my youth. The next building that would stand on that spot would not be provided to "wards of the state" by Indian Affairs, but built by Secwepemc people for their own use.

I do not know what my father felt watching the old house burn from the car. He drove away when the bulldozers moved in. But it was not an easy period for him. He could barely walk by that time and his once crystal clear thinking was clouded. Evidence of this came most sharply when he became embroiled in a dispute with Bobby, who was still serving as band chief. It had something to do with band policy that was so insignificant that I cannot now recall the details.

My father, who was still revered by many, and who by this time had been three times nominated for the Nobel Peace Prize for his work with the National Indian Brotherhood and the World Council of Indigenous Peoples, was being intensely courted and, I believe, manipulated by the opposition. Finally they organized a takeover of the Neskonlith band office, and my father announced he was going to run against Bobby in the band election.

Looking back, it was obviously a confusion in his thoughts, but the whole family and community were affected by this turn of events. In my own mind, and I know for Bobby as well, it reminded us again of the harsh and deeply unpleasant side of politics. Building the gas station became more than a family project, it became a refuge.

My father won the election against my brother, but it was a contest he never should have entered. He would barely serve the two-year term before succumbing to his illness in 1989, the year after my mother died.

Today, despite my father's sad end, I see both my parents as heroic figures. They found strength from some hidden reservoir deep within to withstand and overcome the hardships and adversity that they faced, and went on to build full and rich lives that helped many in their community, in their nation and—in a very real sense in my father's case—the world.

Although I was far from the centre of the political battles, even in this period I was not completely cut off from the fringes. I still did the odd contract for the Union of B.C. Indian Chiefs; one of them was writing speeches for the president, Saul Terry. One in particular put me in touch with the national scene in the late 1980s. It was a speech condemning the Sechelt Agreement, a product of the newly elected Mulroney government, which had begun its own White Paper–style offensive.

The leaked report of Mulroney's policy was offensive to the point that even within the government it was nicknamed the Buffalo Jump for Indigenous peoples. It contained deep cuts in services and the shifting of costs to the provinces. At the same time, it proposed "negotiating municipal community self-government agreements with First Nations which would result in the First Nation government giving up their Constitutional status as a sovereign people and becoming a municipality subject to provincial or territorial laws."[25]

Only the Sechelt had been conned into signing an agreement under these terms. The legislation transferred fee simple title of Sechelt lands to the band and conferred municipal status on the community, placing it under provincial jurisdiction. This was chapter and verse of the White Paper policy of 1969, and many of us were deeply disturbed that the Sechelt leadership would accept it. The speech I wrote hammered the Sechelt municipal government approach, and Saul Terry—the Union president at the time—presented it to the Standing Committee on Aboriginal Affairs in Ottawa.

I gained a renewed respect for Saul when we met some of the Sechelt guys back at the Holiday Inn after the session, and one of them was so angry with our brief he threatened to beat the hell out of Saul. Saul didn't back down. And thankfully, since the guy towered above both of us, Saul didn't turn around and point me out as the speech writer. A small incident, but again a reminder of the passions of our politics.

For most of this period, I was consumed by the business project. It would provide me with an essential education on what the private sector was about, on its strengths and its limitations for Aboriginal people in the reserve setting.

In my family's case, we had jointly inherited both my mother's and father's Certificates of Possession to the land. With the help of a lawyer friend, Wayne Haimila, I set up the Ska-Hiish Holdings company and leased the CP land to it with a twenty-year lease at a dollar a year, basically leasing it to myself.

This was a more or less accepted practice for on-reserve development, but it still required approval from the Department of Indian Affairs. Like almost everything to do with the DIA, it was a demeaning process. My brothers, Bobby and Richard, and I drove down to the Department office in Vancouver to meet with the regional director and a group of a halfdozen officials to ask for DIA approval of our lease. It promised to be a difficult and likely drawn-out affair, except for the fact that my brother Bobby had long since lost patience with these things. As soon as we sat down, he looked the regional director in the eye and said, "I know you have the power to approve or disapprove this lease. Can you let us know right now if you are going to approve it or not?"

There was a moment of silence and sidelong glances, and probably a little disappointment that Bobby was depriving them of the sport of pushing Indians around a bit. The regional director finally answered that he would approve it if all three of us got a legal opinion stating that the Department wasn't responsible for the difference in the real value of the land and the dollar-a-year payment that the lease called for. We agreed and were out on the street minutes later. I mentioned to Bobby that I didn't have money for a lawyer to write up the opinion and Bobby said, "Forget that. We will all just write them saying we won't hold them responsible and that's that."

He was right. Our lease was accepted.

The next challenge was putting together a business plan for the gas station. Though I was nearly broke, I bought a Tandy computer and Lotus 1-2-3—something of a novelty in those days, but a tool I felt was a bit of an equalizer for someone who did not have formal business education. It was well worth the investment. The government business loan I was seeking required 20 per cent private equity, so I went to the bank, showed them my painstakingly assembled and professional-looking Lotus business plan, and asked for the loan. After a couple of their filing cabinets were filled up with plans and background information, both the government and bank loans were approved. From then on, the computer became an essential tool in our house, and I'm sure it contributed to my oldest son becoming a physicist and my youngest an electrical engineer. For Indigenous peoples, the computer has helped break the information monopoly of the dominant society.

With my wife and children and a business to keep me busy, I was enjoying the break from the frustrations of day-to-day politics. I thought at the time that this was it. I would simply do my part in the community. Perhaps I'd use some of my experience to do a few jobs for Indian organizations and raise my children, as all parents strive to, so that they would have pride in their heritage and the skills they would need to find their way in the world.

The gas station and store were opened in 1988. But there was an unexpected hurdle. Soon after we opened, the Progressive Conservative government in Ottawa brought in its goods and services tax, with a provision that the tax had to be prepaid on wholesale purchases. This played havoc with our cash flow, since the government demanded we pay the tax up front, though we sold a large percentage of our gas to on-reserve customers who were tax exempt. As a result, we were put in the untenable position of selling our gas for less than we were paying for it, with the government reimbursement coming only sixty days later.

We were living with an impossibly negative cash flow. It actually took us some time to identify this, and when I showed our financial position to friends and colleagues, the only thing they could think of was that I sell my truck. At the same time, the bank was getting increasingly impatient as we fell behind on our loan payments, to the point where we were beginning to receive threats to shut us down less than a year after opening. Clearly, I needed better business advice. And the most successful person I knew was Ron Derrickson in Westbank.

Already by the beginning of the 1990s, there was something legendary about Ron Derrickson. His success in business and as chief was well known. At the same time, he had also suffered more than his share of slings and arrows, which included—to the shock of all Interior peoples—an assassination attempt.

This had occurred in 1982, when as band chief he was embroiled in a bitter dispute with local white trailer park owners over his aggressive move into business on unused Westbank lands. They felt they were being pushed out of the market and responded by hiring a former police officer to beat him to death.

It was a hot August afternoon when Chief Derrickson heard the knock on his door. When he opened it, he was confronted by a man he'd never seen before who, instead of saying hello, pulled a sharpened crowbar out of his jacket and landed a crushing blow on the side of the chief's head. Half-blinded by the blood pouring out of the gash, Derrickson stumbled backwards. More blows landed on him as he raised his arm to try to defend himself. An artery on that wrist was slashed and it, too, gushed blood. He kept backing up with his arms raised trying to protect his head until he reached his gun cabinet. While blows rained down on him, he pulled out a revolver. The attacker froze, then turned and fled. Derrickson shot him in his front yard through the open window, hitting him in both shoulders. The attacker went down. Derrickson, a bleeding mess by this time, with slash wounds that would require almost 250 stitches to close, still managed to call the police before collapsing in his living room.

When the police came, both Derrickson and the attacker were rushed to the hospital. Both survived their ordeals, and it was soon revealed that

the attacker was not a robber acting independently but an ex–police officer hired by local businessmen who couldn't stand the idea that Westbank
First Nation, under Derrickson's leadership, had moved into direct com-
petition with them. The attacker and one of the businessmen were jailed
for attempted murder. With the escape from the assassination attempt,
Chief Derrickson became even more of a local legend.

But while he was still packing a semi-automatic pistol to deter further
attempts on his life, Chief Derrickson found himself under attack from
within. Just as the band's economic success had drawn the fury of the local
white businessmen, Derrickson's activism had brought the attention of
the Department of Indian Affairs. With the help of political opponents
within his own Westbank community, they began to spread rumours that
he was mixing his personal and business affairs. These rumours grew and,
after complaints were made to the government, an inquiry was launched.
The government undertook an extensive review, with forensic audits of
both his personal books and the band's books, and concluded there was
no substance to the charges. But by this time, for him, too, political life
had lost its lustre. When I drove down to meet him at his trailer office on
the reserve with Bobby and Wayne Haimila, he had been out of politics
for four years and was happy to have it behind him.

At this time, I didn't know Ron that well. His father and mine had been
friends, and Ron and Bobby had been chiefs at the same time and had
developed a friendship as well as a good working relationship. So, while
we didn't really have a personal history, we knew each other through family connections and by reputation.

Bobby and I arrived at his office with a copy of the business lease.
I told him about the bank's threats to close me down before I had time to
straighten the issues out with Revenue Canada. Our backs were against
the wall, I told him. Ron listened, nodded his understanding, then began
studying my lease. After a few minutes he said, "This is a very badly written lease! But I don't think you have anything to worry about. They are
just blowing smoke. They can't shut you down."

Just to be sure, he told me to take the lease to his lawyer, and he called
him up. "I'm sending three Indians over who have a lease I want you to
look at."

The lawyer read it and came to the same conclusion. The lease would
make any bank move against us very difficult indeed. We could forget
about the bank while we fought our battle with Revenue Canada over the

revenues they were withholding from our business cash flow for sixty-day periods.

With the threat of foreclosure lifted, we worked on getting Revenue Canada to reduce its withholding period to a manageable sixteen days. This allowed us to turn over our product and revenues twice a month, which was doable. My cash flow righted itself, and I was thankful that I didn't have to sell my truck. I was also thankful to Ron for helping me buy the time I needed to solve the problem.

His message, essentially, was: *Don't let them bully you.* It is a message that Indigenous businesspeople should have inscribed on the wall where they can see it when they open their eyes in the morning. It is a message that only a few of our people, and even fewer of our leaders, have taken to heart so far. But it is essential if we are going to begin the process of truly decolonizing ourselves.

The business began to run more or less smoothly. Beverly and I still worked long days, but the uphill struggle of the previous four years was over. I had reached the point when I could reduce my focus on the business. And when I looked around, I found a growing crisis in the only issue that could have brought me back to the political struggle: the land issue.

In October 1990, only a month after chaotic fistfights and mass arrests ended the Oka standoff in Quebec, a group of B.C. Indian leaders were in Ottawa for private meetings with the prime minister and apparently looking to pick the fruit of the summer's turmoil. Among the leading figures was Ed John, an Indian lawyer and briefly chief of the Tl'azt'en Nation band, who had been part of the failed constitutional negotiations throughout the 1980s. Ed John is a man of considerable talent—he even served as an appointed cabinet minister in the B.C. provincial government—and he and those who met with Prime Minister Mulroney in the fall of 1990 were determined to settle the B.C. land question at the negotiating table. The immediate result of that meeting was the creation of a tripartite B.C. Claims Task Force made up of First Nations and federal and provincial representatives, which within two years would morph into the B.C. Treaty Commission (BCTC) and the First Nations Summit (FNS) to oversee the negotiation process.

The terms of the negotiations, however, would not be under Section 35 of the Constitution, under which Aboriginal rights would be recognized and affirmed at the beginning of the negotiations. Instead, they would be carried out under the revised Comprehensive Claims policy, which the Mulroney government brought out in 1986. It stated that negotiations would take place under Section 91(24) of the BNA Act, where the federal government had sole jurisdiction over "Indians, and Lands reserved for the Indians."

This policy was not contained in some secret government negotiating strategy, it was explicitly given in the definition section of the negotiating guidelines. The Aboriginal lands under negotiation were defined as lands "held by, or on behalf of, an Aboriginal group under conditions where they would constitute 'lands reserved for the Indians' under section 91(24) of the *Constitution Act, 1867.*"

For us in the Interior and for many Indian nations across the country, it was an astounding retreat by these B.C. leaders. The First Nations Summit was agreeing to begin negotiations by surrendering their Aboriginal title and rights contained in Section 35 of the Constitution Act, 1982, before they even sat at the table. In fact, the government itself referred to this as the "surrender and grant back" policy, with First Nations first surrendering their Aboriginal title and rights while the government decides what to grant them back during the negotiations.

The stated goal of these skewed negotiations was clearly the old ceding and releasing of our rights, to be replaced by what amounted to, in the best case, slightly expanded reserves and the menu of municipal and non-profit organization powers that were defined in the policy.

The basic negotiating model has remained over the years, though there has been some monkeying with the terminology. Instead of speaking of "extinguishment," the government now speaks of "certainty" as the goal of its negotiations. This sleight of hand has fooled no one. Even from afar, it is obvious what has been going on. As the Department of Indian Affairs itself admitted, UN bodies saw that replacing "extinguishment" by "certainty" was meaningless:

> . . . the UN Human Rights Committee called on Canada to ensure that alternatives to extinguishment in modern treaties do not, in practice, extinguish Aboriginal rights. Similarly, the UN Committee on Economic, Social and Cultural Rights expressed concern that the new approaches "do not differ much from the extinguishment and surrender approach," and urged a re-examination of governmental policies and practices ensure they do not result in extinguishment.[26]

The government waited five years to reply to the UN:

Under the modified rights model, aboriginal rights are not released, but are modified into the rights articulated and defined in the treaty. Under the non-assertion model, Aboriginal rights are not released, and the Aboriginal group agrees to exercise only those rights articulated and defined in the treaty and to assert no other Aboriginal rights.[27]

Once you unscramble the bureaucratese, it is impossible to conclude other than that "certainty" means "extinguishment." If an Aboriginal group agrees "to exercise only those rights articulated and defined in the treaty and to assert no other Aboriginal rights," all of those "other" Aboriginal rights are effectively extinguished.

More than twenty years after it was set up, B.C.'s First Nations Summit, which is made up mainly of coastal bands, continues to promote these extinguishment negotiating tables. It is important to note that the Summit itself does not actually carry out these negotiations. The FNS is highly funded by the federal and provincial government as a kind of procurer and public relations cheerleader for the bands involved in the process.

These bands negotiate in secret, on their own, with the negotiations funded by government loans. The negotiations are expensive, requiring costly legal advice and professional negotiators with full-time staff. The bands must pay back this loan money when the negotiation is complete—either through a breakdown or a successful deal. Today, the amount the bands collectively owe on these loans has topped $500 million, with very few deals signed. In a bizarre twist, bands are now negotiating for settlements that might be less than they already owe in negotiation costs. As the international business magazine *The Economist* pointed out in 2012, many "Native leaders fear that the mounting loans will take a big bite out of, or even exceed, any final cash payment."[28] We will look more closely at the disastrous consequences of the B.C. Treaty Process in chapter 15.

As these land and treaty issues arose in the early 1990s, it was already clear that they touched the core of my people's interests and long-term survival. It was becoming increasingly difficult to turn away and tend to my own business, as others promoted our surrender at the negotiating table. But finally, it was the gentle Elder Mary Thomas knocking at my door with a purely local issue that pushed me back into the fray. Mary was for many years a kind of spiritual mother to the whole community. To get me to do what she wanted, she used that unique mix of sweetness and guilt that mothers of all nations have perfected.

She came to see me about a problem with a house for one of her children. She wanted me to run for chief, she said, so I could solve it. I told her that I really wasn't interested in running, that I was busy with my business.

That was all the opening she needed. "Ah, yes," she said. "You have an education and a business." The she paused, smiling sweetly. "You know, you have benefited from the community. Don't you think you need to pay back sometime?"

While I was still telling her that I did not want to run, she assured me that I would not even need to campaign. She had already been talking to some of the other Elders. She would talk to them all and she would take care of it ...

In fact, the idea of one of us running had already come up between me and Bobby. The B.C. Treaty Process had established roots among the coastal peoples and, to the north, Yukon Indians were already coming to agreement on land surrender deals. The pressure was growing on the B.C. Interior peoples to join in, and we both feared there would be a rush to the extinguishment of our Aboriginal title.

We would probably not have much influence on the coastal peoples, but the Interior peoples at least had to stand together against this threat. We needed to denounce the termination of our rights, and the chief would have entry to the rooms where the decisions were being made. Neither of us had much confidence in the current chief. I had suggested to Bobby that he run again, but he said he had taken some soundings and, after the painful divisions created by my father's coup, he didn't think he would be elected. But, he told me, "I think you would have support."

Mary was also convinced of this. A few days later, when I told Bobby that I had agreed to let Mary put my name forward and line up support among the Elders, we both knew what this meant. A few words would be spoken at the sewing circles, at the berry patches, in the kitchens where community suppers were prepared, and in small, dark living rooms where tea was served. And the local political wheels would start turning, whether the designated driver was behind the wheel or not.

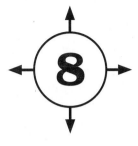

# A Chief's Concerns
## Finances, the People,
## and the Land

YOU QUICKLY LEARN that, despite the government's attempts to make it so, being chief is not at all like being a small-town mayor. As chief, you are expected to be present in the lives of band members from cradle to grave. This includes celebrations like graduations and weddings, and sad events like funerals. The chief is called when a band member is arrested and when a band member succumbs to despair and commits suicide. You are responsible for housing your people and for difficult issues involving child welfare, and for dealing with racial attacks on your children in white schools. And for so many other issues that it is impossible to list them—everything from protecting archaeological sites to hosting visitors.

As chief, you are part of all public functions and you find yourself, even with a salary of six hundred dollars a month, as was my case in Neskonlith, reaching into your pocket to pay for community parties, coffee for council meetings, and the gas you put in your car when you go to off-reserve meetings. But the hardest part of being chief is confronting the real destitution among community members. I was most shaken by those people who were asking for mercy from a really uncaring and unfeeling society. And there was nothing you could do. You can blame them for not doing enough to help themselves, but you know deep down that they are not going to get anywhere unless there is a major change in our society. Without outside help, they will never have the footing to climb out of the situation life has placed them in.

But when you arrive at the band office for your first day on the job, as I did in January 1995, it is the band finances that consume you. As soon as you are elected, you are sent into budget negotiations with Indian Affairs, and they leave you only the smallest room to manoeuvre. Your overall budget is already broken down into line items that the Department controls. And these items often have no relation to the real needs of your community. You are further hamstrung by the fact that you have to compensate for any overruns from the previous year.

This amount of control is not so different from in my father's time, when the Indian agent would come down from his Kamloops office and tell our chiefs to sign a sheaf of documents without even looking at them and take them back to Indian Affairs. My father would tell his chief to stop doing that. "You can't just sign away our decisions. You have to refuse."

This was the situation all over Canada. In fact, very few chiefs in those days could write in English if they even owned a typewriter. So the Indian agent simply took over. My father's first job was to get the chiefs, not the Indian agent, recognized as the leaders of the Indian bands. He wanted the chiefs to lead the way to self-government, though toward the end of his life, he realized that that might not happen.

Today it is often the band manager who plays the controlling role. The manager is in constant contact with the Department of Indian Affairs, and shoves reams of Indian Affairs papers in front of the elected chief for signing. The band manager becomes the de facto Indian agent working in our offices. Often they don't live in the community, and many of them are not even Indian. It was one of our Elders, Irene Billy, who made this link directly. Whenever she needed papers signed by the band manager or had an issue to discuss with him, she would say, "I have to go see Indian Affairs." The band manager, for her, was indistinguishable from the Indian agent of old.

I learned a lot about how the Elders saw the world from listening to Irene. When we went to Ottawa together once on a lobbying trip, I pointed out the giant Indian Affairs skyscraper across the river in Hull. She asked me what floor Indian Affairs was on, and I told her it was the whole building. She could not believe the Department was so enormous, and later admitted to me that she thought when I pointed to the building, it was where the whole government was housed. Knowing how little use they were in the world, she could not imagine that the Indian agents would have such a grand headquarters all to themselves.

When something goes wrong, of course, the Department and its political masters inevitably shake their heads and blame the chief and council for incompetence, or worse, hint ominously at "irregularities." In fact, bands face budgetary surveillance throughout the fiscal year and they are rigorously audited at year-end. Budget problems are invariably caused by the system itself, which forces First Nations to try to satisfy the basic human needs of their people with a budget that simply cannot cover them. There is a reason that while Canada as a whole was sitting in the first rank of world nations when I became chief, Indigenous peoples were living at the seventy-eighth rank—in Third World conditions. It had nothing to do with the administrative skills of chiefs and councils, and everything to do with the fact that our land has been confiscated. In return, we are given what amounts to starvation wages to care for our people. The parentage of our poverty is very clear.

Along with band finances, the chief's own agenda is also largely out of his or her own control. One issue came out of the blue that would later take on an overriding importance in my community—Sun Peaks. When I was elected, Manny Jules, then chief of the Kamloops band, and Nathan Matthew, head of the Shuswap Nation Tribal Council, were working on a protocol agreement with Nippon Cable, which was investing in the expansion of a ski resort on our Aboriginal title land. Along with the rest of the chiefs in the Tribal Council, I signed it without a great deal of thought. It was something I would soon come to regret.

In my initial weeks on the job, plans had to be constantly set aside for the unforeseen. Things like the ramping up of racial tensions between Indian and white teenagers at the local high school in Chase, which occurred while I was still engaged in the budget gymnastics. The council held an emergency debate on the race issue and a long discussion about what we could do. After talking it over for a while, we had to face the fact that nothing had changed since we went to school. We all went through this same kind of trouble when we were younger. I don't know why we initially reacted with surprise, when we knew nothing had changed in Chase over the previous thirty years.

Shuswap Nation Tribal Council, Kamloops, November 2000. Left to right: Chief Ron Ignace (Skeetchestn Indian Band), Chief Nathan Matthew (North Thompson Indian Band), Chief Manny Jules (Kamloops Indian Band), Chief Arthur Manuel (Neskonlith Indian Band), Chief Ronnie Jules (Adams Lake Indian Band), Chief Cherlyn Billy (Bonaparte Indian Band), Chief Rick LaBorde (Whispering Pines Indian Band)

The impoverishment of our people and the racism of the whites had not changed. Even though our people spent several million dollars every year in Chase buying their essentials, and the neighbouring peoples from the Adams Lake and other Shuswap bands spent millions more, there was not even work for us in the service industries in Chase. In the whole village, no Indian youth were given jobs in the shops. No Indian workers were employed in the local assembly plants. We were preparing to take this issue to the town in a co-ordinated way, when, in the late spring of 1995, we suddenly found ourselves facing a much more intense battle on Secwepemc territory, a shooting war.

It began in mid-June when a group of Secwepemc spiritualists and a few non-Indigenous supporters were beginning a Sundance ceremony on our Secwepemc territory near Gustafsen Lake, known as Ts'peten in our language, about three hundred kilometres north of Neskonlith on the Cariboo Highway. The sacred site was located on lands that were fenced by a local rancher, Lyle James, whose claim to the territory was questionable even by the white man's standards. This was Crown land, in fact part of our Aboriginal title land, and James had simply rented grazing rights from the province over a 900-hectare section for $1,300 a year.

The Sundancers were led by Percy Rosette, a Secwepemc faithkeeper. Several years earlier, he had had a vision of the sacredness of that site, and he notified the rancher that he would be holding summer ceremonies there.

This area also has a legendary status with our people. The story goes that Ts'peten was the place where the land commissioner in the nineteenth century had initially arrived with a box of money to purchase our territory. For days, the people politely put him off, saying they were looking for a sign from the Creator as to whether they had permission to sell the land. Finally, after days of waiting, the land commissioner became impatient and insisted the people make a decision. So they said, okay, they would see if the money came from the Creator. But first they had to purify it. They took the box of cash and emptied it onto the fire. The land commissioner watched in horror as the money was consumed by the flames. The Secwepemc then told him that the money obviously didn't come from the Creator, because it had burned in the fire; therefore, the land was not for sale.

This was where Percy was holding his Sundances. They were held at that spot every summer for four years without incident. But the fifth year, after the Sundancers erected a makeshift fence to keep the wandering cattle from trampling their site, the rancher showed up with a dozen ranch hands, several carrying rifles, and ordered the Sundancers to pull down the fence and vacate the land. An argument ensued, and the Sundancers said that one of the hands warned them during the shouting match that "it was a good day to string up some red niggers."

The ranchers returned later and stuck a homemade eviction notice on a ceremonial staff. They returned again when the Sundancers were away from the camp, ripped the door off the ceremonial hut, and walked off with the cooking stove. It was clear to the Sundancers that they were under threat, so they made a call to others to help them as the Defenders of Ts'peten.

The so-called Gustafsen Lake Standoff had begun. Over the next thirty-one days, the RCMP would amass four hundred Emergency Response Team officers complete with armoured personnel carriers. They would fire more than seven thousand rounds at the Defenders, blow up one of their pickups with a land mine, and engage in vile propaganda that even one of their PR officers later described as a "smear campaign." Over the next month, the Sundancers were variously described as being members of a cult, as common criminals, and, finally, as terrorists.

From Neskonlith, these charges seemed bizarre. We knew many of the people at the camp, and they were far from cultists or terrorists. They included, rather, Secwepemc sovereignists like the Elder William Jones Ignace, who was known as Wolverine during the standoff. A member of the Adams Lake Band, he was a long-time supporter of my father and someone I respected for his deep conviction of our people's sovereign rights to our land. He had not initially been with the Sundancers, but after the visit from the armed ranchers, he received a call from Percy Rosette, who told him about the threat. Wolverine headed up to Ts'peten that night and became one of the leading Defenders.

During the standoff, there were several shooting incidents and a few pitched gun battles. It seems a miracle that no one was killed and only a few on each side were lightly wounded. But the barrage of racist attacks in the press and from the police and government officials continued before and after the firefights.

It must also be noted that the Defenders' cause was not helped by the antics of their white lawyer, Bruce Clark; his mental stability was questioned by one judge, who accused him of "delusional paranoia" and charged him with criminal contempt. Clark was eventually disbarred by the law society of Ontario as being "unfit and ungovernable." But it turned out even his delusions were not entirely delusional. The RCMP superintendent in charge of the Gustafsen Lake Standoff, Len Olfert, was quoted by a number of sources within the RCMP as telling Sergeant Denis Ryan to "kill this Clark and smear the prick and everyone with him."

At one point, then national chief Ovide Mercredi travelled to the camp to try to defuse the situation. While he condemned violence from either side, he also dismissed the police and government's attempts to characterize the Sundancers as "terrorists." "These individuals are not terrorists," Mercredi said. "They are people with strong convictions . . . they are not criminals."

The standoff ended with a surrender of the camp on September 11, 1995, after visits from spiritual leaders. Almost all who remained in the camp were arrested and charged. William Ignace, who, as Wolverine, had been given a high media profile during the standoff, was given an eight-year sentence. From his prison cell in Surrey, British Columbia, he had no trouble explaining what the incident had been about. It was clearly and squarely about our right to our land:

> All we want is the respect that we deserve, because we made room in our nations for the non-Indigenous people. And yet where is the respect that we should have? Meanwhile it is the RCMP who is the goon squad for the province of British Columbia to carry on the theft of the resources here in our homeland.
>
> Everyday they are stealing billions of dollars from the Indian people and look where they put our people to where we can only collect welfare and people start squawking about this. But First People have to realize where the tax base starts from, it starts from the Indian land and all the resources. People say we're living off their backs but we're not—they are living off ours.[29]

As is so often the case, the truth of Canada's treatment of Indigenous peoples is more apparent from outside the country. When James Pitawanakwat, one of the Defenders, fled Canada for the United States, his extradition back to Canada was refused by an Oregon U.S. District Court judge, Janice Stewart. After hearing all of the evidence, she said: "The Gustafsen Lake incident involved an organized group of native people rising up in their homeland against an occupation by the government of Canada of their sacred and unceded tribal land." She added, "the Canadian government engaged in a smear and disinformation campaign to prevent the media from learning and publicizing the true extent and political nature of these events."[30]

That, unfortunately, was not news to us. We have been the target of a disinformation campaign since the moment the Europeans arrived on our shores and insisted first that there were no humans here and then, for a time, that the humans who were here were not in fact human. Again, with Gustafsen Lake, we were reminded about how little has changed. Today, James Pitawanakwat remains in the United States in political asylum from Canada. William Ignace recently put me in touch with him. James would like to come home, and I am looking for a legal route to safely bring him back.

One preoccupation of mine that was sidetracked in that tumultuous first year as chief was to counter the centuries of disinformation that began with the doctrine of discovery. Our people had to gain control of their own history. The opportunity to do this in an important way came when British Columbia made available funds for First Nations to do Traditional Use Studies (TUS) of their territories. It was a tool we could use not only to prove our Aboriginal title but also to draw up an Indigenous resource management plan. The goal of the research was not to put together a four-inch-thick book that would collect dust on a shelf, it was to create something we could also apply on the ground when we were exercising our Aboriginal title and rights.

Some of my community members were sceptical about this. "Why do we have to prove that we were here?" they asked. "We know we were here. It is the white guys who should be spending the money to do the research."

I told them that we had to face reality. The federal and provincial governments are in effective possession of our property and our assets. We have to show them in concrete terms that the land we inhabit is ours. And if we hope to manage it, we have to know how, exactly, we are using it today. So our study involved amassing the information from archival, oral tradition, and historical sources through to visiting all of the sites our people use today.

It was important to stress that "traditional use" of our territory did not end after Simon Fraser took his guided tour along what was then known as the Secwepemc River, or after British Columbia became a province in Canada, or after the American loggers arrived to build the Adams River Lumber Company mill in Chase. Traditional use covers a wide range of activities we do today—fishing, hunting, berry picking, and gathering edible and medicinal plants. Many of these activities are still essential for our people, particularly those who must rely on the $175 a month that is given out in Indian social assistance. We know that people cannot get enough day-to-day protein and vitamins on that monthly income; they survive by supplementing it with the traditional economy. So when we speak about traditional use activities, we are speaking not only about something that is ancient, but also about something that is essential today.

At the same time, we needed to look at our historical research to connect our activities with the past and provide ourselves with a detailed history of our Aboriginal title lands.

Gathering this information is not encouraged within the current land claims negotiating structure; in fact, it is actively discouraged. While the government spends millions of dollars a year doing research, for example through the Department of Fisheries and Oceans and the Ministry of Forests' Land Resource Management Plan, we are expected to deal with our land—our title—without any research whatsoever.

When it comes to the land claims process, the government says quite plainly, "You don't need to do research." This is especially the case with the B.C. Treaty Process. It does not even take notice of research, because it does not deal with the rights that flow from possession. If you put rights on the table, they will immediately get thrown off. To enter the negotiation process, all you need to do is take a piece of paper or a B.C. map, draw your territory on it, and have your band council write a letter of intention and mail it in to the B.C. Treaty Commission. *Presto*—you are in negotiation. The BCTC wants us to avoid research and especially to avoid providing a foundation for future resource management.

The government likes this amateurish approach to mapping our territories in another way. Today it is not uncommon for communities to make unresearched maps of their territory that greatly overlap neighbouring Indigenous territories. One of the government's arguments against recognizing title is that it would create economic chaos because of the overlapping claims. This is a challenge that requires serious thought by our peoples. We can at least agree that the land is ours and undertake joint research to address conflicts—something we know that the government has no interest in supporting.

In Neskonlith, we started an ambitious project on our own, but we quickly discovered that we needed outside technical help. A professional job would require professionals. Fortunately, I knew someone who could put together a study combining historical research with traditional use that could serve both as the basis of a resource management plan and as legal proof of occupation of our Aboriginal title lands. That person was Russell Diabo.

Russell is a Berkeley-educated Mohawk from Kahnawake whom I first met when I was living in Montreal. I had gotten to know him when he was a political adviser at the Assembly of First Nations. As with so many things, Russell was ahead of the curve when it came to Indigenous land use issues. When the United Nations released the report of the World Commission on Environment and Development, the so-called Brundtland Report, in 1987, Russell was working with the Algonquins of Barriere Lake in northwestern Quebec in their battle to stop the logging, mining, and hydroelectric developments on their Aboriginal title lands.

The Brundtland Report was the UN's first serious attempt to address the increasing damage to the world's natural environment with a broad focus on population, food security, the loss of species and genetic resources, energy, industry, and human settlements. It recognized that all of these elements were intimately connected in our ecosystem, and demanded that the world turn away from its unsustainable environmental practices. If fact, it was this report that defined *sustainable development* as "development that meets the needs of the present without compromising the ability of future generations to meet their own needs."

Among the Brundtland Report recommendations that caught Russell's eye was that Indigenous peoples should have a decisive voice in resource management decisions that affect them, and that their knowledge should be used in managing in complex ecosystems. He took the Brundtland sustainable development model and applied it to the Algonquin land use battle. Over the next several years, he used it as the basis of tripartite negotiations on co-management of Algonquin title lands with the federal and provincial governments.

Russell and his team managed to draft what he called an "ecosystem-based Integrated Resource Management Plan (IRMP)" with a commitment to the principles of sustainable development, conservation, protection of the traditional way of life of the Algonquins, as well as multiple other uses of the territory, from logging to sports hunting and fishing and other recreational uses. They began with Indigenous knowledge to map the hunting and fishing sites, food gathering sites, sacred sites, burial sites, and other culturally significant areas on the Algonquins' Aboriginal title lands, and then worked out a detailed plan to harmonize the forestry and other activities on the land with the needs of the Algonquins.

In the end, the forestry companies were given a map of areas where they had to leave swaths of varying sizes of the territory intact to protect important ecological and cultural sites. Often, it was only a small corridor that was needed, for example, to leave untouched sixty metres of forest on either side of a portage so the people could find their way when heading to their fishing or hunting camps. Or a similar sixty-metre protected area around bear habitat between November and May when the bear cubs were in the den.

These protections of the living forests called on the Algonquins to be employed as protectors of the land, working closely with the forestry companies and other land users to ensure that their activities did not damage the fragile ecosystem. The Algonquins developed quite a good relationship with the forestry companies based on mutual respect and the reasonable approach that was taken on all sides. The Province of Quebec was also a willing partner. Typically, it was the federal government that finally pulled out of the arrangement, for reasons that were never fully explained. But their withdrawal was consistent with the federal government's slash-and-burn approach to Aboriginal rights over the past fifty years.

In 1996 I called Russell, who was living in Ottawa at the time, and told him that I needed his help with our Traditional Use Study. "When do you need me there?" he asked. "As soon as you can make it," I said.

The next day, he and his wife packed their car and drove across the country. He worked with us for three years with a technical team that included Terry Tobias, a land use and occupancy research consultant, Peter Doug Elias, a university researcher, and David Carruthers, as well as several Neskonlith and Adams Lake band members. Russell and his team produced a study and a series of overlay geomaps that identified more than 7,400 significant sites on our territory and gave a detailed sense of how our people had traditionally organized their economic as well as their social lives. They brought together from all sources a textured portrait of our people and their life on the land from ancient times to the modern day.

The geomaps show more than a thousand cultural sites, 424 traditional camps and base camps, and more than two thousand large and small game hunting sites, fishing sites, trapping sites, and plant gathering sites that our people continue to use today. Together, the overlay maps show a living history of our nation and provide the information we need to successfully manage—in partnership with Canada—the sustainable development of our territory. All that is missing now is that partnership. But the Traditional Use Study remains key to our own plans to build—and more importantly, manage—a truly Indigenous economy with a full range of activities, but carried out in a way that does not do irreparable damage to ecosystems that have sustained us for thousands of years.

While Russell and his team were putting together the study, I was struggling to keep up with the day-to-day needs of my community, and with what turned out to be an expanding role in our nation. I was elected to head the Shuswap Nation Tribal Council, which brings together nine Secwepemc bands in an organization that tries to co-ordinate the political and economic positions of the Secwepemc people. This can be a difficult task. As head of the Tribal Council, you always have to know where your chiefs are on any issue. The government works to undermine your unity by trying to lure individual communities away from your consensus positions. Individual deals are sweetened with that seemingly endless supply of Canadian taxpayer money the Department has at its disposal when it wants to break Indian unity.

I also worked with other Interior chiefs to reconstitute an old organization of the Interior peoples. This Interior Alliance brought together forty-five bands from five Indigenous nations: the Southern Carrier, the St'at'imc, the Nlaka'pamux, the Secwepemc, and the Okanagan. It had its roots in the Allied Tribes organization that had been put together for the Laurier Memorial before the First World War and that Andrew Paull had kept alive in a semi-clandestine form during the dark years from 1927 to 1951. Then as now, it was meant to be a fighting organization. And our main concern as the 1990s came to a close was protecting our lands from the forces of extinguishment.

From the Interior, we watched with alarm as the First Nations Summit communities, made up mainly of coastal peoples, continued to negotiate their title and rights at the B.C. Treaty Process tables. This division between us and the coastal peoples remains one of the greatest blocks to First Nations moving forward in British Columbia. It began in the late 1970s when certain forces, some of them created and supported by the government, began to pull the Union of B.C. Indian Chiefs apart. In recent times, we are most seriously divided over land issues.

The Interior peoples, who have traditionally fought hard against any move to extinguish our rights, are concerned at some coastal peoples' apparent openness to signing what seem to us to be very bad deals with the government. But I recall once being brought up short in a public discussion by the Nuu-chah-nulth leader George Watts saying, "Manuel can speak from a high moral stance because he's got land."

I was reminded that the coastal peoples were not even given basic reserve lands, only tiny parcels pushed against the sea. The colonial authorities decided that instead of land, they could live off the sea. These seashore communities were backed with only a few dozen acres and, as in so much of our history, desperation drives us.

While the divisions on the land issue between the Interior peoples and the coastal peoples are significant, we should not forget that there is also much that should unite us. Many of us, in fact, belong to the same Salish family. Interior people like the Secwepemc share the basic Salish language with many of the coastal people, and at crucial times in our history, as during the time of the Andrew Paull, we have managed to successfully work together. This alliance continued through the friendship between my father and Philip Paul and through most of the 1970s. The hope on both sides is that we will find a way to work more closely together again, to the great benefit of all of our communities.

In the mid-1990s, however, our differences were underlined by our dramatically different positions on Aboriginal title. The emerging symbol at the time was the Nisga'a agreement, a land claim drafted under Mulroney's 1986 "surrender and grant back" policy.

In 1996, however, the broader movement was given hope of coming together by the publication of the Royal Commission on Aboriginal Peoples (RCAP) report, which called for fundamental change between the Crown and First Nations. Then, a year later, by a sweeping Supreme Court decision that had the same effect in moving the struggle forward for my generation as the *Calder* decision had had for my father's. In *Delgamuukw*, the Canadian courts reminded the executive branch once again that Indigenous peoples in Canada have far more rights than the government was prepared to admit.

# Upping the Ante
## RCAP and a Landmark Court Decision

I N ANY POLITICAL MOVEMENT, there are those who insist on their maximum demands and those who are willing to settle for less. To the frustration of the most dedicated activists, movements generally form a consensus around the weakest position. Given this dynamic, one way to advance a cause is to somehow raise the minimum. The publication of the Royal Commission on Aboriginal Peoples report helped our movement do just that. It provided an extensive, thoughtful look at where Aboriginal peoples were in Canada and a detailed historical analysis of how we had arrived at this point. It was then—and remains today—a document that virtually the whole Indigenous movement can rally around.

The Royal Commission was created in the wake of the Oka Crisis in 1990, with a broad mandate "to study the evolution of the relationship between Aboriginal peoples, the government of Canada and Canadian society as a whole."[31] The co-chairs were Georges Erasmus, a former national chief, and Justice René Dussault of the Quebec Appeals Court. In its extensive research, RCAP commissioned dozens of studies, travelled to close to a hundred communities, and held more than 175 days of public hearings. When the report was finally released, it contained 440 recommendations and provided the most detailed analysis of relations between

Indigenous peoples and Canadians that the country had ever seen.

In two areas in particular, RCAP went to the heart of our demands. First, it recognized the need for governments to disavow the doctrine of discovery. Second, it described the true source of the authority of our Indigenous governments.

The first of these, the repudiation of the doctrine of discovery, was among the Commission's first recommendations. The RCAP authors went on to demand that governments issue what would amount to a new Royal Proclamation recognizing our Aboriginal title and rights. In section 1.16, they urge federal, provincial, and territorial governments to begin the process of renewal by "acknowledging that concepts such as *terra nullius* and the doctrine of discovery are factually, legally and morally wrong." The governments should declare "that such concepts no longer form part of law making or policy development" and should commit "themselves to renewal of the federation through consensual means to overcome the historical legacy of these concepts, which are impediments to Aboriginal people assuming their rightful place in the Canadian federation."[32]

It is difficult to overestimate the importance of this move. As we have seen, the doctrine of discovery, a concept from another era, remains the legal justification for the colonial occupation of our lands and our nations. As long as Canada bases its existence on that doctrine, it is hard to characterize it as anything other than a racist state where one race has been given the right to subjugate and confiscate the lands of another. For government to repudiate this doctrine and issue a new one recognizing the reality of the lands we all occupy would benefit not only us, but also Canada. This step would allow Canada to become a moral country, facing its history and the current reality of the peoples within its borders, instead of hiding behind an internationally discredited racist doctrine.

On the second point, the true source of our governments' authority, the RCAP report set out an important consensus position on the inherent right of Indigenous peoples to govern ourselves. RCAP looked to international law and practices to clearly view our place within the Canadian political space. But equally important, it looked at the rights that flow directly to us from Section 35 of Canada's Constitution. In his "Address for the Launch of the Report of the Royal Commission on Aboriginal Peoples," co-chair René Dussault clearly stated: "The right of self-determination finds its foundation in emerging norms of international law and basic principles of public morality. By virtue of this right, Aboriginal peoples are entitled to negotiate freely the terms of their relationship with Canada and to establish governmental structures that they consider appropriate for their needs."

Among RCAP's recommendations are the following:

7. Aboriginal peoples possess the inherent right of self-government within Canada as a matter of Canadian constitutional law. . . . It stems from the original status of Aboriginal peoples as independent and sovereign nations in the territories they occupied, as this status was recognized and given effect in the numerous treaties, alliances and other relations maintained with the incoming French and British Crowns.

8. The inherent right of Aboriginal self-government is recognized and affirmed in section 35 of the Constitution Act, 1982, as an Aboriginal and treaty-protected right. The inherent right is thus entrenched in the Canadian constitution, providing a basis for Aboriginal governments to function as one of three distinct orders of government in Canada.[33]

In simply following the guidance of these two RCAP sections—on the doctrine of discovery and the inherent right to self-government—Canada could have embarked on a dramatic new era in its relations with our peoples, where Canada and Indigenous peoples look at one another not as colonial power versus wards of the state, but as peoples with historical ties and a shared space. We could then have embarked together on a search for a formula for coexistence that meets each other's needs. That was, and remains, the promise of the Royal Commission. We are still waiting for Canada to show up for these talks.

By the time the RCAP report was published, the Liberals were back in power and there was, unfortunately, little hope that they would follow through with the Commission's recommendations. A few years before that, there had been a glimmer of hope that the party was turning over a new leaf. In opposition in the late 1980s, the Liberals had indicated they were prepared to make a major shift in their Indigenous policy. In fact, the reform movement within the party was so strong that it attracted a number of key Indian strategists into an Aboriginal Commission to rewrite the party's Aboriginal program.

Among those lured into the Liberal tent were the Anishinabe lawyer David Nahwegahbow, the past president of the Native Women's Association, Marilyn Buffalo, and my friend Russell Diabo. All three of them, who are among the most principled fighters for Indigenous sovereignty I know, now consider this foray into the Liberal party a bit of an embarrassment. But I think they would agree to my using it as a kind of cautionary tale for those in our movement who might be considering entering party politics to make changes from the inside.

Working within the existing system is a gambit that our people have attempted a number of times with the same result. Either they become co-opted by the parties they are attempting to change, or they quit as soon as they become aware that real change within the political parties is a mirage. In this case, the foray ended with Nahwegahbow, Buffalo, and Diabo sitting with National Chief Ovide Mercredi in a press conference and literally burning the Liberal Aboriginal policy book that they had helped to write.

David Nahwegahbow has given an account of their experience in an article entitled "Chrétien's Legacy: Betrayal and Broken Promises."[34] I will summarize it here because it points out the pitfalls so well.

David first became involved with the Liberals in the late 1980s when the party was in opposition. It had no Aboriginal policy to speak of and no real structure for the organized involvement of Indigenous peoples. He was recruited as the new co-chair, along with Marilyn Buffalo, of a small Native caucus. In Calgary in 1990, at the convention at which Jean Chrétien was elected leader, Nahwegahbow and Buffalo brought forward amendments to the party's constitution to turn the Native caucus into a full-blown commission. The new Aboriginal Peoples Commission was given the job of drafting the Aboriginal component of the Liberal platform. Over the next year, Commission members researched, reviewed, and wrote the Aboriginal platform, which was released in October 1993 as a standalone document. David admits he appeared proudly on the stage with Chrétien when he released it.

The party promised to "engage the provinces in redressing the grievances of Aboriginal peoples over land and resource rights, including negotiating agreements for resource revenue sharing." In addition, once in government, the Liberals promised to "seek the advice of treaty First Nations on how to achieve a mutually acceptable process to interpret the treaties in contemporary terms, while still giving full recognition to their original spirit and intent." Of central importance, the party would at last respect our Section 35 rights in the Constitution.

But when the Liberals won the 1993 election with a massive majority, Prime Minister Chrétien named Ron Irwin, who had little connection with the Aboriginal Peoples Commission, as minister of Indian Affairs. Two years later, Irwin released the federal policy on self-government.

Though it purported to fulfill the Aboriginal platform commitments, the new policy was a riddled with doublespeak. While it recognized the existence of the "inherent right" in the abstract, it refused to recognize that Indigenous peoples actually possessed this right. As in the past, the policy required First Nations to negotiate with the federal government before the right of self-government would be recognized or exercised. Inherent right was not inherent at all but one of those Hegelian potentialities that had to first be surrendered before the government granted back jurisdiction in limited areas. There would be no acknowledgement of our Section 35 rights, no independent claims commission, no meaningful consultation on policy and financial decisions affecting us.

The Liberal Aboriginal program had been forgotten. Not forgotten in the sense that it was left on the corner of someone's desk to be picked up later. It was forgotten as if it had never existed. As if it had been sucked into a black hole where the only evidence of it was the puffs of white smoke from burning the Liberal platform book at Nahwegahbow, Buffalo, Diabo, and Mercredi's press conference denouncing the Liberal party for yet another betrayal of Indigenous peoples.

The lessons learned in this experiment in party politics were the same ones Martin Luther King Jr. wrote about in his famous 1963 "Letter from a Birmingham Jail," where he finally gave up hope of progress coming from what he called the "white moderate." King characterized white moderates as people who claim good intentions but who finally are "more devoted to 'order' than to justice; who prefer a negative peace which is the absence of tension to a positive peace which is the presence of justice." King concluded at the time that "shallow understanding from people of good will is more frustrating than absolute misunderstanding from people of ill will. Lukewarm acceptance is much more bewildering than outright rejection." He could have been talking about our Liberal party.

So it was not really a surprise a few years later when Chrétien tossed the RCAP report into the same black hole. RCAP, after all, called for fundamental change, and the Liberals were interested only in sleight of hand. In fact, after the Aboriginal Peoples Commission was dissolved, the Department of Indian Affairs put together a group known as the SWAT (Special Words and Tactics) team, whose task was to twist the language of Aboriginal title and inherent right to self-government into the delegated municipal authority that was being offered—essentially the opposite of these terms' accepted meanings—and try to sell to our people a wolf in sheep's clothing. That process is still very much alive today. The Liberal party has never been able to bring itself to keep its promises to Indigenous peoples, from shelving the White Paper to reconciling our rights flowing from Section 35 of the Constitution in Canadian law.

In 2005, a new leader, Paul Martin, made no change in fundamental policy. In his Kelowna accord, he promised only to lighten somewhat the load of our poverty with the injection of several billion dollars in additional program spending. But he refused to address the cause of our poverty, the fact that Indigenous peoples control only 0.2 per cent of their territories. For the first time, the government presented an initiative that purposely tried to separate its programs from our rights. This initiative, too, would fall by the wayside when, shortly after the signing of the accord, the Martin government was defeated by Stephen Harper's Conservatives.

While the Chrétien government in the mid-1990s could ignore his party's Aboriginal policy and all 440 of the Royal Commission on Aboriginal Peoples recommendations, it could not so easily ignore the judgment that came down from the Supreme Court in 1997, the *Delgamuukw* decision. This decision would reset the relationship between Indigenous peoples and the federal government to an even greater extent than the *Calder* decision in 1973, because it confirmed that our Section 35 rights in the Canadian Constitution involved real proprietary rights to our lands.

When the decision was released on December 11, 1997, I was at a meeting at the Little Shuswap band. A copy was faxed to us and, as soon as I finished going through it, I called my brother Bobby, Wayne Haimila, and my band council members and asked them to meet at my house at nine o'clock the next morning.

By the time they arrived, I had printed copies for each of them. I knew that this was important enough that we had to gain a firsthand understanding of it.

After everyone had read the decision once, we went through it together section by section, reading it aloud and discussing every point. Although it was clear that *Delgamuukw* was not the silver bullet that would slay the settler vampire, what struck all of us at that first reading was that our Section 35 rights—which had for the past fifteen years been ignored and obfuscated by a series of federal and provincial governments—were alive and well. Paragraph 109 of the decision clearly stated that the Crown's constitutional "Interest" is subject to the Indian constitutional "Interest" so long as the Indian "Interest" has not been sold to the Crown by a valid treaty.

The second thing that struck us was the issue of proof of title. Prior to the *Delgamuukw* decision, we were uncertain what Canadian courts would require as proof of our title. *Delgamuukw* gave weight to historical possession and, equally important, to our oral traditions in determining title. This was an important piece of the puzzle that fit with the Section 35 recognition and affirmation of our title and rights. This decision, fifteen years after the Constitution Act, 1982, recognized our Aboriginal rights and it provided a judicial recognition of those rights that the wretched negotiations with the federal and provincial governments had denied us.

The Interior Alliance had some resources to make a more thorough analysis of the decision on its own, thanks to the funding we had received from National Chief Phil Fontaine. The funding had come to us in a deal we had struck with Phil the previous summer, which in itself provides an example of the internal Indian politics that would soon play out over *Delgamuukw*.

That July I had driven down to Vancouver with Bobby to attend the Assembly of First Nations annual assembly. A series of political twists and turns had led to Bobby presenting himself as a kind of sacrificial lamb in the hotly contested election for national chief, which pitted Ovide Mercredi, Phil Fontaine, and Wendy Grant-John against each other. Ovide was the sentimental favourite of many in the Interior Alliance, but what concerned us was Wendy Grant-John, the former Musqueam chief and wife of Ed John, who was intimately tied to the First Nations Summit organization and its extinguishment process. Wendy had attracted our attention a few months before the July election when she announced that she had the support of 100 per cent of the B.C. bands in her bid to become national chief. To the Interior peoples, who had been fighting against the B.C. Treaty Process, this boast was not only obviously false but also troubling, since she was using it to leverage support in other parts of the country.

To make our point that Wendy's claim of blanket B.C. support was false, we decided to run a candidate whose only role would be to demonstrate that she did not have the support of the Interior bands. It speaks to my brother Bobby's conviction that he accepted to play that role, to run a campaign only to keep our Interior vote together and out of the hands of those who could use the AFN to put added pressure on us to surrender our rights.

When the chiefs assembled in Vancouver for the election, the first ballot gave Ovide Mercredi 127 votes and Phil Fontaine 126, with Wendy Grant-John only four votes behind the leader at 123. Bobby had succeeded in keeping the Interior people together, and his 35 first-ballot votes were suddenly of enormous interest to all three candidates.

Ovide, we felt, no longer had a chance. Though he was in the lead, we knew from the makeup of Phil's and Wendy's support that once one of them was eliminated from the race, the bulk of their support would go to the one still in. Even if Ovide had Bobby's 35 votes, the election would not fall his way; there was too much overlap in Phil's and Wendy's support.

It was then that I went to speak to Phil. I said that we would support him if he would support our fight for Aboriginal title in British Columbia. Knowing that Ovide had no real growth potential, leaving him in a neck-and-neck fight with Wendy, Phil agreed to our demand. Bobby and the Interior bands, as promised, threw their support behind him for the next ballot.

Phil kept his bargain. Within weeks of his election, he sent a contract to the Interior Alliance to set up an Aboriginal Title Committee. But we had not been alone in seeking Phil Fontaine's support. On the second ballot, Wendy saw her chances slipping away as Bobby moved to Phil's camp. She then also went to Phil to ask for support for the Summit and the B.C. Treaty Process. Phil took her offer; she dropped out of the race and threw her support behind him. So he finally won the leadership with the backing of both the opposing forces in British Columbia.

After the election, the First Nations Summit received additional support from the new national chief, and Wendy Grant-John took a job as the associate regional director-general of the Department of Indian Affairs. For our part, we put Phil's funding to work promoting our Section 35 Aboriginal title rights. When the *Delgamuukw* decision came down six months later, we were able to put our own resources into researching it.

Sadly for our family and for so many who knew him, the run against Wendy Grant-John turned out to be Bobby's last campaign. He would pass away the following year. He was someone who throughout his life inspired the love and affection of many and who provided all of us with an important symbol of courage and commitment, along with an enormous well of quiet good humour..At the same time, Bobby was not afraid to challenge those who he thought were selling our birthright to the colonial power. We miss his courage and his conviction. His death was a serious blow to our movement, to our family, and to me personally.

In the months immediately after the ruling, the *Delgamuukw* decision was studied throughout our regional and national Indian organizations. Typically, the federal government responded quickly by claiming that it was an empty box, just as it had tried to characterize Section 35 in the Constitution. In this case, the government completely ignored the decision and all of its implications for our Aboriginal title and their Comprehensive Claims policy. When pressed, they gave a smirky reply that if we weren't happy with what they were offering, we should go back to court, knowing that that was a decades-long process that could cost tens of millions of dollars, while they continued unfettered with their business-as-usual approach.

We did not immediately go back to court, but we did seek a wide range of legal opinions on what *Delgamuukw* meant. Our legal experts identified eleven important points that *Delgamuukw* addressed. These points have also been recognized by those outside of government in law journals and even by those who have long opposed recognition of Aboriginal title. For example, right-wing populist Gordon Gibson described the decision as "a breathtaking mistake" for the constitutional recognition that it affirmed for Aboriginal peoples. What troubled Gibson and gave us hope were the strong points of the Supreme Court decision, which asserted the following:

1. Aboriginal title is a land right or property right.
2. Aboriginal title is a collective right.
3. Where it exists, Aboriginal title gives rise to a fiduciary (trust) obligation on the part of the Crown.
4. Aboriginal title is a right to exclusive occupation.
5. Aboriginal title has an inseparable economic component.
6. Aboriginal title is a broad and encompassing right that is not limited to traditional activities, but includes an interest in all resources

and entitles its holder to a broad range of resource activities.

7. The only limitation on Aboriginal title is that it cannot be used in a manner inconsistent with the Aboriginal connection with the land (for example, you can't put a parking lot in a sacred area). If an Aboriginal title holder wishes to do something that destroys the connection with the land, then title must be extinguished by surrender. Contrary to the federal government's Comprehensive Claims policy, extinguishment or surrender is not a blanket requirement—it is only required in limited circumstances.

8. Prior to 1982, Aboriginal title could not be extinguished by the province. It could only be extinguished by the federal government, through legislation, and only if the government expressed a clear and plain intention to do so.

9. After the passage of the Constitution Act, 1982, neither the province nor Canada can extinguish Aboriginal title without First Nation consent, because of the constitutional protection in Section 35.

10. However, post-1982 Aboriginal title may be infringed by the Crown. In order to so infringe Aboriginal title, the Crown must do two things. First, it must establish that the infringement is pursuant to a valid legislative objective. Second, it must justify the infringement in light of its fiduciary obligation. Generally, the Aboriginal title holder should be involved in the decision-making process. The Court also said that compensation for the infringement will usually be required.

11. Aboriginal title, where it exists, will have to be reconciled with Crown title. The Supreme Court urged negotiations to achieve this reconciliation.

As I said, the *Delgamuukw* decision was not a panacea. Crown title was still clearly derived from the doctrine of discovery—still the only legal precept that the Crown has. And the Crown could still legislate on our lands after consulting us, although in many cases this also required our approval. But *Delgamuukw* did recognize all of the essentials of our title, that it is a collective right to the land with an economic component that could not be extinguished without our consent. And the Court went further, saying that Aboriginal title need not be extinguished and could be reconciled with Crown title through negotiations. It strongly urged the government to take this route in the spirit of "the honour and good faith of the Crown," a phrase that is repeated numerous times in the judgment.

The Interior Alliance's focus in the beginning was to bring the government to the table as the Supreme Court suggested to begin talks to reconcile Aboriginal and Crown title. Initially, we asked the government to recognize and affirm Aboriginal title as stated in the Constitution and affirmed by *Delgamuukw*. From there we believed we could move to new arrangements for jurisdiction over lands and resources, resource revenue sharing, and the type of co-management arrangements that would allow us to build environmentally sustainable Indigenous economies within the Canadian economic and political space.

We tried to strike while the iron was hot, before the government could erect a political blockade. Unfortunately, this didn't happen, and, worse, the material for the blockade was provided by one of our own. In the months after the decision, Satsan (Herb George), hereditary Wetísuwetíen chief and B.C. regional vice-chief of the Assembly of First Nations, went to the government requesting funding for a three-year study of the decision. Herb was, of course, welcomed with open arms and the government quickly allocated just under a million dollars a year to his regional office of the AFN. It was a real coup for the government. While a growing chorus of voices was demanding the government immediately bring its extinguishment claims policy in line with the reconciliation of Crown and Aboriginal title of the *Delgamuukw* decision, the government could deflect them by saying that it was waiting for the results of Herb George's three-year study. After his study was complete, Herb went on to a government appointment to head a newly created First Nations Governance Centre, but those fighting for the recognition of Aboriginal title and rights were left in the lurch.

Despite this setback, the Interior Alliance went ahead with our attempt to pressure the government to follow the path of "honour and good faith" that their own Supreme Court had laid out for them. We held a meeting on *Delgamuukw* in Kamloops in February 1999 to try to bring together all of the nations with unceded Aboriginal title territories. We sought a co-ordinated push to have the government replace the Comprehensive Claims policy with one that was consistent with the legal principles and negotiating framework set out in *Delgamuukw*.

At Kamloops, Herb and I came into open conflict about the significance of the *Delgamuukw* decision. Herb seemed to take the government line of downplaying it. I argued that this Supreme Court decision was the type of breakthrough that should at least give us the power to demand a new claims policy from the government that was in line with Section 35 of the Constitution, which the Court had cited in its decision. After all, I pointed out, the split decision of the Court in 1973 over *Calder* had in itself resulted in a land claims policy, where before there had been none. Our parents' generation had seized on that decision and demanded that the government respond to it. With *Delgamuukw*, it was imperative that we show the government once again that we had far more rights than they had thought.

By the time of the AFN's annual meeting in July 1999 it was clear that we would have to find a means to force the government to respect the Court's ruling with our own strategy for implementing *Delgamuukw*. At the meeting, the AFN set up the Delgamuukw Implementation Strategic Committee (DISC), with Phil Fontaine and me as co-chairs and David Nahwegahbow as legal counsel. DISC was mandated to "encourage First Nation people to exercise the rights flowing from their Aboriginal title and obtain benefits from their land and resources."

The Committee was also directed to try to engage the Government of Canada in a co-operative process of policy review through a panel of experts. Immediately after the assembly, we met with government officials to propose a joint review committee, where we would sit down to review the *Delgamuukw* decision together and explore ways to change the current Comprehensive Claims policy so that it was in compliance with the Supreme Court decision. The government officials said that this could only be done by a cabinet decision and they would get back to us with the answer. They never did.

In January 2000, DISC brought together leaders from across Canada in Vancouver to decide on our next move. In the face of the government's refusal to even discuss the *Delgamuukw* decision, we put together a six-point strategy designed to progressively pressure the federal government.

The first was simply public education, to make sure that key Canadian opinion makers understood the decision and its implication. While we were doing education, we would continue to try to work with the government on a process to make the necessary changes to the Comprehensive Claims policy. If this effort failed, we would begin working on unilateral approaches to an Aboriginal title policy that would be consistent with the standards and principles laid out by the Supreme Court. This could include direct action by exercising our rights on the ground. To give added pressure, we would begin to work internationally, with human rights institutions and non-governmental organizations (NGOs), to publicize Canada's intransigence on Aboriginal title.

We returned to the government in May with our plan, telling them we were now at step two, seeking co-operation from the government. By simply meeting with us to explore together ways to make the Comprehensive Claims policy comply with the Supreme Court ruling, we told them they could avoid us moving on to steps three to six, which involved the courts, direct action, and international lobbying. Representatives from Indian Affairs, the Privy Council Office, and the Department of Justice were present at that meeting. Federal officials once again repeated that there was no cabinet mandate to review the Comprehensive Claims policy. Greg Gauld, director general for Comprehensive and Major Claims, would only agree to take it back for consultations with his bosses. The government, it seemed, was still addicted to its policy of extinguishing Indigenous nations through its Comprehensive Claims negotiations.

It is important to mention that these developments did not occur in a vacuum. While the government was refusing to deal with us on reforming the Comprehensive Claims policy, it was pushing ahead with the Nisga'a agreement, which had been negotiated under the old policy, and trumpeting it as the template for all future land claims.

The Nisga'a Treaty was negotiated throughout the 1990s, with the parties reaching an agreement in principle in 1996. It still hadn't been ratified in 1997 when the *Delgamuukw* decision was delivered, and the government's idea of bringing the agreement into compliance with the Supreme Court ruling was to send in the SWAT team. The Special Words and Tactics unit went into the agreement, pulling out references to "ceding, releasing and surrendering rights" and replacing them with "converting, modifying and transforming." "Extinguishment" was replaced by "certainty." The results would be exactly the same. Aboriginal title and rights would be surrendered, with a tiny percentage of territory and a small package of rights granted back. *Certainty* was therefore achieved for the government; *extinguishment* was still the result for us. There was no attempt to reconcile Crown and Aboriginal title and definitely no sign of "the honour and good faith of the Crown" that the Supreme Court had called for.

The Nisga'a leadership signed the Final Agreement in 1998 and the B.C. legislature gave its assent on April 23, 1999. To our dismay, the

Nisga'a Treaty was then promoted as a breakthrough by the First Nations Summit and the B.C. Treaty Process. At the time, it was predicted that it would be the first of dozens to come. In fact, only a handful have been signed. The resistance most often comes from below, as the people refuse to surrender their birthright for quick cash and a tiny fraction of their traditional lands.

The Interior Alliance denounced the Nisga'a agreement and everything it stood for. In the summer of 1998, we argued that the Nisga'a model completely undermined the legal principles and framework for reconciliation of Aboriginal title with Crown title that the Supreme Court had set out in *Delgamuukw*.

By 1999, the rest of the world was also beginning to notice that something was very wrong in Canada. That April, just as the B.C. legislature was giving its assent to the Nisga'a Final Agreement, the UN Human Rights Committee released a report on Canada that chided the country for not following the Royal Commission on Aboriginal Peoples' recommendations and sharply criticized the government's extinguishment policy as a fundamental human rights transgression:

> . . . the Committee is particularly concerned that the State party [Canada] has not yet implemented the recommendations of the Royal Commission on Aboriginal Peoples. With reference to the conclusion by RCAP that without a greater share of lands and resources, institutions of aboriginal self-government will fail, the Committee emphasizes that the right to self-determination, requires . . . that all peoples must be able to freely dispose of their natural wealth and resources and that they may not be deprived of their own means of subsistence.[35]

The Human Rights Committee then demanded that "the practice of extinguishing inherent aboriginal rights be abandoned as incompatible with Article 1 of the Covenant." This was a hugely important assertion by the human rights body. Article 1 of the International Covenant on Civil and Political Rights, which Canada ratified in 1976, states:

> 1. All peoples have the right of self-determination. By virtue of that right they freely determine their political status and freely pursue their economic, social and cultural development.

2. All peoples may, for their own ends, freely dispose of their natural wealth and resources without prejudice to any obligations arising out of international economic co-operation, based upon the principle of mutual benefit, and international law. In no case may a people be deprived of its own means of subsistence.

3. The States Parties to the present Covenant, including those having responsibility for the administration of Non-Self-Governing and Trust Territories, shall promote in the realization of the right of self-determination, and shall respect that right, in conformity with the provisions of the Charter of the United Nations.

The Human Rights Committee was pointing out that the extinguishment of our right to the land was incompatible with our human rights as peoples. These rights are protected by the international covenant, which Canada is legally bound to uphold.

In August 1999, I found myself heading to Europe to attend a meeting of the UN Working Group on Indigenous Populations, an organization that had been launched in 1982 in answer to the demands by Indigenous peoples to have their issues addressed. I was there to speak on our fight against Canada's extinguishment policy and other issues arising from the *Delgamuukw* decision, and to respond to distortions of the Indigenous reality that Canada offers in international meetings.

True to form, the Canadian spokesperson spun a wonderful tale of partnership between the federal and provincial governments and Indigenous peoples. He spoke of the new federal programs called Gathering Strength and the Healing Fund as part of their Agenda for Action. And he spoke of the Nisga'a Treaty as the highest form of expression of this new partnership.

As the next speaker, I was able to present a far different picture of Canada's relationship with Indigenous peoples. I spoke of the poverty and the racism that was at the core of much of the treatment of Indigenous peoples in Canada and, more specifically, of the government's refusal to accept its own Supreme Court's judgment recognizing our Aboriginal title and rights on our territories. I also spoke of the Nisga'a Treaty, how it was an extinguishment of Aboriginal title and an affront to international law and norms. When I finished, I was pleased to see that my intervention was well received by all but the Canadian delegation.

The world was indeed ready to listen to us. But it was up to us to put our rights into play on the ground.

How to accomplish that? The spark and the example had come in the early summer of 1999 from Grand Chief Ron Derrickson in Westbank. After more than a decade away from Indian politics, Ron had successfully run for chief the previous year. I had been glad to see him back because I knew he had the economic smarts that most of us lacked. But I didn't expect that he would lead us into battle in the forest.

That news came out of the blue. In July 1999, I was sitting in the band office talking with my adviser, Wayne Haimila, when I received a call. It had been in the news that Westbank was going out logging on its off-Indian-reserve territory. This was not so noteworthy in itself; what made it special was that their permit did not come from the provincial government but from the Okanagan tribal council. Chief Derrickson was logging Indigenous logs with an Indigenous permit.

Both Wayne and I expressed surprise not only at this bold tactic but also at its instigator. Up until then, I had known Ron Derrickson as a shrewd businessman and economic development chief who had proved, with his skill at reading people and his powerful determination, that it is possible to overcome the obstacles the Department of Indian Affairs has put into place to ensure our impoverishment.

He was also known as tough negotiator, the type of chief who, when he had a difficult negotiation with the province, would insist that the meeting take place at a Vancouver hotel at 5:30 on a Friday afternoon and continue until an agreement was reached. This tactic was another Ron Derrickson legend in Indian country. His staff said that in these meetings, Ron would have them arrive early to rest up all day and then push the harried bureaucrats, who had worked the day in Victoria and arrived already tired on the afternoon ferry, until two or three in the morning. At that point, they would be so exhausted they'd agree to anything.

But these were still tactical manoeuvres. His logging initiative was a bold assertion of Aboriginal title and rights, exactly the type of action that we would have to take if we were going to force the government to take our rights seriously.

I called Chief Derrickson and told him that the Interior Alliance would support him and his initiative in any way that it could. He welcomed our support, and we organized an Interior Alliance meeting with him to co-ordinate our efforts.

Within the Interior Alliance, we realized that Chief Derrickson was the perfect person to take the lead on this. He had that legendary quality from his past successes that would make the government hesitate to try to slap him down, like they did so many other chiefs. Ron Derrickson was a man that the government and the businesspeople in the region knew you could not take lightly or intimidate with a show of chest-beating. He had survived an assassination attempt and character assassination attempts. Now he appeared willing to take on the government on the issue of Aboriginal title and rights. We were more than ready to follow him into the forest.

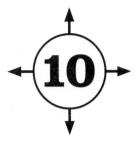

# The Battle in the Forest
## The Trade in Indian Trees

I N 1995, the year that I was elected chief, I had gone to the B.C.
Ministry of Forests office to complain that our people were not
being granted licences to harvest the forests immediately adjacent
to our reserve. I pointed out that some of the licences were coming
up for renewal and Secwepemc people should have a chance to acquire
them. It seemed like a modest request, but the forestry official replied
with a telling nonchalance.

"Sorry, Chief. You're too late. All of the forests have been given out."

This meant that Indigenous peoples, despite having Aboriginal title
to the land and bearing the brunt of logging's impact on hunting and fishing, were relegated for all time to being employees to the non-Indigenous
forestry companies—while facing real racial barriers to acquiring those
jobs. When we go to court over specific logging or other developments,
it is often suggested that we can pick berries or engage in our traditional
economies elsewhere. But in reality, all our lands are allocated to commercial industrial activities. We are left with the unwanted impacts and
none of the benefits.

The lumber industry was, in fact, a big contributor to our poverty.
In British Columbia, it is one of the most profitable industries, yielding
billions of dollars of revenue each year to the national and multinational
corporations to whom the provincial government has given control over
our forests. It was the lumber industry that brought the first significant

wave of settlement to Secwepemc territory when American loggers founded the Adams River Lumber Company in 1907 and built a mill near the town of Chase. To feed the mill, which in its second year of operation was already cutting 175,000 board feet in a ten-hour shift and 30 million board feet over the year, the company engaged in the most rapacious form of clear-cutting. Our people watched as our ancient forests, including now extremely rare interior rainforests, were devastated.

The loggers slashed through the white pine, western larch, and Douglas fir at the bottom level and worked their way up through the western red cedar and western hemlock to the Engelmann spruce and lodgepole pine at the higher elevations. They scarred the land, changed the course of our streams and rivers, and, in many cases, choked off the salmon runs with their sluices and booms. Locally, the Adams River salmon run, the world's largest remaining run of sockeye salmon, is still under serious threat by mining and forestry, while our Elders remind us that all our rivers once had large salmon runs that sustained our peoples and our economies.

I left that meeting with the forestry official with a growing frustration and sense of powerlessness. For a hundred years, we had been left with no say in how our land was sold off and defaced, while we were excluded from even cutting enough wood to build our houses.

Now, Grand Chief Derrickson's Indigenous logging licence gave us, at long last, hope that things could change. After the five-hour Interior Alliance meeting with him, we decided we should raise the stakes by not only supporting his logging operation but also demanding that all forestry companies acquire Indigenous permits to log on our Aboriginal title lands. If they refused, we would threaten an international boycott. We also demanded far more ecologically sound logging practices. We were not talking about simply changing government licences for Indigenous logging licences, but about changing the way the forests were managed.

When the Westbank logging operation, and a second operation launched by the Okanagan band, received stop work orders, Grand Chief Derrickson took the fight to the media. He received an enormous amount of attention for the cause when he announced that, unless the provincial government backed off and freed up licences for every B.C. band, an international boycott of B.C. forestry products would be launched.

That statement led to an emergency meeting with the provincial forestry minister, David Zirnhelt. The minister's message to Derrickson, though, was that the bands were free to bid at the forestry auctions. The only other avenue to a resource-sharing deal, he said, was to enter the B.C. Treaty Commission process. In response, Chief Derrickson walked out of the meeting. As he told the press waiting outside the door, "All that he offered was for us to pay for the trees we already own."

Within weeks, we in Neskonlith and two other Secwepemc bands, Adams Lake and Splatsin, joined the Westbank and Okanagan loggers with our own operations. Like Chief Derrickson had done, we first went to our tribal council to get an Indigenous permit. We were not wildcatting, but embarking on a legal operation based on our constitutional and Supreme Court–recognized Aboriginal title. We announced what we intended to do ahead of time and explained that the profits from the sale of the wood would go to building badly needed housing on our reserves.

We selected the Harper Lake logging site, in the hills a few kilometres from our reserve, by following the small business auction notices. When we saw the Harper Lake logging site come up for auction, we moved in to ribbon it off before the auction could take place.

Harper Lake had been identified by the B.C. Forests Ministry as a bark beetle logging site that was to be clear-cut to protect the surrounding forest. We hired a professional forester from the Adams Lake band, David Nordquist, to supervise the operation. It was, for us, a historic moment. We began with a drumming ceremony and a community gathering on the site. In a clearing in the spruce and lodgepole pine forest, I spoke about what this operation meant for our Aboriginal title and how we were exercising our rights to our land that had been given to us by our Creator and recognized by the Supreme Court of Canada in the *Delgamuukw* decision.

"Some will call us radical," I said. "But we are not radical. We are standing behind one of the most conservative institutions in the country and that is the Supreme Court of Canada. If anybody is radical, it's the premier of the province of B.C., because he's trying not to implement the decision of the Supreme Court. If anybody is being radical, it's the prime minister of this country, because he's not willing to go along with what the highest court in the country says. Because radical just means that you're trying to go against what is the accepted norm, and the Supreme Court of Canada in *Delgamuukw* recognized that Aboriginal title is a proprietary interest. So those of us who are standing behind the Supreme Court in that decision are really just trying to implement the law, and it's the executive branch—the prime minister and the premier—who are the radicals."

Our position gained credibility when the province took out a stop work order against us and then quickly tried to withdraw the order as soon as we raised the defence of Aboriginal title. To keep the province from withdrawing its order, we had to fight on procedural grounds—that once you initiate an action you have to continue to the finish. We believed that this was a case we could win.

After our loggers cut eighty truckloads of the damaged trees, we faced the problem of getting them out of the bush. No one would haul them out because we didn't have a timber mark, which serves the same purpose as a cattle brand in identifying ownership. The province, taking a different tack, advertised the trees that we had knocked down for sale. So we went to court and won a ruling that allowed us to sell the trees ourselves to pay the loggers and the transport to a sawmill and, while the case went to court, put the remaining profits in a trust account with our lawyers.

It was clear to us that our fight against the stop work order would go all the way to the Supreme Court of Canada, because the issues were fundamental ones arising from our Section 35 Aboriginal title and rights and affirmed in *Delgamuukw*. In fact, we had to go all the way to the Supreme Court just to get the province to fund our case. We convinced the Court that this was a case of national importance and, since it was the province of British Columbia that had initiated the legal action against us, it should have to pay our legal fees up front. On December 12, 2003, the Supreme Court of Canada agreed. Our case, which named the chiefs who had been involved—me, Chief Ronnie Jules, Chief Stuart Lee, and Chief Dan Wilson, all of whom had been charged personally and as representatives of our bands—has set the precedent for cost awards in Canada.

The province then tried to create an internal fight between the Okanagan and Shuswap, based on the argument that it can handle only one Aboriginal title case at a time. But it turned out that we would be third, not second, in line when the courts put both us and the Okanagans behind the earlier Tsilhqot'in case that had set out on its journey to the Supreme Court a decade before ours. (The decision on that case, which came down in the summer of 2014, would have important implications for Aboriginal title; we will look at those in more depth in chapter 17.)

The province continues to drag its heels on our case. Ten years ago, it appointed Justice Sigurdson to supervise the case at the B.C. Supreme Court, but it still has not even gone to trial. Our lawyers continue to try to push the case forward, and the money from the Harper Lake operation still sits in a trust account, while the province, knowing that it is on extremely shaky legal ground, keeps bringing motions to limit and stall the case. This is a very telling example of justice, once again, delayed and denied to Indigenous peoples.

This case has also underlined the hypocrisy of the government's taunt that if we are not happy with its policies, we should go back to court. When we do, the government does everything legally possible to keep our cases from actually being heard.

We, however, were determined to be heard. I had already visited Geneva that summer. Over the next three years, the Harper Lake operation would lead us, through a circuitous route, to Washington, New York, and back to Geneva as we successfully fought for recognition of our title on the world stage. This sojourn began with a full-page ad on the logging dispute that the Interior Alliance took out in the *Vancouver Sun*.

The ad informed the public and investors that we were exercising our Aboriginal title and rights in our logging actions, and that henceforth we would demand that forestry companies seek Indigenous logging permits before logging on our territories. We also gave notice that we would allow only ecologically sustainable logging. If the companies refused to comply, we would launch an international boycott of B.C. forestry products.

Not surprisingly, the ad greatly angered the forestry industry. Their spokesperson described the potential economic impact of a boycott as devastating. He also said that it was unfair; the logging industry would be collateral damage in our real dispute over provincial and federal government policies. But nothing could be further from the truth. It is the corporations that benefit from the non-recognition and non-implementation of our Aboriginal title and rights, as they do not have to pay the Indigenous owners of the land and resources. The forestry minister predictably reacted to the ad by portraying us as job killers and gave notice again that our logging operations would not be tolerated.

On the other hand, the ad won us the support of many of B.C. environmentalists who had long protested the unsustainable practices of large commercial industrial logging operations. More importantly in the immediate term, it attracted the attention of the Natural Resources Defense Council (NRDC), the largest environmental NGO in the United States. The NRDC describes itself as an "environmental action group, combining the grassroots power of 1.3 million members and online activists with the courtroom clout and expertise of more than 350 lawyers, scientists and other professionals."

Our NRDC contact was Matthew Price, who was originally from British Columbia and was well aware of the politics here. Through him, I was invited to Washington to meet with the head office staff; I also had an invitation from the Rockefeller Foundation to meet in New York. These contacts were a bit of a godsend, because while Chief Derrickson and I were repeating to the B.C. media that we were going to launch an international boycott, we really had no useful contacts to follow through on the threat. And these meetings would lead us into the Canada–U.S. Softwood Lumber Dispute.

Softwood lumber is one of Canada's largest export products to the United States: the fir, pine, cedar, and spruce harvested from our forests are made into lumber and exported to the United States, where the wood is used mainly in the home construction industry. There is hardly any value added in Canada; often, even raw logs are shipped to the United States, meaning the integrated wood processing corporations profit from taking the timber from our territories. Indigenous peoples do not benefit at all, and Canadians benefit very little.

This longstanding Canada–U.S. trade dispute was flaring up at the end of the 1990s. Canada sold around $10 billion worth of softwood lumber to the United States each year. Because in Canada forestry companies paid only a tiny amount in stumpage fees, the United States accused Canada of unfair competition and subsidizing the forest industry. According to the U.S. Department of Commerce, Canada was collecting stumpage far under fair market value, making it impossible for the U.S. industry to compete with imported Canadian softwood.

In British Columbia, much of the forestry is allocated through large, long-term renewable tenures, such as tree farm licences, to large corporations that both cut the trees and mill the lumber. Much less volume is available to smaller companies, and the best Indigenous peoples can hope for are the very few short-term, non-renewable licences. To further stack the deck, the corporations themselves are now responsible for grading the lumber, which determines the stumpage fees. Hence, minimal stumpage fees of 25 cents a cubic metre abound in the B.C. Interior.

Canada refused to change the system or to review its stumpage fees. The Americans threatened to impose a countervailing duty. The Canadian industry was thrown into a panic and took the last refuge of the scoundrel: beating the patriotic drum. They began to insist that it was a matter of Canadian sovereignty and pride to fight the U.S. duty with all of the force they could muster.

While the battle was going on, I began to focus on the fact that Canadian companies were paying ridiculously low stumpage fees on land that neither they, nor the Crown that was licensing them, fully owned. One fundamental cost that was not included in the stumpage calculation was compensation to Indigenous peoples for the extraction of the timber from Aboriginal title lands.

This angle was part of a new assessment of where we as Indigenous peoples and our Aboriginal title lands fit into the larger economic picture. The *Delgamuukw* decision had acknowledged our title as a proprietary interest that pre-existed and co-existed with Crown title. In addition we had an Aboriginal right to cut trees on our territory to build houses in our communities. Further, our proprietary interest meant that we had a share of the ownership of all the trees in our territory that multinational forestry companies were cutting in gigantic swaths.

With this idea still forming, I led a group of Interior chiefs to Washington to meet with the NRDC in a delegation that included Chief Ronnie Jules from Adams Lake, Chief Garry John from Seton Lake, Chief Dan Wilson from the Okanagan Indian band, and Councillor Chad Paul from Chief Derrickson's Westbank band. Headed by Robert Kennedy Jr., the NRDC had been involved in Canada with the James Bay Cree and the Nuu-chah-nulth on Vancouver Island, who had fought logging on Meares Island in the 1980s. When we met with Liz Barratt-Brown, their senior adviser who had already worked with partners on acid rain issues, the NRDC was already looking at the environmental effects of the cross-border softwood lumber industry.

I had come to sound them out about the idea of an international boycott of B.C. forestry products. While I was explaining our position, I pointed out that, in fact, Indigenous peoples were subsidizing the Canadian softwood industry. Lumber companies were cutting trees on our Aboriginal title land, but they were not paying us anything for them.

The NRDC lawyers at the meeting actually laughed at the idea. But after I returned to Canada, I sent them our file on the industry and the *Delgamuukw* decision on Aboriginal title. A few days later, Matt Price called me. The NRDC wasn't sure what, exactly, they could do with this subsidy argument, but now that they had taken a look at the facts they were very interested in pursuing it with us. During the call, we decided it could be brought before the U.S. Department of Commerce, which had launched a countervailing duty investigation into Canadian subsidies to the lumber industry.

But Price cautioned that it would be a challenge to get it there, because the rules required that the complaint be put forward by an American stakeholder. Usually, this meant an individual or business directly affected by the subsidies. So the NRDC sent their lawyers to work. The solution they found came down to their 1.3 million members. The NRDC went to the Department of Commerce and said that they wanted to make an intervention on behalf of their million-plus members, who were consumers of softwood lumber industry products. The NRDC put forward our submission to the U.S. Department of Commerce. We argued that the Canadian government was providing a subsidy to the forest industry because it did not recognize and implement Aboriginal title and hence did not pay the Indigenous owners of the resource.

This work was international in nature. It was new territory for Indigenous peoples, who had focused on UN human rights bodies, but had never before made arguments under international trade law. Our submissions, which were later also accepted by international trade tribunals, made it clear that Indigenous peoples have their own Indigenous economies, and that their rights have a clear economic dimension that has to be taken into account in the context of the local and Canadian economy, as well as internationally.

Indigenous peoples across Canada quickly took notice. The Interior Alliance nations were joined by the Grand Council of Treaty 3 and the Nishnawbe Aski Nation, whose treaty territories covered more than two-thirds of the province of Ontario. They agreed that the failure to remunerate Indigenous peoples—and in their case, to implement treaty rights—constituted a violation of Indigenous and economic rights.

To reflect this expanded common Indigenous front, we needed a new organization with a larger scope than the Interior Alliance. This new organization, which we called the Indigenous Network on Economies and Trade (INET), would represent international economic efforts and international trade law arguments. Expertise in this area would be provided by our new international legal adviser, Nicole Schabus, an Austrian lawyer specializing in international law who had a particular interest in

Indigenous peoples. INET's initial mandate was to present briefs to tribunals of the North American Free Trade Agreement (NAFTA) and the World Trade Organization (WTO).

Nicole would be central to these efforts. I had met her in Geneva at the UN Working Group on Indigenous Populations in the summer of 1999. Afterward, I went to an Indigenous peoples' solidarity meeting that had been arranged in Vienna, where Nicole was serving as a volunteer interpreter. It turned out that as well as being a lawyer who specialized in international law, she spoke four languages fluently and had a surprisingly good grasp of the issues facing Indigenous peoples around the world. She had just finished degrees in law and international business and was ready to take on the challenge of making international trade tribunals listen to Indigenous peoples and recognize that Indigenous rights have an economic dimension.

Because this area was so new, developing the briefs was a long and difficult process. As we went through it with internal staff, the first draft was, according to all who reviewed it, weak and unfocused. Nicole then took over as lead writer, and we began to make some headway. We decided from the beginning to be frank about what we wanted: international recognition of our proprietary interest in our Aboriginal title forests as a way to get fair remuneration for our people, as well as to ensure that Indigenous peoples have a say regarding the management of our lands and resources with ecologically sound forestry practices, based on our Indigenous knowledge.

We started off with the submission to the U.S. Department of Commerce in its countervailing duties investigation. I was called down to the Department of Commerce in Washington, D.C., in 2001 for hearings in which our arguments were to be strength-tested by the U.S. Trade Representative lawyers. I admit that I was more than a little intimidated when I arrived in front of the massive stone Herbert C. Hoover Building on Constitution Avenue and passed through the towering Greek columns into the Department of Commerce's head office.

But I had prepared my testimony with Nicole in the weeks before, and I knew that I could not allow myself to get sidetracked. The worst mistake I could make was to try to answer any question that was not in our brief. Improvising during questioning can lead to self-defeating statements. One question in particular we had decided I shouldn't answer: the dollar value on our trees. This was, I knew, something that the Americans wanted to hear, so they could calculate it into their countervailing duties. For both the Canadians and the Americans, the trees were simply a commodity to be extracted. For our people, the forests included the salmon streams, the cultural sites, and the hunting and gathering sites. We supported ecologically and culturally sustainable logging, but not the sort of destructive logging that continues to be carried out in our forests. I was not going to allow our proprietary interest in the forests to be reduced to cents per foot of lumber.

As I expected, the U.S. Trade officials at the hearings pushed for a dollar figure. I resisted, and I could see that they were not pleased by that. At the same time, it was clear that the forestry industry was taking softwood lumber worth billions from our territory, and we were not being remunerated; that was where the subsidy sat. So in the end, they accepted our position that although Aboriginal title was too encompassing to be quickly or easily reduced to the price of the lumber, it was nevertheless clear that a large subsidy was being conveyed by Canada.

Interestingly, Canada, in response to our brief, did not ask how much value we were putting on our trees. This was obviously a fight that we would have later, in other venues, north of the border.

The U.S. Department of Commerce decision brought down the hammer on Canada by imposing a 27 per cent countervailing duty on Canadian softwood exports. The collected monies, amounting to over a billion dollars a year, would be held in an account at U.S. Customs. Not surprisingly, Canada disputed the decision before international trade tribunals of both the WTO and NAFTA. Which meant that we would have to follow them there.

We had decided early on that despite the fact that neither NAFTA nor the WTO had much of a record in promoting environmental practices— and were in many cases associated with those destroying the environment and corporate interests—we would let them know we were fighting for environmentally sound forest practices as much as for fair remuneration. In fact, we probably couldn't have hidden it. The Interior Alliance and by extension INET had been part of the massive protest against the WTO in Seattle at the end of 1999, and in our Indigenous Declaration, we had expressed "our great concern over how the World Trade Organization is destroying Mother Earth and the cultural and biological diversity" through its relentless global pursuit of neo-liberal policies. In 2002, we were going to the WTO without apologies for what we wanted and without illusions of the organization's role in the world. We were simply looking for international recognition of our economic rights as Indigenous peoples and Aboriginal title holders. If that meant dealing with the U.S. government, NAFTA, and the WTO, we were more than willing to do so.

We understood that virtually all international trade agreements aim at gaining corporate access to lands and resources. This makes it all the more important that these bodies hear directly from Indigenous peoples, since we have to control access to our lands and resources and be fully involved in all decision-making regarding them. Canada cannot continue to sign international trade agreements without taking into account Indigenous rights. And as Indigenous peoples, we have to make sure that those negotiating with Canada know about our Indigenous and economic rights. Failure to recognize and implement Indigenous rights will cause economic and legal uncertainty for investments.

In our briefs to the international trade tribunals, we began by identifying current logging practices in Canada as unsustainable, and as having a harmful effect on Indigenous peoples who still depended on the living forest for an important part of their livelihood. We pointed out that "most of the extraction of softwood lumber in Canada takes place in the traditional territories of Indigenous peoples and their proprietary interests and rights to control access have to be taken into account."

We went on to tell the story of our constitutional rights and the Supreme Court's recognition of them, and pointed out two ways in which the Canadian stumpage system did not take into account the proprietary interests of Indigenous peoples. First, if Indigenous peoples had a say in land and forest management, logging would have to be conducted in a more sustainable way and restricted, which would limit supply and therefore raise prices in an open market. Second was the omission of payment for the logs that were taken out of our Aboriginal title territories.

Canada argued for the complete rejection of our brief, because it was based on a land dispute within Canada that neither NAFTA nor the WTO had any jurisdiction over. We countered that we were not asking the international trade tribunal to resolve land disputes, but simply to take into account Indigenous rights when it comes to the interpretation and application of international trade law regarding subsidies.

An Indigenous intervention in an international trade decision was without precedent, and we knew that acceptance was far from certain.

This was also the feeling that we received from the WTO Secretariat. At the WTO, we were running into gatekeepers at every turn, to the point where they would not even tell us the submission deadline or procedures. We asked if the submission could be faxed in and they said yes; we asked for the fax number and they did not want to give it to us. But we persisted and figured out the timelines for submissions by parties in order to get ours in on time.

While we were pushing our brief forward, we had more indications of how narrow the door to entry was. The first WTO panel rejected submissions made by industry groups, since they represented the same interest as Canada. They did not even accept briefs by environmental groups. But we remained certain of the justice of our cause and the strength of our arguments. We still could not see how the WTO could dismiss our brief when they looked at it through the prism of both Canadian and international law, something Canada's colonial governments pointedly refused to do.

# Sun Peaks to Geneva

## Playgrounds and Fortresses

**W**HILE WE WERE IMMERSED in the softwood lumber battle abroad, a new ground war was erupting at home, one that would show our people's courage and commitment, but also lay bare some of their divisions. It crept up on me, but it would lead to a number of Neskonlith Elders and youth, including two of my daughters, going to jail in an agonizing battle to protect our land. This was a painful lesson about how fiercely the Canadian government still fights in its war against our people.

The issue was Nippon Cable's Sun Peaks development. I had signed the initial protocol when I was first elected, with an expectation of getting some benefits for our people. I had asked that our Secwepemc communities be given the right to supply gravel for the construction. It would have been a lucrative contract for us, and it seemed within the parameters of the protocol that we be given at least a preferential bid. I had pushed forward this idea in meetings with the Sun Peaks management, but finally we learned that we would be deprived of a preferential bid—in fact, we would not get to bid at all. The contract was given, with no call for tenders, to a white contractor. The Sun Peaks management idea of economic development for our people was to offer us space on our own mountain for an arts and craft store, which we knew would be a money-loser. Nothing more.

This financial snub was a minor issue, however. The deal became truly disturbing when we began to realize the extent of the proposed development. Nippon Cable, the company purchasing the Tod Mountain ski hill, was planning more than an upgrade of the tiny facility. When my children were small, it had been little more than a rope tow with a couple of trailers to warm up in between runs. The company now meant to supplant it with an all-season mega-resort, an instant city of condos, hotels, and restaurants on our territory.

All this was taking place in the area we called Skwelkwek'welt, which is part of our Neskonlith Douglas Reserve 1862 and only sixteen kilometres as the crow flies from Neskonlith. In our language, *Skwelkwek'welt* means alpine region; the area encompasses Tod Mountain, Mount Cahilty, and Mount Morrisey. Skwelkwek'welt also includes the mountain watersheds with McGillivray Lake, Morrisey Lake, Cahilty Lake, Eileen Lake, and all of the systems flowing in and out of these lakes. This area provides us with a variety of plant foods such as roots, berries, plant stalks, mushrooms, and lichens, as well as serving as a home to deer, moose, bear, beaver, lynx, cougar, and wolverine. As one of the last places in our territory where we can still hunt for food, gather medicines, and continue to practice other Secwepemc cultural traditions, it has a special importance to our youth who are learning our traditional ways.

As we looked into the Nippon Cable Sun Peaks master plan, we learned that the proposed resort activities included heli-skiing, cat-skiing, and snowmobiling. These are forbidden in most alpine areas in Europe because of the noise and their impact on wildlife. In addition, artificial snowmaking would be used to create and maintain a full snow cover, using chemicals and bacteria prohibited elsewhere. Many of these activities would not be allowed in European ski resorts. Mass winter tourism as it is presently practised in Canada is not sustainable environmentally, socially, or economically. And all this would take place on our lands just adjacent to the Neskonlith and the Adams Lake reserves.

The extent of the development was only gradually revealed to us. The first phase was to begin as an all-seasons destination with 1,100 employees and 400 permanent residents. Onsite accommodation would increase from 100 beds to over 5,800, and lift capacity would be increased to allow the delivery of 8,000 people a day to the mountains. The next stage called for an increased capacity to 20,000 beds.

This rapid expansion had not been part of our protocol with Sun Peaks, and now this instant city was being implanted on our territory. This land-devouring project was fed by a government land giveaway scheme that sold our Aboriginal title land to the developers at a rate that accelerated with the pace of development. The more land they developed, the more they were given.

This massive real estate deal would turn our territory into a playground for the rich. The pressure of tens of thousands of tourists descending on a mountain ecosystem would be immense; the water, sewage, and garbage needs of the resort would all take their toll, forever changing the plant and animal habitats of these pristine mountain ecologies. To solidify possession, the provincial government even invented a new administrative structure they called a "mountain resort municipality." This designation gave Sun Peaks municipal powers, even though it did not have enough permanent residents to justify them.

As the extent of the development became clear, our Elders became extremely concerned. For many, like Elder Irene Billy, the concern was personal—it was the site of her family trapline. In 1998, the Elders asked for a meeting with Masayoshi Ohkubo, the head of Nippon Cable, to explain to him that the government did not have the right to lease this land to him until the land and title issues in Canada had been addressed or meaningful consultation had occurred between the Neskonlith and Adams Lake bands, the government, and the B.C. Assets and Land Corporation.

It took a lot of pleading on behalf of the Elders, but Ohkubo finally agreed to meet with the people in the Adams Lake community hall. They told him, "We have seen our title and rights ignored, our way of life attacked, our lands damaged and fenced in, the fish, game, and plants we depend on depleted, and we have seen our children suffer because of all this. Our people have suffered and endured poor treatment from the non-Secwepemc for many generations."

They expressed serious concern over the threat to traditional medicines posed by the development. Medicinal plants, which many Elders use and share with their families, are generally fragile, blooming in specific places at specific times. It does not take much to upset the balance. Elders also spoke about it being an unspoiled area where they took young people from the Secwepemctsín language immersion school to show them the traditional ways, making the region a vital link between our past and our future. There was a note of pleading in their voices when they asked Ohkubo to spare the region, or at least to greatly lighten the development footprint.

Ohkubo left the meeting without making any commitments. And ultimately, he made no changes. Nippon Cable went ahead and initiated the $70 million expansion plan without a single concession to our people.

After listening to our Elders' concerns, I sought a legal opinion to review our options. Our lawyer confirmed that such a project on our Aboriginal title lands absolutely required prior consultation with our people and possibly our consent. The fact that no meaningful consultation had taken place certainly put it on shaky legal ground. This was especially the case for the planned expansion that had not yet been built.

Then our lawyer looked at the means we could employ to force the company to listen. There were only two. Get a court injunction to halt construction while talks took place, or take direct action in the form of symbolic informational roadblocks to put political pressure on the province and Nippon Cable to negotiate with us. A court injunction, our lawyer said, would be difficult, because the construction was underway and injunctions were generally given on the balance of convenience. Halting construction would require the layoff of hundreds of workers and cost millions of dollars in delay, something most judges would be reluctant to order.

It was after I came back from another UN Human Rights Committee meeting in Europe in the fall of 2000 that Janice Billy, an activist member of our community who was then working on her doctorate in education, informed me that the Elders and youth had gotten together to put up a small protest camp in Skwelkwek'welt. This action fit with the strategy of proving our title on the ground, and I instantly supported it.

The protest remained peaceful while we tried to initiate meaningful negotiations with Sun Peaks to accommodate our traditional uses and legal rights to the land. We were not successful. The company said it had the approval of the province and that was all that was required.

The following June, the conflict began to escalate when the B.C. Assets and Land Corporation issued a lease to Sun Peaks for the land our camp was located on. Sun Peaks then sought an injunction and, in July, the police moved in and arrested four of our people, including two Elders, charging them with criminal contempt for refusing to leave the camp.

On August 13, our people were physically blocked from access to Mount Morrisey, which is one of our traditional hunting grounds and spiritual places. Our people then set up the Skwelkwek'welt Protection Centre at the entrance of Sun Peaks ski resort to monitor environmental damage, to inform visitors and investors of the ongoing unresolved land issue, and to assert their title and rights to unceded lands.

Over the next several years, five Skwelkwek'welt Protection Centres, two traditional cedar bark homes, a hunting cabin, two sacred sweat lodges, and one cordwood house—home to a young Secwepemc family— were bulldozed or burned down by the resort or by persons unknown. None of these acts of were investigated by the police, who, we noticed, were increasingly acting like hired security guards for the resort.

In fact, the RCMP acted shamefully throughout this incident. The quality of person we were dealing with was reflected in officer Monty Robinson, who went on to media fame as one of the officers who was involved in the tasering of Polish tourist Robert Dziekanski in the Vancouver airport.

The Sun Peaks protest first reached a national audience when the twenty-four-hour music TV channel MuchMusic planned its heavily promoted annual spring break snow festival at Sun Peaks for March 2001. The five-day event was called Snow Job, which somehow seemed appropriate to us. The people at the Protection Centre protested to Much-Music and we ended up in a press release battle with the station founder and owner, Moses Znaimer, who had recently been awarded the Human Rights Centre gold medal for the promotion of tolerance and creative race relations.

In its dealing with our people, MuchMusic was no better than Sun Peaks. In fact, as they issued their public statements, it became clear that they were lifting content from the Sun Peaks publicity department. We asked Znaimer to live up to his reputation, support the human rights of the Secwepemc people, and cancel the MuchMusic incursion onto our territory. He didn't listen. But the Snow Job event ended up giving our people an important national platform to raise our issues.

In retrospect, the protest was perhaps too successful. After Snow Job, the B.C. government and Sun Peaks redoubled their efforts to isolate the youth and Elders at the Protection Centre and increased the use of the police to put pressure on them. At the same time, they launched a Gustafsen Lake–style smear campaign against the protesters, impugning their intelligence and their sanity and whipping up the latent racism against our people in the region.

The government and police dropped any pretense to even-handedness. In the spring of 2001, when twenty members of the Native Youth Movement walked through the village singing traditional Native songs and calling for a moratorium on the development, several young white guys on a bar terrace began shouting racial slurs at them. One of the men strode off the terrace and approached the Native youth shouting, "Fucking Indians, get off our land!" and "You want war? Come on!" He swung several punches in the direction of one of the young men, then directed his attention to my daughter, Niki, shouting at her and, finally, hitting her in the face.

The police moved in and arrested not the man who had committed the assault, but my daughter. Later, a cabin in the woods that the protesters were living in was burned down, and our people began to receive threats of violence if we entered nearby towns. After fanning this local anger, the resort began leading a call for mass arrests of the protesters and went back to the courts to get another round of injunctions against us. Once again, Elders and youth were arrested. It was infuriating for our people to see eighty-three-year-old Irene Billy led away in handcuffs for the crime of occupying her own family trapline.

During this period we pressured the federal government to exercise its duty to recognize and affirm our rights on our Aboriginal title lands, or at least order that we be consulted by the province and the resort before the new developments took place, as was spelled out in the *Delgamuukw* decision. This was, we saw, the only way the dispute could be settled. As the Supreme Court judges underlined several times in *Delgamuukw*, justice depended on "the honour and good faith of the Crown." In Sun Peaks, the Crown made a mockery of both.

We had asked the federal Indian Affairs minister, Robert Nault, to meet with us to discuss the issue. Nault, to our dismay, said that there was no role for the federal government in the dispute because it dealt with provincial lands. In claiming this, he was wilfully ignoring Canada's Constitution as well as the Supreme Court decision on Aboriginal title. We were not the only ones asking Nault to help solve the dispute; the local press were also frustrated by the federal government's refusal to shoulder its responsibility.

As I wrote in a letter to Prime Minister Chrétien, "The Minister's refusal to address the issues surrounding Sun Peaks has meant that a solu-

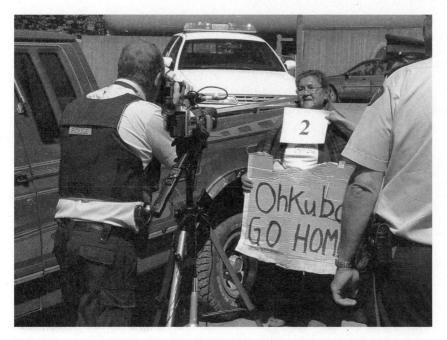

Police photograph Elder Irene Billy during her arrest on May 23, 2001, at Sun Peaks

tion is impossible to reach—even with all of the goodwill of our people and the provincial government."

Unfortunately, the prime minister and his government decided to give over the conduct of Indian Affairs to the RCMP. This was a subject I also addressed with the Mounties. During a meeting at a restaurant in Chase with the officers in charge, I told them that we had a legitimate reason to be up at Sun Peaks. They were doing irreparable damage to the mountain that impacts our hunting and gathering. For us, the RCMP were not peace officers in this dispute. They were Indian agents—government employees with guns—who were not enforcing the law but backing up one side of the argument. And in this dispute, the Supreme Court had already ruled that Aboriginal title and rights had to be taken into account. The RCMP officers made no reply. The arrests of our people continued, and Sun Peaks fanned the flames of racism with calls for increased police violence against us.

By this time, the tensions were not only with the white community, but also within our own. In Neskonlith, and even more so in other Secwepemc communities, people began to have a genuine fear of white backlash and government reprisals. This last fear was felt most acutely by the chiefs. They were in the business of delivering government programs and services, and it is at moments like this that our dependency becomes most evident. Some understand that the only way out is to break that dependency once and for all, to assert our right to our lands and begin to build true Indigenous economies on our territories. Many others test the wind and, if it is blowing too strong, flee back to their subsistence benefactor at Indian Affairs, which pays their salaries as well as the community program funding. I could feel this happening, and I honestly did not know what to do about it.

Finally, a crack appeared in the government wall. The B.C. attorney general and minister responsible for treaty negotiations, Geoff Plant, called and left a message on my phone. He wanted to talk. I was encouraged when he was quoted that day in the press saying that the dispute at Sun Peaks was the symptom of a much deeper problem and admitting that the police "are not the appropriate body to deal with these issues."

I called him back, and we agreed to meet at the Prestige Inn in Vernon. I had never met Plant, but I certainly knew of him as the lead government minister in the recent mail-in referendum against Aboriginal rights in the province. This was a vote on a series of eight ridiculously worded questions intended to strip Indigenous peoples of their basic rights in the province. All of the leading Christian churches, the Canadian Jewish Congress, Canadian Muslim Federation, B.C. Federation of Labour, and a host of other groups had denounced the referendum as racist. Finally only a third of B.C. residents even bothered to vote on it.

I was sitting in the meeting room when Plant strode in and, in a John Wayne voice, said, "All right, Chief, you caused enough embarrassment to Sun Peaks and to the provincial government. It's time to negotiate. What do you want?"

I told him we were not interested in embarrassing anyone, but that tens of millions of dollars of investment was being plunked down on our land and we had to protest or he would say we were agreeing to it.

He thought for a moment. "So you don't want to get caught sleeping on your rights. I see your point. We did use that once against a band on down the coast. What if we provide you with a letter recognizing that you are asserting your rights. Then get the people off the hill and we can start negotiating."

I told him that I couldn't tell the youth and Elders what to do, but I would take his offer to them.

I spoke to Janice Billy. She went up the mountain and came back the next day. She said the protesters said it made no sense for them to leave our land to negotiate whether we had the right to be there, and they decided they will only move off the mountain if he puts a moratorium on development.

I transmitted their decision to the minister. The hammer dropped.

On November 8, Plant broke off all discussions with us. In his letter to me, he said, "The tension at Sun Peaks has escalated to the point where members of the public feel that their safety is threatened, largely as a result of the perception of increased violence and past aggressive behaviour by occupants of the protest camps."

It was a cleverly written introduction to what would follow. Because Plant knew better than to accuse our peaceful protests of being "violent," he states only that "the public feel that their safety is threatened" by the "perception of increased violence." A perception that he and his government, and Sun Peaks, had been doing everything to create over the previous six months. The letter continued:

> In the interests of de-escalating tensions in the area and protecting public safety, both the Skwelkwek'welt Protection Centre and the McGillivray Lake camps must be removed in order to create a climate where negotiations are possible. Given the current climate at Sun Peaks and your community's apparent unwillingness to remove the protest camps, I am regrettably of the view that we have exhausted options to negotiate a resolution. Therefore the Province must look to other remedies.

We all knew what was coming with the "other remedies." On November 13, KAIROS, a coalition of church groups, tried to intervene on our behalf. In a letter to Plant, they said:

> KAIROS has great respect for the restraint displayed by the Secwepemc people, especially those at the Skwelkwek'welt Protection Centre and at McGillivray Lake. Their perseverance, and ability to maintain a peaceful and non-violent presence in an atmosphere thick with racial

animosity, and amid acts of intimidation and provocation, is a testament to the depth of their commitment and dedication. Forcing the Secwepemc peoples out of these areas does nothing to resolve the land rights issue, but serves only to criminalize the Secwepemc peoples.[36]

The plea went unheeded. On November 16, 2001, the police moved in, accompanied by B.C. Assets and Land Corporation, armed with pepper spray and clubs. They beat and then arrested the protesters en masse and seized all of their personal effects at the camps. The Canadian state once again showed its teeth to Indigenous peoples, and soon the police were not just assaulting the people at the Protection Centre, they moved onto reserve land as well.

Among those arrested on the mountain were my two daughters, Niki and Mandy. Mandy was jailed for sixty days. She was separated from her four-month-old baby boy, whom I took care of with help from the child's grandmother.

It was a sombre time. Once a week, I would drive down to Burnaby with the child to visit his mother, with a cooler to carry back the milk she expressed for him every day. But when I arrived at the jail, I had to turn the infant over to a guard who brought the baby to his mother in the meeting room. I could not carry the infant to her directly, because the rule said she was allowed to have only one visitor at a time. I would wait in my truck for the guard to bring the child back out, and I remember feeling not so much anger as shame for the whole system that had produced this situation. This is not just how whites treat Indians, I thought, it is how they treat each other. If I needed any inspiration to continue to try to get back our people's birthright, our land and our independence, taking my grandchild to the Burnaby jail for those brief visits with my daughter was more than enough.

The criminalization of my people continued with more than fifty arrests for inhabiting our own land. It was the Canadian state and its industrial developers at their very worst, brushing aside Canadian law and our constitutional protections and using the police more as goons than as peace officers. The Canadian government reaction to our legal rights has been similar to the nineteenth-century approach of U.S. president Andrew Jackson, who, when Supreme Court Chief Justice Marshall ruled that the Cherokee Nation had title to their lands and internal sovereignty, said, "John Marshall has made his decision—now let him enforce it." The Cherokee were then marched out of their lands on a Trail of Tears.

Fortunately, the twenty-first century is far from the nineteenth and our people, whether the government wishes it or not, are not going to be marched anywhere. While all this was unfolding on our territory, INET was putting forward our brief to the WTO and finding new openings at the international level.

One of the problems with WTO procedures generally, and especially when it comes to amicus curiae submissions, is that those who submit them do not necessarily find out if their submissions have been accepted. Nicole Schabus and I had made it inside the WTO fortress in Geneva because the organization was hosting a seminar for NGOs. As the only Indigenous person in a room full of government and NGO representatives, I was determined to put the Indigenous point of view before the conference. But I spent virtually the entire meeting with my hand up trying to get on the speaker's list.

Like a waiter in a busy restaurant, the chair managed to float his eyes past me every time until the very distinguished fellow directly in front of me put up his hand. When the chair looked at him, addressing him as "Your Excellency," he could not avoid meeting my eyes. I was put on the list.

When I was finally given the floor, I spoke about Indigenous peoples' rights to their land, the need for much greater environmental protection of the forests of the world, and the need to give Indigenous peoples the right to refuse the kind of rapacious development that was being practised by multinationals around the world.

My speech was met by a disapproving silence. Finally, one of the panellists, a fellow with long white hair and a Tom Wolfe–style white suit, seemed to speak for the room when he said that Indigenous peoples should not have the veto over development. As the room gave a general nod of agreement, my heart sank. Faced with attitudes like this, I feared the WTO would never accept our brief.

My misgivings were soon dispelled by Nicole Schabus. She had gone to the front desk and called up to the Softwood Lumber Dispute desk to enquire directly about the status of our submission. The same staffer who had previously put all sorts of roadblocks in our path was now suddenly friendly. She was happy to inform us, she said, that the WTO panel had accepted our submission.

Not only that, but the three adjudicators—who are independent international trade law experts—had decided to circulate our submission to all the parties (Canada and the United States) and the third parties (Japan, India, and the European Commission, which represents European Union member states in international trade matters) for comment. This again was without precedent. It showed that international trade tribunals were taking our arguments seriously and that nation-states would have to start to deal with them.

Another sign of our success came after the seminar. A number of government representatives wanted to talk to us. Those who were involved in the Softwood Lumber Dispute asked us to come to their missions to meet with their trade experts. I was even approached by a representative of the Canadian Mission, who invited me to a reception. But I reminded him that we had an independent submission accepted before a WTO tribunal. If the Canadians wanted to meet, it should be a formal meeting, taking place in our territories.

Our priority at the time was meeting the Americans, the other party directly involved in the dispute. But by the time Nicole and I made it to our meeting with them, it was already after hours. The U.S. Mission was out of town and we had to spend almost all of our remaining cash to get there by taxi.

Entering the mission grounds was like entering a U.S. military base. It was heavily guarded by machine gun–toting marines, who waved the taxi over to where they could examine the undercarriage with cameras. When we were let off, a marine sergeant was waiting at the embassy door. I gave my name and he replied, "Yes, sir, we have been expecting you." He led us to the U.S. Trade Representative's office, where we were greeted by a couple of giant trade lawyers, who towered over us at about six foot six. They took us into a meeting room, which, I noticed right away, was well stocked with peanuts and other snacks, soft drinks, and a surprising amount of alcohol. I hadn't had time to eat that day, and the sight of all those snacks made me realize how ravenously hungry I was.

But the Americans got right down to business. They wanted our input into the bizarre turn Canada's arguments had taken. The Canadian trade lawyers were suddenly trying to evade the whole subsidy issue by recasting their position. On the softwood lumber issue, they said that they really were not calculating stumpage as a payment to obtain ownership of the trees. They suggested that the forest industry in Canada had such long-term forest licences that they amounted to proprietary interests in the forests and that, instead of stumpage, the companies were simply paying a tax on their revenues.

This was an astounding argument, and it was inconsistent with Canadian law. It was clearly crafted to escape the application of international trade law. This position would mean that the forests were no longer owned by the Crown. Not only Indigenous peoples would be excluded from ownership, but the Canadian people would also be tossed from the national forests. Canada was arguing that the Crown had given the country's forests over to the forestry companies—many of which, ironically, were American owned—and was simply taxing their revenues.

The U.S. trade lawyers asked if we understood the new Canadian position in the same way, that Canada was basically saying the companies owned the trees as they grew in the public and Indigenous forests. We agreed that that was what they were saying. So they asked: "And they do not pay you as Indigenous peoples anything for taking the trees from your forests?"

We had to answer a couple of times that, no, our people were not paid a cent. They repeated the question, just to make sure. We were asked the same question by representatives of the European Commission. They all treated us as Indigenous peoples who are the owners of our lands and resources; only Canada denied it. Even in the United States, the tribes are some of the biggest holders of forest lands. They get paid for the trees taken from their lands, and they are actively involved in the forest industry. But they cannot compete with lumber imported from Canada, because here the timber is taken without any compensation for Indigenous peoples.

So Canada was now saying that the forestry companies owned the forests. It was here that our Aboriginal title argument had its most important effect, because it showed that even if the Crown could give over the forests to the forestry companies, they could only give over the Crown ownership portion. They could not at the same time hand over the Aboriginal title, because they did not own that in the first place. Our legal standing, our proprietary interests in the forest, and our submission helped counter the new Canadian assertion that they had given over the forests to the forestry companies.

We left the U.S. Mission and that room full of snacks with growling stomachs and headed onto the street. We didn't have enough money for a taxi back to the hotel, so we began the long trip back to the city on a maze of buses. We knew, though, that we had made an important step. The Canadian government continued behind its fortress of refusal toward us, but big cracks were appearing from outside pressure on those walls. The acceptance of the INET WTO submission[37] was an enormous victory, and it set a precedent that stands today and can be built on by Indigenous peoples from around the world. It recognizes that we do indeed have economic rights that have to be taken into account in local, national, and international economic decision-making.

The solidity of our victory was confirmed when it came to the NAFTA panel. Canada was taking our submission seriously. The Canadian negotiators had hired a U.S. trade law firm, supported by a Canadian law firm, to counter our submission, with a focus on technical and procedural reasons why our submission should not be accepted. They did not even counter our substantive arguments, which we had based on both international and Canadian law.

NAFTA tribunals consist of trade law experts appointed by the two countries involved in the dispute. So it was even more amazing that in 2002 our independent submission was accepted by the NAFTA panel, which had been nominated by Canada and the United States. Canada had spent excessive legal fees on trade law firms (whose bargain rate begins at $1,000 an hour) to counter our submissions, while ours had been prepared on a pro bono basis by Nicole, putting forward arguments based on Indigenous rights and international trade law. This further evidences the strength of our arguments and the weight that international trade tribunals attach to Indigenous rights.

Unable to beat us at the WTO and NAFTA tribunals, the Canadian government looked for ways to put pressure on our base. The chiefs in the Interior Alliance suddenly began getting letters from bureaucrat and Métis lawyer Al Price, "Advisor, Intergovernmental Affairs, B.C. Region DIAND [Department of Indian Affairs and Northern Development]." Price faxed them "a copy of the submission of Chief Art Manuel to the World Trade Organization on behalf of the Interior Alliance." He explained that he was involved in a group of federal officials from various departments who were considering the submission and the government's response.

Price's letter pointed out that "the issue of US countervailing duties on softwood lumber exports is having a devastating effect on the industry and economy generally in B.C. Also as you are aware, many First Nations are struggling to gain a larger share of the industry, market and benefits of timber resources in B.C."

Then he got to the point. "I am asking if your First Nation was aware of this submission, and whether Chief Manuel does, in fact, represent you in this exercise and approach. It will be significant for the necessary officials to have in their minds as we formulate a response, and we want to make sure your voices are not being misrepresented."[38]

With the Softwood Lumber Dispute gaining the stature of a national emergency in Canada and the creaking noises of the government agents moving through the Interior Alliance, we knew that we had to have the best possible support for our case. So to bolster our arguments, we sought out an economist who had the best possible credentials, Joseph Stiglitz. Stiglitz, an American economist at Columbia University, New York, had won the Nobel Prize in Economic Sciences in 2001. He had been a senior official at the World Bank and chaired President Clinton's Council of Economic Advisers. *Time* magazine and others who rate such things routinely list him as one of the hundred most influential people in the world.

I was able to put our case directly to Professor Stiglitz in 2003. The meeting was arranged through one of Nicole's contacts, Anton Korinek, a young Austrian acquaintance of hers who was one of Stiglitz's senior academic assistants. We sent him information outlining our dealings with the U.S. Department of Commerce and requested a meeting. With Anton's help, we were invited to meet Stiglitz at his office at Columbia University.

We thought that we had been invited for an informal discussion, but when we arrived, Stiglitz was all business. He wanted the unvarnished facts of our WTO case so he could make up his own mind. I summarized our position on Aboriginal title and described the *Delgamuukw* decision.

This was not new territory for Stiglitz. A couple of years before, as chair of the Council of Economic Advisers to the U.S. president, he had dealt with the previous round of the Softwood Lumber Dispute, but he noted that the Indigenous arguments added a different dimension. Earlier in his career, he had also provided expert evidence and an independent economic analysis for the Seneca tribe when the lease they had given settlers over the town of Salamanca, New York, expired and the tribe did not want to renew it. Stiglitz calculated that the difference between the present discounted value of what was paid and a fair market rent was enormous, amounting to hundreds of millions of dollars. As a result, the federal government was forced to pass a bill providing past compensation of over $300 million and increasing annual lease payments from $57,000 to $800,000, with future increases built into the deal. Those settlers who refused to pay the increased leases were evicted.

When I finished making my case, he said, "Okay, now I see. You have proprietary interest in the trees."

As former senior vice president and chief economist of the World Bank, he understood that the failure of the Indigenous peoples to receive remuneration for the resources on the land in which they had had a long-standing interest was not only unacceptable, but also destructive to their economy, lives, and livelihoods. This failure, he said, also raised serious and complicated questions for assessing the impact of Canadian softwood lumber management policies, potentially including those at issue in the dispute. Since the real benefactors of the failure to provide remuneration of the Indigenous peoples were the forestry companies, the issues of fair trade and distortion of trade could not be ignored.

Stiglitz agreed that it will be important in the future to provide just remuneration to the Indigenous peoples, and he showed that he understood the complexity of the issue. In assessing the amount of compensation for past use of Indigenous land, he said, you will have to look at the core economic, environmental, social, and cultural values that Indigenous peoples associate with it, then determine the true economic worth of the land and its resources, and give value to both current and cumulative past infringements. This was a clear validation of our position from one of the leading economic lights of our generation. We left New York with a sense of vindication. And of hope.

The endorsement of our economic arguments by Stiglitz showed yet again how out of step Canada was becoming with the world. We began to ask ourselves how long Canada would be able to hold out in its nineteenth-century policies toward Indigenous peoples. The answer, we now understand, is that it will hold out as long as we, the Indigenous peoples, allow it to.

But international trade law is one area that we must continue to revisit. Unlike many of the world's human rights treaties, trade law has real sanctions that can be used to force a change in economic policies.

During the last round of the Softwood Lumber Dispute, between 2001 and 2006, the United States alone collected over four billion dollars in countervailing duties. Canadian industry was pushing hard to get these monies returned, but U.S. industry did not want to see them go back to their Canadian counterparts who had been subsidized in the first place. They did indicate, though, that they would be ready to return part of the monies to Indigenous peoples, since we had been the ones paying the real price, having our trees removed without our consent or remuneration. We are talking about a billion dollars a year for the forest industry alone—add up similar subsidies to other industries and you know why Indigenous peoples remain poor. And with billions of dollars in revenue for access to our lands and resources, we could also ensure more economically and environmentally sustainable development.

In the end, the Canadian industry pushed for and accepted a negotiated settlement of the Softwood Lumber Dispute in September 2006, where part of the monies was returned and they agreed to Canadian exporting provinces either collecting an export tax that ranges from 5 per cent to 15 per cent as prices fall or collecting lower export taxes and limiting export volumes. In other words, they accepted increased taxes rather than sharing with Indigenous peoples. It is up to Indigenous peoples to hold them accountable and make sure that, in the future, Indigenous proprietary interests are remunerated.

# Taking It to the Bank

## Accounting for
## Unpaid Debt

OUR SUBMISSIONS to international trade tribunals continued
to draw attention to INET and the new reality that Indigenous rights are not simply human rights, they are economic
rights as well. We were approached by academics who were
looking at what this development might mean for Indigenous peoples in
other countries and internationally. In 2002, a greatly respected Indigenous rights activist and academic, Professor Russel Barsh, organized a
seminar for Nicole and me at New York University, and in 2003, I was
invited to a NAFTA seminar in Mexico City. In 2004, Nicole and I were
asked to draft a paper on our Indigenous submissions to trade tribunals
for the *Chapman Law Review*.

Given the evidence, international economic institutions were recognizing what Canadian governments refused—that we indeed have
economic rights on our territories. The question then was: What does
Aboriginal title mean for the larger Canadian economy, and what are the
real implications of Canada's refusal to recognize it? As INET grappled
with this question, I found myself back in New York City in 2003, check-
ing into the Vanderbilt YMCA on East 47th Street, for a meeting at Standard & Poor's head office in the Financial District.

Standard & Poor's is near the top of the world's financial pyramid. It generates more than two billion dollars in revenues, and more than $1.5 trillion in assets are connected to S&P's indices. The company describes itself as "the world's foremost provider of independent credit ratings, indices, risk evaluation, investment research, data and valuations." It has offices in twenty countries, including in Canada, but I was determined to speak to the head office first. I believed that they would be able to give me a more independent assessment of our claims.

My ticket to New York had been paid by the World Council of Churches, which had invited me to a seminar in the outskirts of New York. The churches were looking at the impact of globalization and they had invited me to give the Indigenous peoples' perspective. It was an interesting meeting and our cause found an encouraging amount of support from the churches—a nice change from our original relationship with Catholic priests and other Christian pastors who arrived on our territories. But I must admit that during much of the event, my mind was on my upcoming appointment with Standard & Poor's.

It had not been an easy one to arrange. Nicole Schabus had called the Standard & Poor's office as soon as my World Council of Churches trip was confirmed. They put her in contact with the analyst at the Canadian desk, and it would be an understatement to say that he was surprised to hear about a Canadian Indian who wanted to meet with him to discuss Aboriginal title. He tried to brush Nicole off, but she is a determined woman. She pushed back. It took her forty minutes on the phone to wear him down to the point where he said, "Okay, okay, send me your information and I'll meet with Mr. Manuel."

When the World Council of Churches event was over, the organizers dropped me off in front of the Vanderbilt YMCA. I spent the evening in my room preparing for the Standard & Poor's meeting as if it was a law school exam. I intended to put this question to them: If Canada had this outstanding debt to First Nations on Aboriginal title lands, something the WTO had recognized, where was it in Canada's books? We knew that the government wanted "certainty" by extinguishing our title for a small amount of land and a cash payment, but what was the value of those unextinguished lands?

I wasn't expecting anything like a dollars-and-cents answer, but I was curious to know if the credit rating agencies would agree in principle that our Aboriginal title to our lands should somehow be reflected in the government's accounting.

I rose early that morning and took a swim in the Y pool, then headed underground to puzzle my way through the New York subway system. An hour later, I succeeded in popping up into the sunshine amid the glass towers on Wall Street and made my way to the Standard & Poor's head office. I was not at all sure of what sort of reception I would get. I had assumed, given the fact that the official had needed to be pressured to meet, that he would be neutral at best. But I feared that I would get a continuation of the hostility that Nicole had initially encountered on the phone.

My fears turned out to be groundless. Several officials met me in the conference room. The lead was Joydeep Mukherji, director of the Sovereign Ratings Group. He introduced me to Roberto Sifon-Arevalo, research assistant, Latin America Sovereign Ratings, and explained that his own primary responsibility was to financially analyze Canada and that Mr. Sifon-Arevalo was responsible for Latin American countries. The fact that they had brought in the Latin American expert suggested that they were looking to see if the Indigenous angle was transferable to other parts of the hemisphere.

From their initial questions, it was obvious they had read our submissions and the *Delgamuukw* decision, and they were interested in exploring the matter further. I told them quite directly that I thought that financial monitoring agencies needed to pay greater attention to matters regarding Indigenous peoples. I said that it is important to report accurate information to investors, and Canada and British Columbia are in a serious case of conflict of interest in reporting on it. I wanted to bring them up to date about this situation based upon my interpretation of the facts.

I then outlined the legal and constitutional issues regarding Aboriginal title. I was very frank, describing the strengths and weaknesses of our case. I explained that the primary responsibility for dealing with Aboriginal title resides with the federal government, and that officially close to 60 per cent of the Indian bands in British Columbia were negotiating— some of them since 1993—but that more than 40 per cent of us were not negotiating. I explained that the negotiators were represented by the First Nations Summit, and that the rest were represented by the Union of B.C. Indian Chiefs.

I told them that we had had two major meetings during the last six months, one in Kelowna and one in Prince George, where the First Nations Summit and the Union came together in an ad hoc Title and Rights Alliance, because the negotiators themselves were dissatisfied with the lack of progress. I explained that we were all seeking recognition and reconciliation of our Aboriginal title with Crown title. Existing federal government policy sought only to extinguish our Aboriginal title for very limited treaty rights. But up until that point, only the Nisga'a Tribal Council had accepted the government offer.

I also outlined our Harper Lake logging case and how it fit in with the jurisdiction issue. I told them that we had just won our case on receiving provincial funding at the Supreme Court of Canada. I briefly outlined our successful submissions to the WTO and NAFTA and said that our economic arguments had the backing of a fellow New Yorker, Nobel Prize winner Joseph Stiglitz.

While I was speaking, they listened closely, interrupting only to ask for more details. I was impressed with their thorough knowledge of Canada. They were familiar with the country's political leadership—cabinet members as well as the provincial premiers—and it was interesting to see how they integrated the new information on Aboriginal title and rights into their overall picture as I spoke.

When we got down to the question of accounting for Aboriginal title and uncertainty on the books, I provided them with a copy of the Summary of Financial Statements of the Province British Columbia, March 31, 2002. It showed that since 1997, when the *Delgamuukw* decision came down and when the Nisga'a Treaty was reaching the Final Agreement stage, the B.C. government had reported that it manages its liability for Aboriginal title through negotiations under the Comprehensive Land Claims Policy and the B.C. Treaty Commission's Treaty Process. The province told independent financial monitors that the majority of bands were involved in Nisga'a-style negotiations and the minority are contending they have other rights, and that this issue will likely have to be addressed in court.

I suggested that this report did not accurately describe the economic trouble British Columbia is in, since the Aboriginal title holders of a large percentage of B.C. territory had no intention of surrendering their title under any circumstances. They were demanding that their ownership be reconciled with Crown title as the Supreme Court of Canada had outlined in *Delgamuukw*.

I pointed to the accepted accounting procedures contained in the International Accounting Standards Board regulations, particularly number 37, which demands that *contingent liabilities* and *contingent assets* be disclosed with sufficient information "to enable users to understand their nature, timing and amount." The Government of British Columbia was withholding vital information by basing its contingent liability solely on the Nisga'a deal and not taking into account the more than 40 per cent of B.C. bands that were not even inside the process and the rest of the B.C. bands that, while inside the process, had refused to accept the Nisga'a model for more than twenty years. The B.C. books did not offer anything close to the "sufficient information" demanded by international accounting principles.

When we had gone through the material, Mukherji connected the dots himself. Canada, he said, did seem to have some substantial hidden liabilities when it came to Aboriginal title.

In subsequent visits to both the New York S&P office and the Canadian S&P office in Toronto, we were told that what we needed to do was to begin an alienation study to account for all of the timber, mineral, oil and gas, and other resources that have been taken off our Aboriginal title lands, not just in British Columbia but across Canada. With that we will have a figure to begin future discussion with.

It is this case that we must make with greater force at the international level and within Canada. Canadian federal and provincial governments are telling their citizens and the world that everything is under control and that the only problem with Indigenous peoples is some sort of governance problem. They are trying to ignore our rights to self-determination and to economic control over our territories. But in the twenty-first century, the world is not in tune with Canada's nineteenth-century colonialist approach.

While we were moving forward on the international front, troubles at home were increasing. My absences played a role in this. But the issue that was raising the most concern continued to be the Sun Peaks battle. The protests continued throughout 2002 with the youth and Elders at the Skwelkwek'welt Protection Centre returning to the mountain after every eviction. They kept the camp going through hot summers, rainy falls, and cold winters with a heroic determination to protect our land. I was proud that among the strongest defenders of the camp were my twin daughters, Mandy and Niki. They had grown up in the struggle.

With Hubert Jim at his Sutikalh sovereignty camp near Melivin Creek, May 2010

When they were just four years old, they had ridden with Beverly on the Constitution Express to Ottawa for the protests that led to the inclusion of Section 35 in the Constitution. They had grown up knowing we have Aboriginal title and rights to our territory, and they were determined to defend these rights at Skwelkwek'welt.

The Native youth and the Elders at Skwelkwek'welt were not alone. There were several battles like this going on in Canada at the time. In 2000 Hubert (Hubie) Jim, a Lil'wat from the Mount Currie band in the mountains to the west of Neskonlith, set up a camp on traditional lands at a place they call Sutikalh, halfway between Lillooet and Mount Currie, to keep former Olympic gold medallist Nancy Greene and her husband, Al Raine, from building a ski resort in the mountains behind the camp. Greene, now a Conservative senator, is a big promoter of the Sun Peaks development and owns the Cahilty Lodge, a hotel in Sun Peaks, so there was an instant solidarity between the camps.

Hubie, a warrior to the core, has always been supported by Mount Currie activists like Rosalin Sam and Alvin Nelson and others, but he was

also often the lone fighter staying at the camp. He and his friendly dogs
have stayed in the camp through thick and thin, despite having shots fired
at them, and he remains there today. It is always a pleasure to visit him
and, on the second of May, the date that the camp was set up, people from
all around the nearby communities join him for a feast.

Around this same time, in December 2002, the people of Asubpeeschoseewagong Anishinabek (Grassy Narrows First Nation) in northwestern Ontario, led by activists Steve Fobister and Judy DaSilva, also
launched a blockade. They and other young people from the band went
out onto a road leading past their reserve and stopped the logging trucks
carrying away trees cut on their territory. "It was the last thing we could
do because everything around us was disappearing," Judy said. "The
clean water, the clean air, our way of life, our traditions, like the wild rice
picking and even blueberries were disappearing."

That battle, too, continues today. I have visited the community many
times, usually with a gift of traditional foods from my people, and I have,
whenever possible, brought their case to international meetings.

In the B.C. Interior, however, our defenders at Sun Peaks were under
increasing pressure. With every passing month, businesspeople and the
local media upped their rhetoric, demanding harsh measures to deal with
our people on the mountain. This clamour reached a crescendo when
tour bus operators threatened to pull out of Sun Peaks because they were
afraid of being confronted by information pickets on the road leading
to the resort. Behind the scenes, the provincial government was working overtime to pressure, or simply bribe, local chiefs away from their
support of the protest. In this climate, local racist elements felt embold-
ened, and more and more verbal and even physical attacks were directed
at Indian people at Sun Peaks and throughout the region.

I visited the Skwelkwek'welt camp often and worked closely with
Janice Billy, one of the main leaders of the protest, who had recently
received her doctorate in education. I defended them in the press and
praised their commitment to our land. As chief, I offered whatever support I could to their cause. But I was aware of a growing fear among the
people of the rising white backlash, a fear that was reaching a level I had
not seen before. It says a lot about our vulnerable position in the world
that many of our people, rather than confronting the mounting racism
head-on, began to question the protesters for bringing it to the surface.
The leading voices in fuelling this opposition were a number of local

chiefs, and their motives were not hard to assess. Some were looking to make deals with the province, and all were receiving an unequivocal message from the provincial and federal governments to back off from any confrontation with the developer.

The first to break ranks with us was Bonnie Leonard from the Kamloops Indian Band. Chief Leonard criticized the Elders and youth at Skwelkwek'welt in the press, and in response, Janice Billy sent her an eloquent letter saying that now, more than ever, was the time "to protect our traditional knowledge, language, and culture, all of which is based on the land." The letter continued:

> If we lose this, we cannot consider ourselves true Secwepemc. Maintaining our connection to the land and our language is the only way we will remain as a strong Secwepemc Nation.
>
> We not only want to protect the land for our traditional use but are protecting our survival as Secwepemc. We are dismayed that you, as a Secwepemc person, cannot see and respect our position.

A few months later, I received a direct warning shot from Chief Nathan Matthew of the Simpcw band, whom I had replaced as leader of the Shuswap Nation Tribal Council. He pulled me aside after a Tribal Council meeting and told me his band was considering leaving the Tribal Council because of the racism that the Sun Peaks protests had unleashed on all Indian people. He said it was affecting even the Indian guys who were working at the mill. A climate of fear was being created.

"Why are you blaming the victims?" I asked. I pointed out that in trying to protect their land, and standing up against the ever-expanding resort, the youth and Elders at Skwelkwek'welt were not responsible for white racism. They were the first victims of it. So I told Nathan we should be battling against the developers who were stealing our land, not against our people who were defending it. But even as I spoke, I could sense that this was just the beginning. Deals were being made in back rooms. Forces were being put in motion, and Nathan was not speaking only for himself. I called an early election of the Tribal Council.

This suspicion was confirmed when on March 12, 2002, Geoff Plant, the B.C. attorney general, announced to the media that he had met with five of the six chiefs in the region "but not with Art Manuel because he has a separate agenda. We have proposed five or six resolutions," he said, "but we needed the First Nation members to cease their occupation first. Art Manuel did not seem interested in problem-solving."

The news that the chiefs were meeting behind the back of the chair of the Tribal Council to undermine their protest infuriated the people at Skwelkwek'welt. They fired off a letter to all of the chiefs demanding an explanation. But the die had been cast. Within two weeks, Nathan was re-elected chair of the Tribal Council. At the time, I couldn't resist pointing out that it was Plant who appeared to be the real chair, but today I better understand the forces that keep our chiefs beaten down. Our government band councils live off the crumbs thrown them by the federal and provincial Indian Affairs departments, and they live in fear that any bothersome noise will get them all booted from the room. It is naive to expect people to bite the hand that feeds them, especially, as in the case of many of the chiefs, if they are individually being very well fed by Indian Affairs.

Discontent, however, was also seeping into my own community. In late fall 2002, my brother Richard, who was on the band council, came to see me. Trouble was brewing, he said. Supporters were drifting away. Opponents—and there are always opponents—were saying that I was too often away and making accusations that I was living the high life in world capitals. Richard knew the truth, that my fancy hotel was actually the YMCA with the bathroom down the hall, but he thought I should be warned.

It's not so serious yet, he told me. But it could be. He suggested I simply do what chiefs often do when support is wavering. Just before the election, you offer some carefully selected band members temporary jobs and you will get their vote, as well as the votes of their family and extended family. It just takes a handful of minimum wage jobs to the right people—that is another measure of the desperation our people live with. But I knew that what Richard was saying was true.

For me, it was a time for soul-searching. The political eruptions were coming at the same time as my personal life was changing and my marriage was ending. That is a particularly difficult thing in a small community where everyone is involved in some way in your personal life.

On the political level, I knew that continuing to serve as chief while dropping the larger battle for our land rights would not do our people a service. As chief I could only continue to manage our people's poverty. It was a time when I badly missed my brother Bobby, who had always been the one I turned to at moments like this. He understood better than anyone the hard personal choices that are often part of political struggle.

Finally I told Richard I would rather lose the election than win it with the tired old fraud of vote buying with jobs that only reminded us all of our helplessness. Richard nodded and said he'd see what he could do.

I didn't bother campaigning or anything like it for the vote in January 2003, but I could feel the turning away that Richard had predicted coming to pass. On election night, I stopped by the community hall and glanced at the first numbers. After having won the previous four elections for chief, it was over. I went home, and Beverly called me around midnight with the final number. The local Kamloops paper, which had been one of the loudest voices in attacking the Sun Peaks protesters and my support of them, must have held the presses until after midnight, because they had the final count on the front page of their morning edition under a headline celebrating my defeat.

It was bitter medicine for me, but it was, indeed, medicine. I was freed to focus on my work with INET and on the larger issues that mattered to my people. Perhaps the people had seen that with the chief's duties and those of the larger struggle, I was stretched too thin. Whether intentionally or not, they provided me with the remedy.

Nothing important changed in my community. The people were not at all interested in entering the extinguishment negotiations offered by the B.C. Treaty Commission process, and the new chief was pressured into quietly supporting our youth and Elders at Sun Peaks, though in a far less visible way than I had.

Still, I wouldn't be honest if I didn't admit that after receiving the call from Beverly, I slept fitfully. The human ego is not so easily silenced. It was a long dark night of the soul. But in the morning, the sun comes up. You get up and you go back to work. After eight years as chief, there were many files that had to be wrapped up and prepared to hand off to the incoming administration.

In the months after the election, I spent more time working with the protesters at Skwelkwek'welt. The people continued to build permanent camps and even log houses on our territory in the mountains, and the resort continued to use the RCMP to move in, tear down the structures, and arrest our youth and Elders. But the Skwelkwek'welt protesters also began to link with other activists who were focusing on British Columbia's 2010 Winter Olympics to bring attention to the province's unsettled land claims. During this period, we picked up an important friend and ally when Naomi Klein covered both the Sun Peaks battle and the Olympics protest in an article she wrote in July 2003 for *The Guardian*. As usual, she was able to cut to the heart of the matter:

> Let's be clear: this is not about a ski hill. It is about a plan to build a small city in the mountains, a place for urbanites to have a weekend getaway—and for developers to make a killing on real estate. Let's be clear about something else: the massive expansion of the Sun Peaks Resort is an act of violence. British Columbia's First Nation peoples have already been robbed of so much. It is the duty of all Canadians living on stolen land to join in the struggle to defend what is left.[39]

Naomi had interviewed me about the Olympics protest, and I told her that we were seeing the same kind of split there that we had seen locally with Sun Peaks. On one side were the chiefs and entrepreneurs who saw the Olympics as an opportunity— a chance for a new community centre, some affordable housing, a way to sell West Coast Indigenous art. On the other was a growing grassroots movement of people who still hunt and fish, and see industrial-scale tourism as a threat to their survival. They are the ones, not the chiefs, who depend on hunting to meet their needs. More tourism is going to take food off their tables, and they are going to end up on Vancouver's Hastings Street. That's what happens when you force Indian people off their land.

Over the next few years, Naomi came out to visit the Protection Centre several times. In our conversations, I learned a great deal about the wider struggle she was committed to. She has set an example on how to forcefully push for change in a principled way, and still not lose your sense of humanity or—to the delight of her friends—your sense of humour. She is not at all intimidated by power and showed herself quite prepared to work with the people who are resisting and trying to make fundamental change in society. We had several occasions to speak publicly together, and I was always amazed at how well she understood our issues. At one gathering at the Vancouver Library, where we were on the same panel, she said:

> Arthur talks about extinguishment. It is one of those bureaucratic phrases you hear when people talk about treaties. I think . . . it is

deliberately bureaucratic so that people kind of tune out. But if you think about the word *extinguishment*, this is a violent term . . . it is not a bureaucratic term. Extinguishment is the snuffing out of life, the snuffing out of an entire culture.

That is what you see—extinguishment in process, you actually see extinguishment in process, except for there is a moment when you can actually intervene and stop the extinguishment before it is too late. That is the moment we are in right now. This is the truth time.

Are you going to sleep, are you going to stay asleep on your responsibilities, our responsibilities and duties, or are we going to wake up with Irene over there and strut down main street in Sun Peaks.

For the activists who were even then taking a spiritual and, too often, a physical beating, it was balm to their souls. Her personal support helped to carry the weary protesters onward.

In fact, we prepared everywhere for long battles. On the logging issue, we continued to push our Harper Lake initiative through the courts in defence of our Aboriginal title and rights, and we continued to make our case to the world through INET as we built up our network with increasing support from Indigenous nations in Central Canada. And we found that, in our battle for our lands and our right to self-determination, we were gaining new allies at almost every turn—in Canada and around the world.

By this time, Nicole Schabus and I had become a couple. She had moved to Canada to work with INET and had taken courses at the University of British Columbia to get her Canadian accreditation as a lawyer. We have remained together as partners in struggle and partners in life, and she has contributed immeasurably to both. Now a law professor at Thompson Rivers University in Kamloops specializing in Aboriginal law, she continues to make a major contribution to the work of INET, and to my family and community. A woman with a brilliant mind and a generosity of spirit, she has thrown herself with enthusiasm into the task of spoiling my grandchildren and serving community members with free legal help. Meeting Nicole has been one of the great unexpected benefits of my political work.

# The Fourth World

## A Global Movement

NE OF THE RECURRING THEMES in our struggle has been the attempt to find justice on the international stage when it has been denied at home. This is not merely a matter of seeking sympathetic listeners abroad. It is deeply imbedded in our legal and political fight. I have spoken about the advances of the *Calder* and *Delgamuukw* decisions by the Supreme Court of Canada, and in chapter 17 we will look some more at the recent *Tsilhqot'in* decision. All three have clearly shown that we have far more rights, even within the Canadian system, than the governments were prepared to acknowledge— a large part of our struggle is simply to have governments obey their own laws in regard to Indigenous peoples. But the judges themselves have recognized that there is a limit to the justice they can dispense. On the fundamental question of Crown title and sovereignty, vis-a-vis Indigenous sovereignty, the Court itself is in conflict of interest.

This conflict stems from the fact that the judicial branch, along with the executive and legislative branch, is part of the Crown. If you ask the Court to judge the legality of the Crown assuming sovereignty over and title to Canadian territory on the basis of the travels and sightings of a few passersby in the seventeenth and eighteenth centuries, the Court, as one of the three branches of the Crown, cannot. It is as if you are asking the Court to determine if it has the right to exist or to judge the very sovereignty under which it was established.

This is not merely theoretical; it has been addressed by Commonwealth courts. In the *Mabo* decision (*Mabo v. Queensland* (No. 2) 1992) in Australia, a case similar to *Delgamuukw*, the Indigenous peoples had questioned the colonial doctrines in terms of acquisition of sovereignty. The High Court of Australia found: "The acquisition of territory by a sovereign state for the first time is an act of state which cannot be challenged, controlled or interfered with by the courts of that state."[40] They said the issue had to be addressed at the international level.

It is for this reason that Indigenous peoples have looked to the international level—and must continue to do so—as an essential part of our struggle for recognition of our land title and sovereign rights. Indigenous peoples have sought this recognition for more than a century. And over the past ten years, we have made important advances.

Historically, one of the most important attempts at an international hearing was made by a Six Nations Iroquois, Deskaheh, a hereditary chief of the Cayugas. In 1923 he travelled to Geneva on a Haudenosaunee passport to address the League of Nations. Deskaheh demanded that the Europeans respect Iroquois sovereignty as set forth in the Two Row Wampum Treaty they had originally made with the Dutch in New York. He then formally requested League of Nations intervention in the Six Nations land dispute with the Canadian government. His speech to the League was initially received sympathetically. The newly created world body had a mandate to recognize and support the self-government rights of all nations. But Canada, through its British representation, was deeply alarmed by the international support for Deskaheh. It was only through intense British lobbying that the League's formal support was denied to the Haudenosaunee nation.

Deskaheh went home empty-handed. But the Canadian government was not going to let his challenge go unpunished. The following year, the RCMP dissolved the traditional government of the Six Nations, confiscated important documents and wampums, and declared an immediate election to overturn the traditional government, which was replaced by a Department of Indian Affairs band council. Deskaheh died less than two years after addressing the League. Before he did, he summed up the Canadian and American Indian policy as follows: "Over in Ottawa, they call that policy *Indian Advancement*. Over in Washington, they call it *Assimilation*. We who would be the helpless victims say it is tyranny. If this must go on to the bitter end, we would rather that you come with your guns and poison gases and get rid of us that way. Do it openly and above board."[41]

In 1927, in response to international challenges and growing legal challenges in Canada to Ottawa's colonialist policies, the federal government brought in the Indian Act amendments that made Indian organizing on the land issue illegal. It was thus our parents' generation who took up the issue of international recognition, after the restrictions were lifted in the 1950s.

While activists of our parents' generation were trying to build unity at home, they were also building new relationships with Indigenous peoples around the world. They understood that they were part of what my father called "the Fourth World," Indigenous nations trapped within states in the First, Second, and Third Worlds who had been kept isolated and voiceless for too long. (This concept was an important one for our movement, and my father used it as the title for his 1974 book, *The Fourth World: An Indian Reality*.[42]) The first step, they decided, was to build an organization that would give Indigenous peoples visibility and voice on the international stage.

In the early 1970s, my father, as leader of the National Indian Brotherhood, was offered a place on a government trip to New Zealand and Australia led by Indian Affairs Minister Jean Chrétien. There, he was able to meet with Maori and Aborigine leaders. He later travelled to Scandinavia to meet with the Sami people. These contacts would eventually have an impact in his personal life. He established lifelong friendships with Sami people and eventually met a Sami woman, Maria Sofia Aikio, who travelled with him for some time. They went on to have a son, Ara Manuel, who is now part of the international wing of our family.

My father also visited Central and South America to meet with Indigenous peoples, and he even made it to Africa to meet with small Indigenous peoples and with world leaders like Julius Nyerere in Tanzania. As a result of these contacts, representatives of Indigenous Maori (New Zealand), Aborigine (Australia), Muisca (Colombia), Inuit (Greenland), Sami (Norway) peoples and my father from the National Indian Brotherhood met in Guyana in 1974 to plan the founding meeting of the World Council of Indigenous Peoples for the following year in Port Alberni, British Columbia. Angmalortok Olsen, an Inuit representative from Greenland, described this Guyana meeting in itself as a major achievement. "It dawned upon us that even though we sit in the far corner of the world, there is a movement through the whole world of ideas and of peoples and it seems to us that maybe we could do our little bit to humanize the present world as it is."[43]

The WCIP founding meeting, in 1975, was hosted by the Nuu-chah-nulth people on Vancouver Island with Indigenous representatives from North, Central, and South America, Europe, Australia, and New Zealand—a total of 260 participants including members of the world press. By all accounts, it was a historic event, with Indigenous peoples from around the world, often in their traditional dress, meeting one another for the first time. It was so new that the first item of business was to seek agreement on the proper name for the organization and for their collective existence. The identifying terms *Indian* and *Aboriginal* were both discussed; in the end, an old and respected Indigenous leader from Colombia who had just listened to the debate for days got up and said, "Indian and Aboriginal were colonial terms. We are people indigenous to our territories, so Indigenous is the term that should be used."

The conference agreed, but then participants had to decide who, exactly, were Indigenous peoples. They settled on this definition: "Indigenous peoples are peoples living in countries which have a population composed of differing ethnic or racial groups who are descendants of the earliest populations living in the area and who do not as a group control the national government of the countries within which they live."

This naming exercise is not as simple as it seemed. You will have noticed that in this book, I occasionally use the term *Indian*. It is a term that Indigenous peoples often use among themselves in a sort of self-derogatory way, and that is still commonly used at the grassroots level. For me it has a special significance, because it reminds me that decolonization has not yet come to our peoples and our lands. But *Indigenous* was adopted by our people at the world conference, and Oren Lyons, a chief and faith-keeper of the Onondaga Nation for whom I have great respect, told me that it was in 1977, after it was approved at the World Council meeting, that they brought the term *Indigenous* to Geneva and asked that it become the term used at the United Nations, as it now is in the UN Declaration on the Rights of Indigenous Peoples.

The next item on the conference agenda was, naturally enough, the land issue. Even though this resolution was put together forty years ago, it could have been written yesterday. That is how consistent Indigenous peoples have been, not only over the past forty years but also over the past two hundred years. On the land issue they said:

The WCIP believes that the traditional land rights of Indigenous peoples worldwide have been overpowered by the domination of Colonial powers. They no longer have the supreme and absolute power over their territories, resources or lives and have been forced to accept the Colonizer's imposed concepts of Indigenous Rights.

In order to rectify this injustice, the WCIP has recommended the following:

1. that the International community recognize Indigenous sovereignty and entitlement to traditional lands.
2. that the UN recognize the treaties that Indigenous Nations around the world have signed as binding under International Law.
3. that the International community and the UN honour its responsibility to the Indigenous Nations of the world by establishing the necessary mechanisms and instruments to protect their rights to self-determination with their lands and resources.[44]

With that baseline statement of rights established, the Conference elected my father, George Manuel, as chair, and the great U.S. leader and thinker Sam Deloria as secretary general. It was also agreed that the WCIP would take over the National Indian Brotherhood's observer status at the United Nations, which the NIB had acquired in 1975.

During the late 1970s and through the 1980s, the WCIP played an important role in establishing and cementing relationships among Indigenous nations around the world and in presenting the Indigenous point of view at the United Nations. Its influence waned in the 1990s, because of state pressures and internal divisions, and some of its functions have been replaced by more direct access for Indigenous peoples to the United Nations. But there is still a real need for such an organization to bring together Indigenous peoples in our own organization between international meetings to set our own agenda and develop and implement common strategies in the decolonization struggle.

For Indigenous peoples, the international bodies also present an essential link to the world. I know Canadians consider that they have one of the most benevolent governments in the world, and it has indeed shown benevolence in many instances, but never toward Indigenous peoples. When our issues are on the table, the government is ready to defy international law and even its own national laws. When Indigenous peoples have pushed Canada to live up to its ideals and its rhetoric, the retribution has always been swift. If the complainer has been receiving funding support, it is cut off and redirected to those who can be convinced to play the government's game. Many of those who stand fast find their names dishonoured; those who dare to try to protect their land quickly face armed assaults and mass arrests. A number of times over the past twenty-five years, this has been preceded by shootouts in our forests.

The criminalization that we saw of the Secwepemc people in our attempt to guard Aboriginal title and rights at Skwelkwek'welt was far from an isolated case. During the decades of the 1990s and 2000s, there were more than two hundred arrests of Indigenous people across Canada in land disputes, with charges ranging from criminal contempt to mischief to intimidation and obstruction of a peace officer. In Oka and Gustafsen Lake these disputes escalated into shootouts.

Indigenous peoples have found little sympathy and even less justice in Canada, so the applications we were able to make to international bodies like the Geneva-based UN Committee on the Elimination of All Forms of Racial Discrimination (CERD) and the UN Human Rights Committee take on an even greater importance.

At CERD and other world bodies we can present evidence of Canada's failure to uphold international human rights standards when it comes to Indigenous peoples. Canada is then forced to respond to our assertions. In our submissions, we have been able to chronicle the criminalization of protest as well as the RCMP's use of land mines at Gustafsen Lake at a time when Canada was championing the treaty to ban land mines from the world. We also gave evidence on the very disconcerting number of Indigenous deaths in police custody, many of them unexplained and never thoroughly investigated.

We put forward evidence showing how Indigenous activists are often subject to surveillance, their privacy invaded and their conversations and actions illegally recorded. Indigenous leaders and activists who stand up for their rights are often subject to bitter attacks on their honour and reputation. One example of this was the slander against me personally by a federal member of Parliament who described me as an "economic terrorist" for promoting our proprietary interests in our lands. The UN Human Rights Committee gives us a forum to show the world the face of Canada that is often kept hidden even from its own people, that of the bitter colonial state fighting on all fronts to preserve its dominance over Indigenous peoples.

An important new international institution was created in 2002—the UN Permanent Forum on Indigenous Issues as one of three UN bodies that are mandated to deal specifically with Indigenous peoples' issues. The others are the Expert Mechanism on the Rights of Indigenous Peoples and the Special Rapporteur on the Rights of Indigenous Peoples.

The establishment of the Permanent Forum was an important breakthrough for Indigenous peoples. It moved us a step forward from our previous status of an Indigenous Working Group. The next advance on the road to full recognition of our nationhood has to be at least observer state status at the United Nations.

The main limitation of the Permanent Forum is that the states with whom we are fighting for recognition of our rights still have a heavy influence. But it does give us a focal point for pushing our cause forward at the international level. Most of this work is done by the Global Indigenous Caucus, which meets before and during the annual meetings to take common positions. For Indigenous peoples from Canada, it is also essential that we are there to counter the steady stream of falsehood that Canada delivers to obscure its blatant colonialism over the Indigenous nations within its borders.

The inaugural session of the Permanent Forum in 2002 was opened by Secretary-General Kofi Annan, who proclaimed that the world's Indigenous peoples now had "a home at the United Nations." Delegates came forward with issues related to land rights, human rights, economic and social development, education and culture, the environment, women's rights, and Indigenous children and youth. The Permanent Forum has taken on one of these broad themes each year, as well as finding a space for Indigenous peoples in existing UN initiatives such as the Millennium Development Goals.

The first official Indigenous representative for North America was Wilton Littlechild, an Alberta Cree lawyer who went on to become a member of Parliament in Canada. He was also made the rapporteur of the session. I was honoured to be invited to speak at that first meeting, and I used my time to recall the organizing work of Indigenous peoples themselves in building the new international relationships, particularly our parents' generation having brought Indigenous peoples together in the World Council of Indigenous Peoples. Afterward I was very touched when Elders from around the world came to speak to me about my father and his role in building international solidarity.

Over the years, I have played various roles in the Indigenous caucus, from regional to global co-chair, and I have watched it move slowly—as everything to do with the United Nations does—to push the debate forward as states become more educated about our issues.

By mid-decade, the Permanent Forum work was bolstered by one of the most important documents ever drafted on Indigenous rights: the UN Declaration on the Rights of Indigenous Peoples. This document had a particularly tortuous history; it was twenty years in the making, with experts, member states, and Indigenous representatives battling over every point. Even referring to us as *Indigenous peoples* was a battle with the state representatives who wanted us referred to as *Indigenous populations*. That term would have kept us outside of the protection of the UN's basic human rights covenants, which offer special protection to all of the world's "peoples."

During this extended process, the longest negotiation of any human rights instrument in the UN's history, there was a great deal of tension between UN member states and Indigenous peoples' representatives, particularly over the issue of self-determination.

When observers speak of the reluctance of member states, they are really referring to four states in particular. Not surprisingly, they are the world's main anglo colonizers, the United States, Canada, Australia, and New Zealand. From the beginning, these states have fought the world at almost every turn. Yet despite their best efforts, the Declaration on the Rights of Indigenous Peoples was passed by a large majority by the UN General Assembly in 2007. With some important gaps, which I will discuss below, it was a historic breakthrough. For those interested in the state of Indigenous rights today, the UN Declaration on the Rights of Indigenous Peoples is an essential document that should be closely read.

The Declaration begins by noting that Indigenous peoples "have suffered from historic injustices as a result of, inter alia, their colonization and dispossession of their lands, territories and resources, thus preventing them from exercising, in particular, their right to development in accordance with their own needs and interests."

The preamble acknowledges "that the Charter of the United Nations, the International Covenant on Economic, Social and Cultural Rights and the International Covenant on Civil and Political Rights, as well as the

Vienna Declaration and Programme of Action, affirm the fundamental importance of the right to self-determination of all peoples." This opening links the right of Indigenous peoples to self-determination directly to the binding international treaties that recognize the right to self-determination of all peoples. After decades of debate the world community has now agreed that Indigenous peoples have the right to self-determination, which is spelled out unequivocally in Article 3 of the UNDRIP:

> Indigenous peoples have the right to self-determination. By virtue of that right they freely determine their political status and freely pursue their economic, social and cultural development.

I am including the full Declaration in the appendix to this book. If you go through it, you will see that Canada is in flagrant violation of virtually all of the core provisions regarding Indigenous self-determination, Indigenous land rights, and the requirements for governments to acquire Indigenous peoples' free, prior, and informed consent before initiating any developments on their land or any legislative and policy changes that affect us.

You will see that Canada's current land claims policy violates virtually every clause in articles 26, 27, 28, and 32. By explicitly refusing at the outset of land claims negotiations to acknowledge that "Indigenous peoples have the right to the lands, territories and resources which they have traditionally owned, occupied or otherwise used or acquired" (article 26), Canada is in violation of the Declaration on the Rights of Indigenous Peoples.

Canada is the only country in the world to have twice voted against the UNDRIP, first in the UN Human Rights Council that adopted the draft declaration as one of its first substantive decisions. After that Canada actually managed to reopen the text and after trying again to weaken the Declaration section by section, went on to lead the quiet opposition to it on the General Assembly floor. To influence the world body, they went to developing countries trying to raise fears that Indigenous self-determination could break up their countries, and worked with the United States, Australia, and New Zealand to have the world body vote it down. At the time, we feared the Canadians might succeed, like the British had in blocking the originally strong League of Nations support for Deskaheh and the Haudenosaunee Confederacy. But when the final vote came in September 2007, it was the rights deniers who found themselves in stark isolation.

Many developing countries, the Third World, had achieved decolonization through exercising the right to self-determination; they were not convinced by Canada to vote against it. The UN General Assembly supported the Declaration on the Rights of Indigenous Peoples by a vote of 144 to 4, with 11 abstentions. The four countries voting against were, of course, Canada, the United States, Australia, and New Zealand. Two years later, Australia and New Zealand reversed their vote, and Canada and the United States grudgingly followed. Canada, though, tried to muddy the waters by announcing only its "qualified" support for the Declaration, suggesting it supported the Declaration only insofar as it did not actually require Canada to change any of its current laws or policies against Indigenous land rights, self-determination, and prior informed consent.

But the UNDRIP, overwhelmingly supported by the international community, cannot be so easily ignored. Today its provisions are recognized principles of international law and a unifying document for Indigenous peoples around the world. Within Canada, it is something that the Assembly of First Nations and the First Nations Summit, INET, the Defenders of the Land, and Idle No More can get behind and together demand that the Canadian government respect. It is what the world expects. It is what Canadians should expect.

Despite its imperfections, the UN Permanent Forum has allowed us to continue to push forward in our bid for justice. After the Declaration on the Rights of Indigenous Peoples, the most important statement by the Permanent Forum on Indigenous Issues came in 2012 when it condemned and rejected the doctrine of discovery—the basis British and other European powers used to claim our lands and sovereignty over them.

I had been elected co-chair of the Global Indigenous Peoples Caucus that year, so I was given the honour of addressing the Forum on the doctrine of discovery. The text was put together by representatives of Indigenous peoples from around the world meeting over two days in New York. Each paragraph in these documents goes through an exhaustive discussion. If there is a dispute on any item, those who disagree are sent off to resolve it. If they cannot, the caucus won't put the paragraph in the document. So it is truly a consensus statement.

In the 2012 text, we recommended "that the Permanent Forum acknowledge that the doctrine of discovery, both in theory and in on-going practice, constitutes the subjection of peoples to alien subjugation, domination and exploitation. It is the denial of fundamental inherent human rights, is contrary to the Charter of the United Nations and is an impediment to the promotion of world peace and cooperation."

The Indigenous peoples of the world demanded that the Permanent Forum acknowledge and transmit to other UN agencies that:

> The doctrine of discovery is an expression of racism, xenophobia and discrimination—that it represents a regime of systematic oppression and domination by one racial or religious group over another, and it is committed to the intention of maintaining that regime. As such, the continuing operation of the doctrine of discovery should be recognized as a crime against humanity and should be condemned as such.

In concrete terms, we asked the Permanent Forum to launch a study on the cascading effects of this doctrine on Indigenous health, physical, psychological, and social well-being, human and collective rights, lands, resources, medicines and titles to such lands, resources, medicines.

We also noted that the modern state extension of the doctrine of discovery could be clearly seen in the extinguishment policy pursued by Canada and other states.

> "Extinguishment", in the context of indigenous peoples' rights to lands, territories and resources is inconsistent with the contemporary understanding in international law, specifically the peremptory norm of the absolute prohibition against racial discrimination. No other peoples in the world are pressured to have their rights "extinguished".[45]

We ended our statement by recommending that permanent seats at the United Nations General Assembly be established for Indigenous peoples. This idea is in its infancy, but it is a vital one in ensuring that we take our place where we belong, among the nations of the world, to speak directly to the family of nations without the interference or outright suppression that we have endured from the member states. After the massive vote in favour of the UN Declaration on the Rights of Indigenous Peoples, we know we would find friends there.

Like my father before me, I have been privileged to visit Indigenous peoples around the world, and I find them without exception committed to the principles set out in the Declaration. Their political commitment

With Russell Diabo and two Sami activists, Alta, Norway, June 2013

is bolstered by their spirituality, which has survived centuries of colonization. My friend Lix Lopez—a Mayan who first worked with my father at the WCIP and now lives in Canada, where he leads Mayan ceremonies—arranged a trip to Mayan territory in Guatemala for me. There I experienced the great pre-Columbian Mayan spirituality in the highlands of their country. I was fortunate enough to be present for the beginning of the thirteenth Baktun, the changeover of the Mayan calendar. In our political fight, where the spirit easily becomes dry and parched, it was a cool glass of water and another realization of what we are fighting for as we enter into this new era of the spirit.

My travels also sometimes help to bring me full circle. Recently in Alta, Norway, at a preparatory meeting for the 2014 World Conference of Indigenous Peoples, Wilton Littlechild introduced me as the son of George Manuel, one of the pioneers of the international movement. I was pleased to be able to tell Wilton that I was not George Manuel's only son there. My Sami brother, Ara, was also present, and he too was invited up to the stage. Today we fight our father's fight along with his fellow Sami activists like Maria Sofia Aikio and Niillas Somby, and our Indigenous brothers and sisters from around the world.

# Line of Defence

## Side by Side for
## Mother Earth

**T**O SAY THAT INDIGENOUS PEOPLES are environmentalists is a redundancy. We are, after all, the children and the defenders of the land. Our Indigenous economies have been based on cultivation, herding, hunting, gathering, fishing—and their related technologies—all integrated into the natural cycles of the earth. For Indigenous peoples, the air and water, the forests and animals are eternal values, the things that sustain life itself. If you damage any one of these to satisfy your immediate needs, you are literally harming yourself. Watching today's rapacious industrial development of the land by the Western world is like watching a person with a serious mental illness causing self-harm. But our people, because we are so deeply connected to the land, are generally the first to feel the pain.

Our duty to protect our lands is primordial, and the assault on our lands and resources today is unprecedented. In places like the Alberta tar sands, the scarring can be seen from outer space and the pace of development is accelerating. According to Canadian government estimates, more than $650 billion (yes, billion) in resource extraction investment is expected to pour into Canada over the next twenty years. The great majority of that investment will be targeted on our lands.

Extractive industries seem to view our land as if it was a vast Walmart where they can endlessly go up and down the aisles picking things up—or digging them up—and taking them home. The economic system today looks at Mother Earth and sees only profits; the rest it sees as simply garbage. As if the land had no value of its own and no limits on what it can give. But at the same time, an increasing number of people around the world, including many of our Canadian friends and allies, are coming to understand that this understanding is false. If the old industrial model of viewing the land simply as a resource base for production leading to profit persists, the damage will soon be beyond repair. The planet cannot sustain the damage we are inflicting on it. In some respects—like global warming—we have already passed the eleventh hour.

In the struggle to protect the land, Indigenous peoples are the first and last line of defence. But fortunately, we are not fighting these battles alone. Over the last two decades, Indigenous peoples have been increasingly working in partnership with non-Indigenous environmentalist individuals and organizations. In many ways, this is one of the most hopeful Indigenous/non-Indigenous alliances we have had in any sphere, and it is crucial if we hope to spare the earth from irreparable destruction.

To understand the historic importance of this relatively new alliance, we have to realize that it was not at first a natural one. For more than a century, the environmentalists, previously known as conservationists, with whom we came into contact did not seem to share our fundamental values. Just like the state authorities did, these colonial-minded conservationists often ignored, dismissed, and in extreme cases even attacked our people.

One reason was that the conservationists were not motivated by any profound attachment to the land. They seemed more motivated by aesthetics than by genuine concern for the health of the planet. In a way, early environmentalism was simply an adjunct to the system of production, with an interest in cleaning up or hiding the mess.

Conservationists ensured that toxic materials were buried out of sight. Old growth forests—incredibly complex and diverse habitats—were clearcut and replaced with acres of monoculture seedlings, ignoring the real, permanent damage to the ecosystem. Production moved on and the damage to the earth continued unabated, with the conservationists plodding along behind, performing a kind of janitorial service for the resource extractors.

This type of conservationism is still evident in most of the world's carbon-trading schemes. For example, the UN's Reducing Emissions from

Deforestation and Forest Degradation (UN-REDD) program, adminis-tered by the World Bank, allows polluters in the developed world to con-tinue spewing carbon into an already overheated atmosphere as long as they pay a few cents to save a tree in the Amazon. These carbon-trading schemes are like trying to play three-card monte with the Creator, but ultimately, it is impossible to trick the Creator. This type of environmen-talism is built on expediency, a way to try to extend the life of rampant con-sumerism when the earth is demanding a rest. The self-injury continues.

If you go back far enough, you will even find times when the forerun-ners of environmentalists and Indigenous peoples were in open conflict. The hostility was most pointed in the late nineteenth century during the creation of national parks, where the settler environmentalist "cleanup" included removing Indigenous peoples from their homelands. The most infamous and violent example came in the early 1870s, when the U.S. government answered the call of environmentalists by making Yellow-stone a national park. The problem was that it was the territory of the Shoshone-Bannock people. So the government simply ordered their removal. No thought was given to the fact that these lands belonged to the Indigenous peoples, and there was no reflection that the "pristine wil-derness" was in such a state because the Shoshone-Bannock had been taking care of it for thousands of years. The attempt to remove the people sparked a guerrilla war that resulted in more than three hundred deaths, all in the name of "conservation."

We have also seen numerous examples in Canada where misguided—in fact, perverse—attempts at securing "protected" lands have resulted in tragedy for our people. The most recent deadly example was the 1995 killing of Dudley George, an unarmed Anishinabe youth in Ipperwash Provincial Park, during a protest aimed at returning the land, which had been gradually confiscated from the 1920s to 1940s, to the Stony Point First Nation. Since then, the World Parks Congress has recognized "the rights of Indigenous Peoples with regard to their lands or territories and resources that fall within protected areas," but governments have almost universally refused to return these confiscated lands to our people.

It is not surprising, then, that Indigenous peoples were isolated from this type of settler environmental movement. But that does not mean we were inactive. We have fought to protect our lands in Canada from the very beginning, and on the international scene, we were present during the first international conference on addressing the world's fragile ecosystems.

That meeting came in 1972 when the United Nations sponsored the landmark Conference on Environment and Development in Stockholm. My father, George Manuel, attended as the head of the National Indian Brotherhood, not as part of the official Canadian delegation or by invitation of Canadian environmentalists, but representing an NGO under the aegis of the Canadian Labour Congress.

The NIB had put together an Indigenous environmental position paper that my father intended to deliver to the conference in Stockholm. But he found himself completely ignored by the official Canadian delegation, including by the Canadian environmentalists, and was given no place in the agenda to address the conference. What saved the trip for him was the fact that the Europeans were intrigued by the presence of a Canadian Indian, and one of the Swedish newspapers offered to fly him up to Samiland to meet with the Sami people in a staged meeting of worlds. While in Samiland my father was able to win support for the idea of a World Council of Indigenous Peoples, and the contacts he made in Sweden led to future funding support for the organization.

The final report of the Stockholm Conference put forward 26 principles and 109 recommendations that largely reflected the production model of the environment, stating things like "Natural resources must be safeguarded" and "The Earth's capacity to produce renewable resources must be maintained." In environmental principles for protecting Mother Earth, Indigenous peoples were miles ahead.

For the rest of the world, the realization of the extent of the damage being done to the earth's ecosystems came gradually. But by 1987, when the former Norwegian prime minister Gro Harlem Brundtland produced her UN report on the world environment entitled *Our Common Future*, there was a new urgency in the tone and content of the environmental plan. It also, for the first time, recognized an important role for Indigenous peoples in protecting the earth's environment. The Brundtland Report observed:

> Tribal and indigenous peoples will need special attention as the forces of economic development disrupt their traditional life-styles—life-styles that can offer modern societies many lessons in the management of resources in complex forest, mountain and dry land ecosystems. . . . Their traditional rights should be recognized and they should be given a decisive voice in formulating resource development in their areas.[46]

The last sentence signalled the beginning of international environmentalists' awareness that Indigenous peoples were not only potential partners in environmental protection, but must also be the decision makers in protecting their lands.

By the time of the 1992 UN Earth Summit in Rio de Janeiro, Indigenous representatives from around the world were present in large numbers to sound the alarm to the international community. The Rio Summit also turned out to be an important landmark for the world when the Convention on Biological Diversity and the UN Framework Convention on Climate Change, which led to the Kyoto Protocol, were first agreed to. The Summit also gave important recognition to Indigenous peoples. A whole chapter of its political action plan was devoted to "Recognizing and strengthening the role of indigenous people and their communities." And the Summit significantly expanded the Brundtland Report's position on the Indigenous role in environmental protection:

> [Indigenous peoples] are repositories of much of the traditional knowledge and wisdom from which modernization has separated most of us. They are custodians, too, of some of the world's most important and vulnerable ecosystems—tropical forests, deserts and arctic regions. We must hear and heed their voices, learn from their experience and respect their right to live in their own lands in accordance with their traditions, values and cultures.
>
> Full and informed participation of people through democratic processes at every level, accompanied by openness and transparency, are essential to the achievement of the objectives of this Conference.[47]

From the Rio Summit onward, Indigenous peoples have remained central in the international struggle for sustainable development. We have seen this not only in the Amazon forests of Brazil and the tundra of Samiland, but also here in Canada in the boreal forests of the east and the rainforests of the west. It has reached the point today that when governments and multinationals see Indians and non-Indigenous environmentalists getting together on an issue, they become very worried.

At the same time as environmentalists were recognizing the essential role of Indigenous peoples at the international level, environmentalists and Indigenous peoples in Canada were taking the first steps toward working together on the ground. We saw this in a series of battles, starting with the 1984 Nuu-chah-nulth Meares Island logging road blockade and in court challenges to the massive Clayoquot Sound logging protests in the early 1990s. Indigenous and non-Indigenous activists, including my friends Steve and Sue Lawson, stood side by side to protect the old growth forests in a battle that took on international dimensions.

My experience in working with non-Indigenous environmentalists began when I worked with the Washington-based Natural Resources Defense Council on the logging issue. Then, in 2001, I was invited by Maude Barlow to a historic international conference on water protection that the Council of Canadians was organizing in Vancouver. At the time, we were fighting to protect Skwelkwek'welt from Sun Peaks overdevelopment, and it seemed like a good way to promote our cause to the world.

The conference was called Water for People and Nature: A Forum on Conservation and Human Rights. When we first discussed my participation in the conference, Maude was very open to the idea of having an Indigenous component. What impressed me about her was that she understood that water is not only the property of humanity, it belongs to all living things—to all of the flora and fauna of the world. She agreed that Indigenous peoples should not be compartmentalized, but should be an important part of the conference mainstream.

We were given the means to invite dozens of Indigenous peoples' representatives from around the world, and Indigenous delegates met together on the day before the conference began. I was asked to chair the meeting, and we set the goal of drafting an Indigenous position on water rights.

Our declaration listed the attacks on water from chemicals, pesticides, untreated sewage, and nuclear waste as well as the diversion of water for unsustainable resource and recreational developments, and condemned any and all treatments of water like a commodity that can be bought, sold, and traded in global and domestic economies. Water for our peoples is profoundly sacred, and in our declaration we supported the fight of Indigenous peoples and grassroots peoples around the world to protect this special gift from the Creator.

I have remained active in the cause of protecting our water since then. Along with alliances with non-Indigenous environmentalists, I have developed true friendships and have profited greatly from allies' knowledge and solidarity. This spirit has generally marked the movement that has emerged over the past decades. We have learned a great deal from each other.

Our effectiveness in the environmental battle has been increased as courts have recognized our legal status on our Aboriginal title lands. The recognition of our Aboriginal title in *Delgamuukw* allows us to challenge the most irresponsible types of development in court. In fact, *Delgamuukw* gives us a legal duty to protect the land since, according to the Supreme Court, the only way we can lose our Aboriginal title is if we engage in activity on the land that destroys our ecosystem economy for future generations.

Another important breakthrough was the *Haida* decision in 2004. That case involved a series of transfers of timber licences by the province to forestry multinationals, including one to the logging giant Weyerhaeuser in 1999. Since the land was in Haida territory, the Haida went to court to claim that the province had no right to give out the licences without first consulting with them. The challenged the governments' business-as-usual approach following *Delgamuukw*. The Supreme Court agreed. Chief Justice McLachlin wrote the unanimous decision that found that even though the timber licences were merely being transferred from one multinational to another, the province still had a duty to consult with Indigenous peoples and that that consultation had to be meaningful, which might—depending on the strength of the Aboriginal title and rights claim—include consent.

I was at the Supreme Court for the hearing, and I was interested to see that several of the non-Indigenous municipalities on Haida territory intervened on the side of the Haida, seeing in the Haida a kind of protector of the region from the out-of-control industrial development of the multinationals. At the time, I was working with one of the most important Haida leaders in the battles in the forest, Guujaaw, who was for many years president of the Council of the Haida Nation. Guujaaw, along with Naomi Klein, accompanied me on a second visit to Standard & Poor's. Naomi wrote about this encounter in her recent book *This Changes Everything*, remarking that S&P understood that we had never surrendered our title but their attitude was, "We know you never sold your land. But how are you going to make the Canadian government keep its word. You and what army?"

At the meeting, Guujaaw, who always understood the importance of pushing our agenda in the international sphere, presented S&P with the Haida Nation's statement of claim that he had filed before the Supreme Court of British Columbia. We took a common position on many of the important issues facing our peoples, and I was honoured to be invited on several occasions to address the Haida people at their meetings.

In recognizing that even before Aboriginal title was proven in court, consultation with the Indigenous peoples was required, the *Haida* decision was a direct challenge to the government's business-as-usual approach. It also put Aboriginal title and rights in a new light for non-Indigenous environmentalists. As Jessica Clogg of the West Coast Environmental Law centre sees it, Indigenous peoples and their rights—once ignored and at times even dismissed by environmentalists—must now be at the forefront of the environmental movement.

> The Supreme Court of Canada has made it clear that there is an obligation to engage honourably with First Nations peoples when decisions are made about land and resources. . . . But beyond this, First Nations own legal traditions place responsibilities and obligations on them to safeguard the well-being of land and water in order to sustain their cultures, laws and governance systems. These laws and responsibilities are both a source of, and an interconnected part of the First Nations inherent title. In my opinion, the duty on the Crown to accommodate the Aboriginal Title includes an obligation to accommodate these legal traditions in decision-making about the land and water.
>
> Finally, justice and equitable distribution of benefits and resources is a fundamental element of sustainability. There can be no sustainability that is based on the injustice and denial of Aboriginal Peoples.[48]

Clogg touches on the core of this new alliance between Indigenous and non-Indigenous environmentalists. As we have seen, the non-Indigenous activists have considerable financial and international organizational support, and Indigenous peoples have the legal rights on the ground that allow us, in many cases, to actually stop unsustainable rampaging development. This new alliance of Indigenous and grassroots environmentalism has had a number of important victories. We continue to work together on initiatives like opposing the pipeline and tanker export of Alberta tar sands oil through our territories and waterways on the west coast. But at the same time, we still find ourselves on divergent paths with those environmentalists who do not understand the central importance of respecting our Aboriginal title in the long-term protection of the land.

This was illustrated in the battle to protect the Great Bear Rainforest, the largest intact coastal rainforest in North America. In 1994, the Nuxalk

Nation, led by the great hereditary Chief Qwatsinas, invited non-Indigenous environmentalists to their territory to oppose large-scale clear-cut logging.

Qwatsinas was a dear friend of mine—in a friendship that, in a sense, extended back a generation. My father had been very close to the Nuxalk people, and they had presented him with a button blanket that he had cherished. After he passed away, I brought that blanket back to them, since I knew that I did not have the right to possess it. But I was greeted with great emotion, and I sensed the affection they felt for my father. The people put the blanket on me in a potlatch as I continued my father's work and they always invite me to sit with the hereditary chiefs.

From there, our friendship grew and as I learned from him, I developed great esteem for Chief Qwatsinas. I watched as he worked with the outside environmentalists to build a campaign to save the forest with road blockades and a boycott of Great Bear Rainforest timber. Chief Qwatsinas was one of the first arrested, and he spoke for himself in front of the judge. "I am charged with contempt of court," he told the judge, "yet there is continuous contempt of our culture, our heritage, our lands, and our rights. Logging companies coming to our land without our consent show contempt of our laws, our land, our people."

Qwatsinas would be arrested three times, and in jail he would declare himself a political prisoner. But his campaign was working. The loggers were shut out of the forest until February 2006, when Greenpeace and Sierra Club announced they had made a "historic agreement" with government and industry to bring an end to the "war in the woods" in the Great Bear Rainforest. Without consulting the Nuxalk people, they agreed to protection of one-third of the rainforest and to allow logging on the rest of the thousand-year old ancient forest. The sense of betrayal felt by Qwatsinas and the Nuxalk people was profound, and it served as a reminder that in some sectors of the environmental movement, the old "conservationist" attitude remains. Qwatsinas described the deal as a process that allowed the companies to "talk and log." Nothing changed.

Tragically, Chief Qwatsinas passed away after a brief illness in 2010. It was a great loss not only to the Nuxalk but to all of the Indigenous peoples of British Columbia.

Throughout this period the real enemy, however, was a familiar one, both at home and abroad. The battle hinged on the principle that Indigenous peoples would have to give their prior informed consent before any development could take place on their lands. And the state that stood most fiercely against this recognition was, of course, Canada. This battle was fought most directly at the UN Convention on Biological Diversity conference in The Hague in 2002.

The issue of requiring prior informed consent of Indigenous peoples had been opposed by Canada even before The Hague meeting. At a preparatory meeting in Montreal in February 2002 that I attended with Elder Irene Billy, Canada was already trying to undermine the "prior informed consent" clause that was supported by the European Union and countries in Latin America, Africa, and much of the rest of the world.

I remember that meeting well because we were up in the theatre seating while the bureaucratic jargon flew back and forth across the stage, and I thought that Irene was probably not understanding much. But she sat quietly listening during a five-day meeting, as the Canadians tried to dramatically weaken our protection by substituting *consultation* for *consent*. As soon as the meeting closed, she leapt out of her chair and down to the exit where she could head off the departing Canadian delegation. I watched with delight as Irene—this small, dynamic Indigenous woman—ripped into them, bringing up their repression in Sun Peaks with the arrest of the youth and Elders there who were only trying to protect our forests and mountains. She told them that she had listened to the debate and that prior informed consent meant that "we have to say *yes* to a development and we never agreed to the expansion of Sun Peaks." Other delegations stopped to listen at this unprecedented scolding of the Canadians, who tried to escape by handing her their business cards and telling her to contact them after the meeting.

Later, I was with Irene in the lobby where all of the delegates were milling around. We were standing not far from the escalators that led down to the street, and I watched with great amusement as the Canadian delegates practically tiptoed around us to get to the escalators without Irene seeing them. Less amusing was the fact that before fleeing the wrath of Irene, the Canadians at that meeting managed to have brackets inserted around the "prior informed consent" clause to have it reviewed at The Hague meeting in April.

The Hague conference started out well, with the majority appearing to hold fast to the principle of prior informed consent of Indigenous peoples. This stance was not purely altruistic. The world had taken note that while Indigenous territories make up one-third of the earth's surface, they contain over two-thirds of the planet's biodiversity. Removing Indigenous consent would open the door to wild-west industrial development on the most precious lands remaining on the planet.

But then Canada went to work. On Monday, April 15, 2002, Canada, Australia, and Malaysia officially opposed reference to "prior informed consent," supporting *consultation* in place of *consent*. That Thursday, the day before the conference closed, the text submitted to the working group by a group of Friends of the Chair, which included Canada but excluded Indigenous peoples, had changed "prior informed consent" to "prior informed consultation." This change had come about after an intense all-night session, where Canada had threatened to oppose all other decisions of the conference if the wording change was not made.

This was a stunning setback for our cause. The official Canadian delegation was made up of government officials and hand-picked Indigenous representatives from national organizations. My travel costs were being paid for by Canada but my status was as a member of the International Indigenous Forum on Biodiversity (IIFB), not a member of the official delegation. When I arrived at the meeting, I asked fellow Secwepemc Fred Fortier, who co-chaired the IIFB, what could be done about the altered text. He explained that changing text from the Friends of the Chair was pretty hard, if not impossible, because we are not a nation-state and the conference now seemed to be locked in to the position.

I could not accept this.

I went to talk to John Herity, director of the Biological Convention Office at Environment Canada and chair of the Canadian delegation. Herity told me that he required the change to *consultation* because of the need to protect the power of the federal government to expropriate lands. He also said that he had the support of the Canadian Indigenous representatives.

This is where I, and the other delegates at the conference, learned of Canada's deviousness and dishonesty in claiming that "Canadian Indigenous representatives" supported his position. I told Herity that I, for one, did not support the Canada position.

"Well, you are just one chief," he said.

Spotting Peigi Wilson, the AFN representative, high up in the gallery, I pushed my way up through the narrow aisles to speak to her. I asked Peigi if she supported the Canadian "consultation" position. She said that she was aware of the change and she had not supported it, but she had not really opposed it either. I told her that Herity was telling everyone that Indigenous peoples from Canada supported Canada's position and suggested she go down to tell him that this was not the case.

When I spoke to other Indigenous representatives from Canada, I found that their response was similar to Peigi's. They had not really spoken up about the change and Canada was trying to use their silence as approval, lying to the chair in saying that Indigenous peoples from Canada supported the change. I told them to all head down there and tell him that they did not agree. Others joined Peigi at Herity's desk in a chaotic scrum.

On my way toward them, I was stopped by an official representative from Ecuador who asked me to join her and a number of other Central and South American representatives. She told me that they were getting mixed signals from the Canadian Indigenous groups. She said that they had been fighting to get prior informed consent included in this document but we were sending very mixed messages. They pointed to some Canadian Indigenous representatives who started their statements thanking Canada although they opposed our position, when they should be thanking the countries who supported Indigenous prior informed consent.

When I reached Herity's desk, I was surprised to see Rigoberta Menchú Tum, the Guatemalan Nobel Peace Prize recipient, standing at the edge of the group. Rigoberta was one of the keynote speakers at the conference. I had spoken with her while she was touring Canada earlier that year. She had met my father when he was in Guatemala with the World Council of Indigenous Peoples and said he had been an inspiration for her. When Nicole saw Rigoberta in the rotunda outside the meeting room, she told her about our struggle on the floor against Canada's attempt to water down the "prior informed consent" clause. I was surprised and, I must admit, delighted, when she approached me with her arms outstretched asking me what trouble was being caused to our Indigenous peoples. I told her that Canada was trying to change *consent* to *consultation*, and showed her the text. She said that this was shameful and, within earshot of Herity, exclaimed that if Canada did not change its mind, Rigoberta would immediately hold a press conference and denounce them to the world.

Then Rigoberta was on her way to the stage to talk to the chair, distinguished Jamaican environmentalist Elaine Fisher. Rigoberta marched right up the front stairway and motioned me to join them. I was hesitant to follow, so she brought Dr. Fisher to the side stairs where we could talk. Fisher said that the reason she approved the above text was because the Canadian delegation had assured her that they had the support of the Indigenous peoples of Canada. I told the chair and Rigoberta that they did not have my support, nor did I think they had the support of the other Canadian Indigenous representatives who were still surrounding the hapless Herity.

Faced with the vocal Indigenous opposition, and the overt display that his claim for Indigenous support had been untrue, Herity backed down. He told the Indigenous representatives that he would reverse Canada's position and took the floor first accepting prior informed consent. The EU and Norway supported the proposed compromise.

> Where the national legal regime requires prior informed consent of indigenous and local communities, the assessment process shall consider whether such prior informed consent has been obtained.[49]

I addressed the issue of Canada's bad behaviour in my closing statement for the IIFB. I said that traditional knowledge and prior informed consent were causes my people were going to jail for back home at Skwelkwek'welt, and that Indigenous peoples in Central and South America were dying for. I said that Canada's behaviour cannot be accepted and that I would support any statement that notifies the international community that we will take any threat to our rights seriously.

Some Indigenous representatives from Canada, I later heard, worried that making a strong statement against Canada would jeopardize funding for the next international meeting. It is a variation of the argument we have been living with for years: we cannot fight for our rights or for justice because if we do, the crumbs that we are given by governments may be taken away. This argument guarantees our oppression and impoverishment.

On the morning I was leaving The Hague, I had a pleasure that I doubt I will ever have again. As I mentioned, I was not an official representative in the Canadian delegation but Canada was paying my hotel bill, and I was at the front desk when Herity stopped by to take care of the bill. He did it without a word to me, saying to the clerk "I'm here to pay this man's bill," as he thrust the government credit card across the counter. It was the first and the last time my participation in an international meeting through the forum was funded by Canada. But as a representative of INET, I have found a way, without government funding, to attend and speak out at every major biodiversity conference since then. What use is it to be part of the Canadian delegation if you cannot speak for your people and their rights, but only parrot the Canadian line?

This instance is typical of the way Canada behaves on the international stage regarding anything touching on Indigenous rights. Canada has a colonial addiction when it comes to Indigenous peoples. It should be noted that The Hague conference was at the time of the Liberal government, which was generally considered a boy scout in international affairs. This reputation might have been valid on other issues, but when it came to Indigenous rights, the Liberals have been determinedly adversarial, relentlessly subverting our cause and protecting their colonialist hegemony.

Since the Conservative government came to power in 2006, it has openly flouted world opinion on everything from climate change to the rights of the Palestinians, at the cost of Canada's credibility in the world. Ironically, this has helped our cause. After almost a decade of the Harper government, Canada is seen as a self-centred anti-social country. Its interventions against Indigenous peoples are now viewed by the world as simply another manifestation of this approach, and Canada is increasingly isolated.

Even the World Bank, certainly one of the world's most conservative institutions, now sees a major role for Indigenous peoples in protecting the planet's remaining biodiversity. The bank, never a friend of Indigenous peoples, now proposes "as the next logical step to develop natural resource and biodiversity conservation and management plans" with the Indigenous peoples themselves given the responsibility of enforcing those plans. As the bank sees it:

In contrast with hired outsiders, Indigenous peoples already live on the land, reducing the cost of a labor force to maintain and protect the area. The existing decision-making structures that govern indigenous communities lead to greater local buy-in on the decisions reached. Local populations have a far greater stake in the successful outcome of conservation and management initiatives on their territories—a critical consideration for initiatives to maintain protected areas over the long term. Traditional resource management systems tend to incorporate the long-term perspectives required for sustainability.[50]

This is precisely what Russell Diabo was working on at a local scale in his Barriere Lake resource management plan in the 1980s, and what we hoped to achieve with our Traditional Use Study for the Secwepemc people in the 1990s. And it is precisely what Canada fights to avoid in international forums, and even more so within the country, with its extinguishment treaties that aim to remove our lands from us forever and capture the resources and the biodiversity of the land for unregulated industrial extraction by multinationals.

The world understands clearly that stripping Indigenous peoples of their land puts at serious risk the vast majority of the planet's remaining biodiversity. Canada fights against the tide in attempting to retain its full colonial power over the Indigenous peoples within its borders and exclusive control of lands that it does not fully own.

Canada—and in fact, all nations of the world—could learn from Bolivia's Indigenous president, Evo Morales, who has enacted a law protecting Mother Earth that sets out seven specific rights that Mother Earth and her constituent life systems, including human communities, are entitled to. They include the right to the diversity of life, to clean water and clean air, to the natural equilibrium, to live free of contamination, and to have damaged systems restored. The law gives legal personhood to the natural system, and may allow citizens, as part of Mother Earth, to sue individuals and groups in response to real and alleged infringements of its integrity. This law expresses, in modern legal form, the essence of our Indigenous values.

In the environmental battles, the art of a successful campaign is the art of increasing your forces, so we have looked to sympathetic people in all walks of life. It has been encouraging for our people to see non-Indigenous support for our cause. One of those who responded to our call and who has supported us without condition is film director James Cameron.

I first became aware of Cameron when I was working on a contract for Kitchenuhmaykoosib Inninuwug (KI), a large fly-in community on the shores of Big Trout Lake in Northern Ontario. KI was engaged in a bitter dispute with Platinex, a mining exploration company that was moving into its lands. I was in Thunder Bay with Jacob Ostaman and KI Chief Donny Morris when Cameron's blockbuster *Avatar* came out. The two of them liked the movie for its obvious parallel to their fight to protect their forests from mining company exploitation. Chief Morris and the entire KI council had been jailed for six months over their protest and opposition to Platinex's exploration activities. So when I was invited to meet with Cameron in May 2010 when he was attending the UN Permanent Forum on Indigenous Issues meeting in New York, I was thinking more of Chief Donny Morris and his Kitchenuhmaykoosib Inninuwug people's courageous stand against Platinex than Cameron's ten-foot-tall Na'vi people battling the mining company on Pandora.

We had heard that Cameron was focused on the Amazon rainforest, but several of us were determined to bring him to Canada to support our struggles. The meeting took place at his suite in the Ritz-Carlton Hotel, and it was, of course, a bit of a zoo with all sorts of people with all sorts of causes trying to meet with the famous director. I was part of the delegation of the Seventh Generation Fund, whom Cameron had contacted when he was challenged by a young Indigenous person to support our cause. I was let in and we ended up having a very good discussion about our economic and environmental struggles. The world has come to know Cameron as a deep sea explorer as well as a film director, and I must admit we were impressed by the man and his sincere wish to support our cause.

After several months of ongoing discussion, his intervention in Canada came the following spring in the form of a tour of the tar sands and onsite meetings with the Athabascan people in the region. I was invited along with a group of Indigenous and environmental activists, and I confess it was a little surreal when we toured the devastated landscape in a convoy of two helicopters.

The tar sands development had turned these Cree and Chipewyan lands into a hell on earth, and at least for a day, Cameron was able to bring international attention to the environmental devastation. My only regret was that, because of a scheduling problem, Chief Donny Morris was unable to accompany us. As someone who had already been jailed for protecting his land, he would have added something to the tour.

There is a personal coda to this story. In a subsequent email exchange with Cameron, I mentioned that my son Ska7cis was an engineer. Cameron was intrigued by the name, which means grizzly bear in our Secwepemc language, and asked me to ask my son if he could use it in one of the upcoming *Avatar* sequels. My son agreed, thinking it was good to make the Secwepemc language more well known, and Cameron assured him the character would be a powerful warrior. For Indigenous peoples in the Americas, James Cameron is a friend as well as a powerful voice for a new understanding in the world.

# No Half Measures
## The Price of Uncertainty

**O**UR PEOPLE ARE READY to fight for their rights, but the question that echoes through our meetings these days is where, exactly, are our leaders? What has happened to them? Why are they not leading?

Nothing has revealed the poverty of our current Indigenous leadership as much as the willingness by so many of them to surrender our fundamental rights by negotiating under the government's discredited extinguishment policy. The sheer madness of this was driven home to me in the fall of 2010, when I received a call from Darrell Bob, chief of the Xaxli'p First Nation, a St'at'imc community on the Fraser River, about 225 kilometres west of Neskonlith.

Chief Bob wanted to talk about the B.C. Treaty Process. Xaxli'p had entered into the negotiations in 1994 and signed a Framework Agreement in June 1997. Then the negotiations stalled. Xaxli'p, like virtually all of the negotiating bands, ran up against the brick wall of extinguishment. Many bands believed that they could negotiate their own agreements with the government that would not force surrender of their Aboriginal title and rights. The Framework Agreement seemed to allow for this in article 2, which stated that everything was negotiable. Unfortunately, Xaxli'p, like all of the rest, discovered that no matter how much they protested, the government negotiators insisted they check their Aboriginal title and rights—which are recognized under of Section 35 of the Canadian

Constitution—at the door. The only way to exit these negotiations was through extinguishment of Aboriginal title and rights.

Xaxli'p balked, pointing out that article 2 said everything was negotiable. But the government side held that the final result had to be "certainty" as defined by a "modified" rights framework that extinguished Aboriginal title and all of the rights not specifically described in the agreement. This was stated clearly in the government's negotiating guidelines, and the government negotiators had no power to bend on it. Extinguishment of Aboriginal title and rights was, and remains, a federal cabinet-level policy.

Unlike many others who are trapped in these dead-end negotiations, the Xaxli'p leadership went back to their people to consult with them. When they called a community meeting in March 2001, Elder Irene Billy went to the meeting. She was connected to the community by marriage and some of her children and grandchildren are members of Xaxli'p. Irene spoke both the Secwepemctsín and St'at'imc languages, and in her younger days had served as a translator for respected Elder Sam Mitchell, who always took a strong position on Indigenous rights. Irene reminded everyone of the importance of standing strong. The people clearly rejected the extinguishment negotiation process and voted to have Xaxli'p withdraw from the B.C. Treaty Process. It was then that the truly pernicious aspect of this process came to the fore.

The way the negotiations work is that provincial and federal governments loan the band money to pay the costs of the negotiations. The money is used for lawyers and consultants, most of them non-Indigenous, and their hotel rooms, per diems, and travel budgets. Repayments of those loans are to be made from the settlement money paid to First Nations as part of the final treaty or, if the band pulls out of the negotiation, from the band's general revenues. Overall, the negotiating bands in British Columbia today are in hock for well over a half a billion dollars in negotiating loans, an amount that increases day by day.

Xaxli'p is a poor community, but they would not buckle under to a negotiated surrender of their Aboriginal title and rights. So, five years after they pulled out of the process, they received a letter from Allan Price, their Department of Indian Affairs funding services officer, saying that their B.C. Treaty Process negotiating loan of $2,430,444 had come due and had to be repaid over five years at 4.3 per cent interest. The payments would be $27,291 a month. Price then mentioned, almost casually: "In the 2004/2005 audit review, we calculated your working capital ratio to be -4.46%. This year, the addition of the treaty loan ($2M) to current liabilities reduced the Band's working capital calculation to -72.87%."

The chief understood the fiscal message. The demanded repayment of the treaty loan would drive the band into insolvency and, for First Nations, this generally meant government-imposed third-party management. In other words, the penalty for pulling out of the negotiations was bankruptcy and an outside takeover of the band.

Chief Darrell Bob went to the leadership at the First Nations Summit who had gotten them into this mess, the people who with the government had set up the framework of the negotiations and who had promoted them across the province as the solution to the B.C. land question. Surely they would not accept the fact that simply participating in the B.C. Treaty Process should drive First Nations into receivership? The only response he received from the Summit was their offer of "moral support." No concrete help. Nothing. Chief Bob went to the Union of B.C. Indian Chiefs and the Union referred him to me.

Even though this reckoning was clearly coming for all the B.C. negotiating bands—who shared a more than $500 million debt to the government—it came as a shock to hear what was happening to Xaxli'p. When I spoke to the chief and he told me that the Summit had washed their hands of this problem, I told him the only thing I could think of was to take the issue to the international level and try to embarrass the government into backing off. I told him INET was preparing a brief to CERD and that I would add their case to the submission.

When we put the bizarre situation of the Xaxli'p band, and in fact all of British Columbia's negotiating bands, before CERD, Canada came back with a surprising assertion. They told CERD:

> In regard to the Xaxli'p First Nation, the Xaxli'p First Nation accepted loan monies to participate in the Treaty process and elected to withdraw from Treaty negotiations in 2001. Canada restates that Canada has written to the Xaxli'p First Nation to state that the obligation to repay the loan amount has been placed into abeyance and thus loan repayment is not being sought by Canada.[51]

In our follow-up report to CERD, we pointed out Canada's blatant lie with an email from the new Xaxli'p chief, Art Adolph, indicating that they had received no communication from the Government of Canada indicating that the loan had been placed in abeyance. On the contrary, even though Chief Adolph had told Indian Affairs that the community would not be repaying the loan, the Department continued to send the band statements of accounts on the loan, with ever-accruing interest.

But the Canadian assertion to CERD had an immediate benefit for Xaxli'p First Nation. With the government letter informing the band that the loan was due, the Xaxli'p auditor had been obligated to put that amount on the books. The band was therefore already considered drowning in debt, even though they were not making payments. But the Canadian assertion at CERD that the loan was to be held in abeyance was enough for the Xaxli'p management to get the auditor to reverse the entry on the books. Chief Adolph had asked for a formal letter confirming the new government position but, of course, he never received it. The last thing that Indian Affairs wanted other bands to know was that there might be a way out of the government negotiation loan extortion scheme.

The news of Xaxli'p's plight was not only causing waves on the international sphere but also causing unrest among grassroots people in British Columbia, who suddenly became aware of the real economic danger the B.C. Treaty Process was exposing their communities to. Most bands had already borrowed millions of dollars to pay for legal fees, researchers, and flights and hotels for negotiators, and the people were beginning to ask their leadership pointed questions. With a public relations nightmare brewing, the Department of Indian Affairs, which administered the loans, quickly kicked the problem down the road by giving all of the negotiators a five-year extension on their loans. But the loans keep accumulating. By the time they fall due again, the total debt of the negotiating bands will be close to $700 million and heading steady toward the billion-dollar mark.

As time goes on, a number of bands that are still formally in the negotiating process are there in name only. They stay at the table to avoid having the government swoop down to collect on their loans, but they are no longer seriously negotiating. They are biding their time in the hope that when the whole thing collapses, they will be able to make an escape in the confusion.

Not surprisingly, a sense of frustration and open cynicism with this flawed and fundamentally unjust process permeates all of the B.C. Treaty partners. At the outset, in June 1991, the Summit leaders and their government partners optimistically claimed:

Modern-day treaties will form the basis of a new relationship between Canada, British Columbia and First Nations. . . .

As history shows, the relationship between First Nations and the Crown has been a troubled one. This relationship must be cast aside. In its place, a new relationship which recognizes the unique place of aboriginal people and First Nations in Canada must be developed and nurtured. Recognition and respect for First Nations as self-determining and distinct nations with their own spiritual values, histories, languages, territories, political institutions and ways of life must be the hallmark of this new relationship.[52]

In 2011, the head of the B.C. Treaty Commission, Sophie Pierre, said British Columbia should abandon its 140-year-old quest for treaties with First Nations if it cannot find the will to make and meet targets for treaty settlements. Ms. Pierre said that pace is unacceptable. The commission, and the entire treaty process, should be jettisoned if both the provincial and federal governments won't commit to firm targets.[53]

By its twentieth anniversary in the fall of 2012, only a handful of agreements had been signed and even fewer had passed the community ratification of the dozens of bands locked into the process. The Summit's own assessment was announced in a press release:

"Unfortunately, some 20 years after the start, many First Nations remain frustrated by the growing debt and slow pace of the current treaty negotiation process," said Grand Chief Edward John of the First Nations Summit political executive.

"Further, Canada and British Columbia must abandon and renounce their colonial policies to seek certainty through the extinguishment or surrender of Aboriginal title and rights." As Chief Joe Mathias said 20 years ago today, "the negotiations, in our view, will not be based on that tired old notion of extinguishment. We will not tolerate the extinguishment of our collective aboriginal rights! Let us be clear about that today," added Chief White.[54]

Extinguishment, however, is exactly where these negotiations lead. During the past several years, it was not just Xaxli'p who contacted me. Bertha Williams from Tsawwassen First Nation, just south of Vancouver, was following her people's treaty to its unhappy conclusion. The

Tsawwassen First Nation had voted to accept the final draft of the treaty in 2007, but Bertha and many others believed that the process was rigged from the start. For one thing, the backers of the treaty were given a $1.5 million slush fund to sell the treaty to the people, using everything from slick brochures to "signing bonuses" to anyone over the age of sixty. Treaty backers justified these payouts so "Elders could benefit from the treaty before it was signed," but opponents saw them as crass vote buying. When asked about the payouts by the local media, the provincial Aboriginal relations minister Mike de Jong simply responded "guilty as charged."

It was clear that the government was ready to pay any price for the treaty. Bertha also joined our submission to CERD, and the UN committee took issue with the inappropriate procedures in the treaty vote. Despite the international criticism, the vote backed by the payments passed and the agreement was implemented by the federal and provincial governments.

The consequences of signing the treaty were exactly as predicted. Commercial industrial developments immediately began increasing in the territory of the Tsawwassen people. One of the developments is the South Fraser Perimeter Road, a major infrastructure venture in the Greater Vancouver Area. The route resulted in the destruction of sacred sites, including Tsawwassen burial sites. Bertha, a descendant of the hereditary leadership, brought a legal action to challenge the development. In its response to the application, the provincial government tabled in court the provisions of the Tsawwassen First Nation Final Agreement. They said Tsawwassen no longer had a claim to their territory. By agreeing to the B.C. Treaty, the Tsawwassen people had been given four hundred hectares of land and a cash settlement of $16 million in return for the extinguishment of their Aboriginal title and rights and the abrogation of their Section 35 rights under the Constitution. "Certainty" was indeed extinguishment.

This is what happens, as we had been saying for twenty years, when you accept the deal offered by the government. But what happens when you vote no? Well, as the Lheidli T'enneh First Nation discovered when they rejected that final agreement in a community vote, the B.C. Treaty Process will not take no for an answer. As soon as the Lheidli T'enneh rejected the treaty, proponents were back demanding another vote. When there was no immediate mechanism for another vote on the treaty, they demanded a vote on whether to proceed with a second vote. And, as we have seen, the government is not shy in supporting the treaty promoters with slush funds in cash. In the past, the government has been able to live quite well with these endless negotiations that go nowhere. As they followed their business-as-usual approach, the unending negotiations became part of a risk management strategy. They contain First Nations claims against Crown land within negotiating tables that have more or less fixed outcomes modelled on the Nisga'a Treaty. The government has clearly stated that that was the only possible outcome to these negotiations, so any First Nations still negotiating would have to be willing to accept a similar deal that extinguishes Aboriginal title and rights. While the negotiations go on, the meter on the loans to First Nations keeps increasing. With ever-increasing indebtedness, it becomes ever more difficult for Indigenous communities to walk away from the table without signing off on the government's cash-for-land deal.

I know of the stress communities that are trapped in the negotiations feel, because I often receive calls from them when they are dealing with Aboriginal title and rights issues and trying to cope with the B.C. Treaty Process and the Comprehensive Claims policy. I try to help, and I have gone to speak at Lheidli T'enneh, Port Hardy, Port Alberni, and Sliammon, to mention only a few. I go to as many of these communities as I can to rally support, and to champion the defiance of the people of Xaxli'p in walking away from the national disaster that the government is serving us on their negotiating tables.

For opponents of the extinguishment process, there are no four-star hotel rooms, per diems, or plane tickets. We take our pickup trucks and count on someone at the end of the meeting passing the hat to pay for our gas. It is like in my father's time when they were building the movement, before the creation of the government-funded national organization. Recently in Stó:lō Territory, an Elder told me how they had raised money so my father would have a suit to wear when he lobbied for Indigenous peoples. Today we need to rebuild our movement, until it is once again independent from government and the new Indian agents who administer the government's will.

For communities that have refused to enter such negotiations, or that wish to withdraw from them, there is no official alternative to the Comprehensive Claims process. We tried to achieve a change in the policy one last time under Shawn Atleo. I met with him at the AFN meeting in

Calgary in July 2009 at the urging of the Neskonlith chief, Judy Wilson, while he was running for national chief. .

As soon as Judy saw me come through the door, she said "You should meet with Shawn."

I asked her why. After all, only chiefs had votes in the election for national chief, and Shawn and I had been on different sides on a number of important issues so we probably wouldn't have much that was positive to say to each other.

But Judy persisted, I think, because she wanted to make sure that I did not actually oppose Shawn. She didn't want to find herself in a different camp from me after the election. Eventually, because she was so determined, and because I greatly respect her, I agreed to a quick meeting with Shawn in the hallway.

While we spoke, I asked Shawn if he would support an AFN committee to yet again review the government's Comprehensive Claims policy and suggest an alternative process for bands to follow. I knew Shawn worked closely with the First Nations Summit people, but as often happens in leadership campaigns, he seemed open to the idea of a new battlefront. In the hallway at the Calgary convention centre, he agreed to set up a Comprehensive Claims policy review committee if he was elected national chief.

Shawn kept his word. After he was elected, he gave me a relatively free hand in framing the committee's mandate and bringing together the people I wanted to work with. My idea was to keep it small and staff it with those I knew would be serious about finding ways to push the government away from the Comprehensive Claims policy. The initial membership was me, Chief Harry St. Denis, an Algonquin from Wolf Lake in Quebec, Chief Wayne Christian from Splatsin First Nation, Chief Judy Wilson from Neskonlith, my friend Russell Diabo, and Robert Morales, with the national chief as ex officio member. The only representative of the Treaty Process people was Robert, an Aboriginal rights lawyer and negotiator from the Hul'qumi'num Treaty Group. He had been part of the Common Table discussions of Indigenous communities that were involved in the treaty process but were unhappy with the form and format of the negotiations.

While we came from different positions, Robert was always blunt about what is actually going on inside the process and we had some very fruitful exchanges. I even travelled to Washington in 2011 to support his Hul'qumi'num people in their formal complaint to the Inter-American

Commission on Human Rights that neither the B.C. Treaty Process nor the Canadian courts gave them an effective remedy for their land rights issues. Some of the Hul'qumi'num Elders present knew my father from his time in Cowichan, and they must have mentioned I was his son because Robert suddenly asked me if I was related to George Manuel. I told him, yes, he was my father, and Robert nodded. "Ah yes," he said, "a second-generation leader." We do respect each other, even if we have different positions on some issues.

According to AFN rules, committees also have to include a vice-chief as their chair. In our case, the position was claimed by B.C. Regional Vice-Chief Jody Wilson-Raybauld, who had a much different vision than the rest of the committee. She was a former B.C. treaty commissioner, and has since announced that she will be a candidate for the federal Liberal party in the Vancouver Granville riding.

Our review began with a new analysis of the Comprehensive Claims policy and its obvious flaw that allows Canada to have its cake and eat it, too: demanding that First Nations be willing to extinguish their Aboriginal title and rights before they enter negotiations. The way the policy works, Canada concedes nothing but gains everything before the negotiations even start. This bears no resemblance to the process of recognition and reconciliation that the Supreme Court has called for, and everything that is wrong with the negotiations flows from this. Since Canada does not admit to the existence of Aboriginal title, there is no recognition that Indigenous peoples actually own the lands and resources within their territories.

The "resource revenue sharing" components that sometimes accompany the Comprehensive Claims agreements therefore do not acknowledge the real book value of our assets. Instead the First Nation "share" of resource revenues is arbitrarily determined by citing "comparability" with other claims and available budgets (which in turn are established unilaterally and arbitrarily). Again, this is in opposition to the Supreme Court's findings in *Delgamuukw*, which confirmed that Aboriginal title is a property right with a real value, one not to be given up without "valuable consideration." In addition, the Comprehensive Claims policy explicitly denies that First Nations own subsurface resources—which is also at variance with the findings of the Court in *Delgamuukw* that Aboriginal title does indeed include minerals, oil and gas, and other subsurface resources.

Under the smokescreen of being "forward looking," the existing Comprehensive Claims policy explicitly prohibits any compensation for past losses, damages, infringements, or foregone revenues. This, too, is contrary to the Supreme Court's findings. The Court has made it clear that in cases of infringement, depending on the degree, compensation is due.

When our committee finished its review, we began to formulate a response that would help our people to break free of these surrender negotiations. But the moment we headed down this road, we found a sudden burst of interest on behalf of the vice-chief and the B.C. First Nations Summit leader. Our committee was soon to find its wings clipped, with Ed John and Jody Wilson-Raybauld calling for the government to be given a last chance to comply before we acted. The AFN leadership was now talking about a Plan A and a Plan B, and we suddenly found any direct challenge to the government listed as Plan B. Our committee was being undermined before it had really begun to do its work.

I remember looking across the table at Russell Diabo. He had a smile on his face. This Plan A and B nonsense was an obvious way to ensure nothing changed in the national organization's approach. For him, it was over with the AFN. The fact that they could not even consider challenging the government on such a fundamental issue as title to our lands, which had been recognized in the Constitution and by the Supreme Court, suggested that it was indeed over. For Russell and most of the original members of our committee, it symbolized exactly what was wrong with the AFN and the First Nations Summit: their complete dedication to not rocking the boat, to going again and again to government with hat in hand to request justice, which was always denied.

At the same time, of course, the government was always delighted to meet with them, to take part in this charade, to fund their organizations that, in turn, paid them handsome salaries and generous travel expenses to turn around in circles year after year and decade after decade. Business as usual. It served the government's purpose and provided lucrative salaries and per diems to our compromised leaders.

Plan A turned out to be nothing but more meetings over terrain the two sides had been covering for decades. These new meetings were called the Crown–First Nations Gathering. The first one was held on January 24, 2012, and in a surprise, the parties grandly committed to making sure federal negotiation policies reflected the principles of recognition and affirmation mandated by Section 35 of the Constitution. But then, during the follow-up meeting in April 2012, Jean-François Tremblay, assistant deputy minister of Treaties and Aboriginal Government, told the gathered First Nations that actually he had no mandate to change the federal Comprehensive Claims policy, despite what had been suggested in January. In one fell swoop, Plan A was dead in the water. But the AFN and the government participants bravely promised to produce a "progress report."

Then, in September 2012, the AFN members of the Crown–First Nations Gathering learned that they themselves had been tossed overboard by the government. With no consultation whatsoever, and not even any warning, Indian Affairs Minister John Duncan announced the government's new "results based" approach to modern treaty and self-government negotiations. The core of this approach was to skip most of the negotiation and force the First Nations at the ninety-three negotiating tables across the country to agree on all of the essentials before the negotiations even began. Those essentials included reaching "certainty" through extinguishment and the awarding of municipal powers under the name of "self-government." To remain at the negotiating table, a First Nation had to accept the following:

- the extinguishment (modification) of Aboriginal title
- the legal release of Crown liability for past violations of Aboriginal title and rights
- the elimination of Indian reserves by accepting lands in fee simple
- removing on-reserve tax exemptions
- respecting existing third-party interests (and therefore, alienation of Aboriginal title territory without compensation)
- assimilation into existing federal and provincial orders of government
- funding on a formula that would be reduced if First Nations' own-source revenues rose

For those First Nations that would not immediately agree, negotiations would end. This was the first part of the government's power play. The second was the announcement of severe cuts to Indigenous peoples' regional and national political organizations. All organizations would have their funding capped at $500,000 annually. For some regional organizations, this resulted in a funding cut of a million dollars or more. First Nation Band and Tribal Council funding for advisory services would be eliminated. In essence, the federal government was continuing to turn Indigenous organizations into service and program delivery vehicles for the Department of Indian Affairs.

These new policy measures were on top of the suite of crippling legislation the Harper government continues to impose on First Nations, a change to band elections in the Indian Act that shifts power away from community members, and a devastation of Canada's environmental protections.

The government was also considering a new law making it possible for Indian bands to opt into a scheme to turn all of their land into fee simple real estate, an initiative that had already been condemned by the overwhelming majority of them. This idea has been promoted by Manny Jules, who, in conjunction with the Fraser Institute and its leading Indian fighter, Tom Flanagan, have enthusiastically backed the so-called First Nations Property Ownership legislation. This legislation would dissolve our reserves into real estate that could be purchased outright by local developers and, of special significance today, by pipeline companies seeking to push their lines across the country.

We have seen that the proponents of this approach are not interested in an open debate with our people, because they know we will never agree with their plan. They are closer to the government and Department of Indian Affairs, which funds them and shapes their agenda, than to the people they pretend to work for. They are used to making back room deals and pushing an agenda that is not endorsed by our people. At the 2010 AFN General Assembly, a resolution condemning the fee simple plan was overwhelmingly endorsed, with only three chiefs supporting fee simple land ownership for our communities.

The government, as we have seen, never stops pushing its assimilation agenda. But at the same time, the business-as-usual approach is becoming more and more difficult to sustain.

Treaty negotiations are continually teetering on collapse, because the people do not want to extinguish their title for a tiny piece of land and a tiny amount of cash, even though their leadership is, in many cases, urging them to do so. You only have to look at the recent glum twentieth anniversary of the B.C. Treaty Process to see how the government process is running out of steam. The Harper government offensive, with its suite of legislation and aggressive "results based" negotiations, has the air of a desperate gamble to try to regain traction in pointlessly spinning negotiations.

The desperation is also seen on the side of the provinces, which have hundreds of billions of dollars of resource investment knocking at the door but no land claim deals to give their investors the "certainty" they need to make the investments. As a result, the B.C. government has been peddling its Recognition Framework Agreements (RFA) and Strategic Engagement Agreements (SEA), which attempt to sidestep the failed treaty process but still open the door to resource development by recognizing the province as the final decision makers on our lands.

· The process demands that we set aside our title and rights in return for an "engagement process." There are absolutely no economic guarantees or securities for Indigenous peoples, and the process is under the exclusive powers of the province under Section 92 of the BNA Act. The province remains the sole decision maker regarding access to our lands and resources. We want a process based on the recognition and affirmation of Aboriginal rights under Section 35 of the Constitution Act, 1982. We want to be decision makers regarding access to our lands and resources, precisely what the province is trying to avoid under these agreements.

While governments continue to try to entice us to surrender with half measures, uncertainty is increasing around the land question. Major resource sector investors rev their engines on the sidelines, or quietly drive out to meet us to try to do a deal directly. They are aware of the recent study by a former government consultant, Bill Gallagher, that listed more than 150 Aboriginal rights and title court cases—on everything to land ownership to fishing, hunting, and logging rights—that have been won by Indigenous peoples in Canada. Gallagher does not at all ideologically favour our cause, but nonetheless, his view is that "until [Canadians] have true resource-power sharing with natives, the fate of Canada's resource sector will be in the hands of native strategists in their new capacity as resource rulers."55

Gallagher and his allies do not see the solution as acknowledging our title and rights and coming to an honourable agreement with us. Rather, they seek to enter into low-cost resource-sharing agreements that pay us a kind of rent while a mine or other extractive industry is operating, then cut and run and leave us with our poverty and Aboriginal title over the tailings pond after they have made off with the gold.

Today more than ever, it is time to push away from what my friend Russell Diabo calls the "termination tables," which have as their stated goal the reduction or elimination of our rights. This is, essentially, what the First Nations Summit and its supporters call Plan A. But at long last, it looks like Plan A is reaching the end of its course. As we saw at the end of 2012 with the sudden rise of Idle No More, the people are moving back into the equation for the first time since the Constitution Express. And it is the people, finally, who hold the key to their own liberation.

This is Plan B. That we respect our territorial integrity and our internationally recognized right to self-determination and proprietorship of our lands—something that our Elders knew in their blood and the leaders of Andrew Paull's generation and my father's generation fought for, but that many of our current leaders seem to have forgotten. We have to rekindle that spirit of resistance and seize the new tools to fashion a new Indigenous economy. And I believe we have seen the first stirrings of this movement in the rise of activists groups like Idle No More.

# Days of Protest

## Young Activists
## Come Together

O NE OF THE IRONIES of the name "Idle No More" is that most of the key activists behind it have not been idle at all. Indian resistance has not stopped in Canada, but it had, for several decades, been cut off from the leadership. In fact, activists, many of whom would be more comfortable in describing themselves as *sovereignists*, were disowned by our leadership to the point where we recently learned that the Assembly of First Nations was secretly working with the RCMP to contain protests at the community level.

Journalists have turned up documents revealing that the AFN and the RCMP held biweekly meetings and synchronized their press releases during the 2007 Day of Protest, which the AFN was working behind the scenes to undermine. As Russell Diabo described it to the *Toronto Star*: "The Canadian government managed to get the AFN to work against its own people, using them to contain discontent of First Nations and to try to prevent it from spilling into a broad social movement."[56]

Around the time of the Day of Action, I had been speaking to Russell about the need for some kind of cross-country group of activists to support each other on an ongoing basis. During the Skwelkwek'welt protest, in the informal network of contacts that my children were part of, I had met many young people dedicated to the cause. I often saw new faces at the protest camp, generally young people from as far away as the east coast who had come to show their solidarity (although some of the young men, I suspected, were hanging around because they had developed crushes on my daughters). But for the most part, young activists were scattered across North America working in isolated communities and often facing the same sort of police harassment and criminalization of their protest as our people faced at Skwelkwek'welt. They were obviously not getting help and support from the national organizations—which were, at times, actively working to undermine them.

Russell told me a group was trying to form just that sort of activist alliance, and he asked me to work with him to help them out. With the assistance of a phone account provided by my friend Judy Rebick, we organized a conference call with dozens of Indigenous activists from across the country. Many of them were young people who had gone off reserve to get an education and had returned with some idealism to work with their communities, only to find chiefs and councils who saw themselves basically as administrators of Department of Indian Affairs programs and services. At the same time, the young people saw resource companies moving onto their lands and leaving a swath of destruction in their wake, with no recognition of Aboriginal title and rights. It was these young activists, in isolated pockets across the country, who had risen up in the summer of 2007. Now they were seeking to link together to defend their people's lands and Aboriginal rights.

What was most striking from that first call was how little respect these activists had for their chiefs and councils. In most cases, their attitude was that if you dealt with the chiefs, you might as well phone Prime Minister Stephen Harper and the RCMP directly. To our leaders who seemed so willing to negotiate away our rights, they suggested they should just move to town, become settlers themselves, but not destroy the last vestige of our sovereignty.

. The majority of these activists were young, but they had also sought out some seasoned veterans to offer them counsel. Among those on the initial conference call were long-dedicated people like Milton Born With a Tooth, who had spent four years in jail after the 1990 battle over the Oldman River in Alberta; Sam McKay, who had been jailed during the KI (Big Trout Lake) mining protests; and Tom Goldtooth, president of the Indigenous Environmental Network. There were also many second- and third-generation activists like Norman Matchewan from Barriere Lake and Dustin Rivers, the great-grandson of Andrew Paull. More than half of the activists were women, including Judy DaSilva, Heather Milton Lightening, and Carol Martin and Cleo Desjarlais from Northern Alberta. The important and often leading role of women in our struggle has been common since at least my father's day; this includes women Elders like Irene Billy, who was one of the Secwepemc participants at the first meeting. At a follow-up meeting, she was joined by her daughter-in-law Janice Billy, and by Elder William Ignace, the famous Wolverine from Gustafsen Lake, who is better known locally these days as an excellent organic farmer who gives away fresh vegetables to the people in our communities.

Among the young activists, I noticed something that turned out to be typical of youth movements today: a true sense of solidarity. The group was firmly Indigenous and sovereignist but it also had a number of active non-Indigenous supporters, bright and multitalented young people like Shiri Pasternak, who was studying at the University of Toronto (and now has a doctorate in geography), Corvin Russell, a young and savvy activist, and researcher Emma Feltes. These young people understood that justice for Aboriginal people would not only make things better for us, but it would also make a much better Canada.

In British Columbia, we were also in contact with the young South Asian activists Harjap, who works with the Council of Canadians, and Harsha, who is a popular educator rooted in migrant justice. Both are strong supporters of Indigenous peoples. These young activists even crossed the English-French divide. At an Ontario meeting organized by a national trade union, I found the Quebec contingent, led by the charismatic student leader Gabriel Nadeau-Dubois, to be among the strongest supporters of the Indigenous peoples and our rights, at a time when the union leadership was offering us only partial support. The active assistance of these youthful non-Indigenous supporters is yet another reason I have hope for our collective future.

That first conference call ended with a plan for the founding meeting of a new organization, the Defenders of the Land, to be held in Winnipeg in the fall of 2008. The group raised sixty thousand dollars in small amounts from Indigenous organizations and unions to pay for travel and hotel expenses, and worked on a draft charter over the Internet.

The Defenders of the Land described itself as a network of Indigenous communities and activists in struggle across Canada, including Elders and youth, women and men. It was, its website said, the only organization of its kind in Canada: Indigenous-led, free of government or corporate funding, and dedicated to building a fundamental movement for Indigenous rights.

The Defenders would be both nationalist and protectors of Mother Earth. As their charter put it:

> We are sovereign nations. We have the inherent right to self-determination. We will determine our own destinies in accordance with our own customs, laws, and traditions—not in a way dictated to us by Canadian and provincial governments, and without interference by these governments. . . .
>
> No development can take place on our lands without our free, prior, and informed consent. "Self-government" that does not include control of our lands is not self government at all. A "duty to consult" that does not allow us to say no to development is meaningless.[57]

Today the Defenders of the Land includes several hundred activists from more than forty communities who are ready to take on the fight to protect our lands at the ground level. They continue to have a remarkable ability to build alliances with non-Indigenous youth, who can become official supporters of the Defenders by pledging: "when Indigenous peoples stand to defend their land and to protect Mother Earth, we will stand alongside them."[58]

At the inaugural meeting in Winnipeg, the Defenders were given the opportunity to engage in their first national protest when we learned that Prime Minister Harper was in town for the Conservative party's annual general meeting. We drafted a letter condemning his policies and marched through the cold November rain to the Winnipeg convention centre to give it to him. Of course, the prime minister did not come out to see us—but we did present it to his security detail. If nothing else, it served as a calling card for the new organization.

In the fall of 2012, when Stephen Harper's legislative offensive against Indigenous peoples was in full swing, the Defenders were joined by a much more broadly based movement. It began, like so many important events in the world, with the women. Namely, four Prairie women: three Indigenous, Jessica Gordon, Sylvia McAdam, and Nina Wilson, and one non-Indigenous, Sheelah McLean. These four remarkable women launched the Idle No More movement, a movement that would "call on all people to join in a revolution which honours and fulfills Indigenous sovereignty which protects the land and water."

Their alarm had been raised by the introduction in Parliament of the Conservative omnibus bill C-45 on October 18, 2012, which gutted Canadian environmental legislation. Among other changes, it cut the Navigable Waters Protection Act and replaced it with the Navigation Protection Act, which excluded more than 98 per cent of the country's lakes and rivers from federal environmental oversight, thus unlocking them for abuse by resource extraction companies and opening them up for the passage of oil and gas pipelines.

The four women organized a teach-in in Saskatoon on C-45 and its implications for First Nations peoples. They called this session Idle No More and launched a Facebook event page to spread the word. The name struck a chord among a generation that felt Indigenous peoples had been left standing idly by as their leaders frittered away their sovereignty and allowed developers to despoil their lands. A week after the first Idle No More information session in Saskatoon, there were similar events in Regina, Prince Albert, and North Battleford, Saskatchewan, and in Winnipeg, Manitoba. Then that spectacular political fission took place, with Idle No More actions spontaneously springing up across the country and even across the world.

The sense that it was time to act seemed to infect some of the chiefs as well. In early December, a group of chiefs in Ottawa for an Assembly of First Nations meeting—led by Chief Wallace Fox from the Onion Lake Cree Nation in Saskatchewan and Grand Chief Derek Nepinak from the Assembly of Manitoba Chiefs—tried to enter Parliament to demand that the government withdraw its legislation and consult with First Nations before taking any action that might affect us or our lands, as required by UNDRIP. The Idle No More organizers, seeing the rising enthusiasm, called for a Day of Action on December 10 that saw thousands of Indigenous people and non-Indigenous supporters rally in Vancouver, Whitehorse, Edmonton, Calgary, Saskatoon, North Battleford, Winnipeg, Thunder Bay, Toronto, Montreal, and Goose Bay–Labrador.

The day following the Day of Action, Chief Theresa Spence of the Attawapiskat First Nation in Northern Ontario announced her support of the Idle No More movement, and began her hunger strike in Ottawa. She promised it wouldn't end until Prime Minister Harper and Governor

General David Johnston agreed to sit down and talk about the fundamental problems in Canada's relationship with First Nations.

Chief Spence's principled and dignified move further galvanized the Idle No More movement, and actions from round dances in shopping malls to information pickets erupted across the country. In a measure of the movement's growing influence, dozens of members of Parliament and senators felt compelled to visit Chief Spence on Victoria Island on the Ottawa River, along with political celebrities like former prime minister Paul Martin, who described her as an inspiration. In fact, the only people who were having difficulty dealing with Chief Spence and this new high-energy grassroots movement were the Harper government, the chiefs who were closely tied to the government and, it seemed, the AFN leadership.

If nothing else, the Idle No More movement showed how alarmingly out of touch most of the leadership was with the people. This hit me most forcefully when, after the prime minister caved in to pressure from across the country to meet with the Indigenous leadership, I was invited, along with dozens of others, to take part in an AFN conference call. The purpose of the call, I was astounded to discover, was for a panicky AFN to decide what to put in front of the prime minister as our demands. The organization was almost forty-five years old, and it had apparently so badly lost its way that it didn't even know what it stood for. Finally, it patched together an eight-point plan that had something for everyone but lacked, as we soon found out, the means to pressure the government to act on any one of them. It was presented like a half-hearted wish list that focused almost exclusively on process, with no thought to results. To give you an example of the tortured bureaucratic phrasing, item number one on the AFN list of demands was the following:

1. Commitment to an immediate high level working process with Treaty Nation leadership for establishing frameworks with necessary mandates for the implementation and enforcement of Treaties on a Treaty by Treaty basis, between the Treaty parties Nation-to-Nation.

Jesus, I thought when I read their tortured prose, they are asking for nothing at all—except more process.

The AFN leadership had their meeting with the prime minister on January 11, 2013. Ironically, that was the same week they had been scheduled to meet in their high-level Crown–First Nations Gathering to announce the utter failure of the previous year's high-level process, which had begun in January 2012 and had already collapsed by April. The result of the January 2013 meeting with Harper was yet another hopeless high-level process, now called the Senior Officials Committee.

As it had been doing for decades, the AFN consolidated around the weakest position. In the run-up to the meeting with Prime Minister Harper, the stronger elements of the AFN had announced that they did not want to attend a meeting without assurances that it would lead to concrete actions by the government. But the weaker elements insisted that it was important to "engage." The problem is, the government controls the outcomes of those discussions by refusing to change any of its policies. And why should it when our leadership is willing to spend year after year—and decade after decade—discussing these policies without ever demanding they be changed?

When criticized, our leadership came back to us, as they always do, to say that if we did not "engage" we would not have this "process." But since it is the government process, which has absolutely nothing to do with our demands, participating has become, objectively, a form of acquiescence.

We should also be aware that for many Indigenous leaders, process has become its own reward. They negotiate to create processes because processes ensure them jobs and money, since government processes come with government funding pots. These kinds of opportunists are, unfortunately, more widespread in the movement than many of us like to admit. It was, after all, how the B.C. Treaty Process was created. B.C. leaders flocked to Ottawa in the fall of 1990 to get a "process" immediately after the Oka Crisis. And this twenty-plus-year process has resulted in millions of dollars paid to First Nation negotiators and the First Nations Summit and other consultants, but it has gone virtually nowhere. What makes it worse is that these millions—these hundreds of millions of dollars—have to be paid back by impoverished Indigenous communities. But the professional Indian negotiating class continue to have privileged, extremely well-paid careers at government negotiating tables.

I know there are some who will take offence at the frankness of these observations, but it is something that must be said. Many of our leaders have too long dodged responsibility for their actions by claiming that any criticism, no matter how mild, shows a lack of respect and is somehow therefore not Indigenous. It is a self-serving position that we should not accept. Those who put themselves in front and who accept millions of dollars in direct and indirect government pay to act on our behalf must be ready to answer to the people.

This refusal to answer shows a profound lack of respect toward our people, in whose name the leaders are supposed to be acting. I have been at meetings where someone begins to speak against the Treaty Process, and those who are involved in it, instead of defending their position, leave the meeting claiming the person raising the criticism is showing a lack of respect. At other meetings, I found that when someone spoke in very general terms about the government policy, everyone unanimously rejected it. But soon as they suggested that the negotiators pull out of these talks, the negotiators took great offence and said they are being shown a lack of respect. In the worse cases, I have seen speakers literally drummed out of meetings where someone complaining about the leadership's participation in government negotiations was suddenly surrounded by drummers, who misused our sacred drum to silence the discontented and prevent open discussion in the meeting.

It is time for those in leadership to explain to the people exactly who, other than they themselves, is profiting from their decades of failed negotiations on the Comprehensive Claims policies and engage the people in a discussion of where, at last, we should be going from here.

Today, the people themselves are demanding this. In January 2012, the AFN had embarked on a meaningless process. But in January 2013, the AFN was no longer the lone player in the field. The AFN leadership was denounced by some of their own chiefs for heading down the same old garden path with the government, while Idle No More ridiculed this new and pointless process and continued to demand fundamental change in the way Canada addresses Indigenous issues. This was manifest in another Day of Action on January 28, 2013. Parliament came back into session after its Christmas break as Idle No More rallies took place across Canada, in the United States, and even in Europe. Idle No More also received endorsements from student groups, unions, and the movement's old friends, including Judy Rebick, Naomi Klein, and Maude Barlow.

More importantly, Idle No More received the support of key chiefs who themselves began to call the AFN national chief and his executive to account for continually caving in to the government's demands. A number of these chiefs, who stood with Idle No More protesters and insisted that the national chief seek more than "process" from Canada, would later force Shawn Atleo from office over his support of the government's First Nations Education bill.

Another sign of the new grassroots spirit of activism was the joining of forces of Idle No More and the Defenders of the Land after the January 2013 Day of Action. As a symbol of their joint struggle, the Defenders and Idle No More named a joint spokesperson and put forward a common position. In mid-March, the Defenders and Idle No More demanded the following of Canada:

1. Repeal provisions of Bill C-45 (including changes to the Indian Act and Navigable Waters Act, which infringe on environmental protections, Aboriginal and Treaty rights) and abandon all pending legislation which does the same.

2. Deepen democracy in Canada through practices such as proportional representation and consultation on all legislation concerning collective rights and environmental protections, and include legislation which restricts corporate interests.

3. In accordance with the United Nations Declaration on the Rights of Indigenous Peoples' principle of free, prior, and informed consent, respect the right of Indigenous peoples to say no to development on their territory.

4. Cease its policy of extinguishment of Aboriginal Title and recognize and affirm Aboriginal title and rights, as set out in section 35 of Canada's constitution, and recommended by the Royal Commission on Aboriginal Peoples.

5. Honour the spirit and intent of the historic Treaties. Officially repudiate the racist doctrine of discovery and the Doctrine of terra nullius, and abandon their use to justify the seizure of Indigenous Nations lands and wealth.

6. Actively resist violence against women and hold a national inquiry into missing and murdered Indigenous women and girls, and involve Indigenous women in the design, decision-making, process and implementation of this inquiry, as a step toward initiating a comprehensive and coordinated national action plan.[59]

These are the type of demands that the AFN should have been making in its January meeting with Stephen Harper instead of their process-dominated demands. For our leaders today, the first step is to recognize the utter failure of Plan A and to move, finally, to Plan B.

It is time now to do what our leaders refused to do then: withdraw from all negotiations with the government that do not begin with government recognition of our Aboriginal title and rights under Section 35 of the Constitution. By simply pulling out of the negotiations, we will send a powerful message not only to the government and the Canadian people, but also, equally importantly, to the bond rating agencies and the investors, that things are definitely not under control in Canada. It will no longer be business as usual until the government is prepared to sit with us for nation-to-nation discussions that begin and end with respect for our fundamental constitutional rights.

Grand Chief Ron Derrickson will look at the possible content of these negotiations in more detail in the Afterword, but they must include substantial change in our political, economic, and environmental relationship with Canada. Before we begin, both sides have preparatory work to do. In Canada's case, this work was largely completed in its 1996 Royal Commission on Aboriginal Peoples report, which is still waiting for implementation. It is as simple as that. All the government has to do to begin real and substantive negotiations with Indigenous peoples is to follow the recommendations of its own Royal Commission, which repudiated the racist and internationally discredited doctrine of discovery and recognized our right to self-determination.

It is important to recall that the title of the Royal Commission report was *People to People, Nation to Nation*. As RCAP pointed out, our right of self-determination is based on international law, and under this right, Indigenous peoples "are entitled to negotiate freely the terms of their relationship with Canada and to establish governmental structures that they consider appropriate for their needs."

Respecting its own Royal Commission, its own Constitution, and its own Supreme Court rulings is all that the Canadian government has to do to set up nation-to-nation negotiations that can begin the historic and too-long-delayed process of decolonization for both Indigenous peoples and Canadians. It would be an enormously important first step for Canada in its rendezvous with its own past and with an honourable future.

It is unlikely, however, that Indigenous communities simply withdrawing from the current one-sided negotiations will be enough to bring Canada to the table. We will need a more active strategy that includes public education, direct action/assertion of rights, and a strong international campaign.

Ongoing public education is essential. It is not an accident that what launched the Idle No More movement was that first public education meeting in Saskatoon held by the activist women. Similar events, often described as Idle Know More, have been just as important as protests in building support for our cause. Before you can have community participation, you must have community education. This is especially the case in the struggle for recognition of Aboriginal title, which, after all, resides collectively with the community.

At the same time, we have to educate Canadians on our rights and our demands and seek allies there. This is also essential. As we saw during the Constitution Express, when Canadians are made aware of the issues—and of the injustices that are being committed in their name—they can demand that their political representatives find honourable solutions. Already today, we can count on friends and allies in the environmental movement and increasingly among Canadian popular organizations, churches, trade unions, and community activists to stand alongside us and to help us to get the message of justice for Indigenous peoples to the Canadian people.

There is no question in my mind that direct action—that is, asserting our Aboriginal title and rights on the ground—will also be necessary before the government finally agrees to sit down and negotiate with us. Public education is important, but I am not so optimistic as to think that it alone will be enough to turn the massive ship of state from its course. For 150 years, the government has been trying to rid itself of the "Indian problem" by ridding itself of Indigenous peoples through assimilation.

To send a clear message that the days of surrendering our fundamental rights are over and that we are ready once again to take charge of our land and our lives, we will have to show our seriousness with our deeds. I know that asserting our rights on the ground is a contentious issue because, as we saw at Skwelkwek'welt, some people get extremely nervous about the tensions direct action can create. And I know that direct action requires the ultimate and personal commitment of those of our people who take a stand in the face of blatant racism and the threat of criminal prosecution. But as a people, we have a just cause and we cannot simply surrender because demanding justice will create tensions in society.

After decades of waiting, of engaging in process, of losing rather than gaining ground, it is clear that to kick-start true negotiations, we will have to signal our seriousness. This signal of peacefully exercising our rights, of refusing to sit at the back of the economic bus, of ceasing to stand by while our Aboriginal title lands are wantonly destroyed by unsustainable development will send a powerful message to the Crown, to the people of Canada, and to international investors.

Just to be sure that there is no doubt on this issue, I am speaking without exception of non-violent protests. But this does not mean I do not support our warrior movements, which are rooted in our nations. Our Warriors, properly trained in non-violent resistance and connected to the local Indigenous peoples' decision-making structure, are essential for protecting our Aboriginal title and rights. The strength of the Warrior is her or his understanding of the anti-colonial struggle for the restoration of the world of the Two Row Wampum. The Two Row Wampum recognizes our national rights as equal to those of all other nations, with no other nation having the right to hold sway over us.

The Warriors are there to stand against the RCMP and provincial police officers who are committed to the old colonial model of decision-making in Canada. This model treats Indigenous peoples like inanimate baggage to be bulldozed aside with injunctions and aggressive police tactics. We saw this most recently at Elsipogtog in New Brunswick when Mi'kmaq Warriors, joined by Warriors from other nations, stood their ground against the RCMP, who were armed with sniper rifles, tear gas, pepper spray, and riot guns firing rubber bullets. They stood against this massive police violence to block a Houston-based gas fracking company from drilling test holes in their watershed. In an important sign of the times, the people of Elsipogtog First Nation and their Warrior protectors had the support of many in the non-Indigenous community.

We also know that the RCMP and the national security forces work tirelessly to infiltrate our organizations with *agents provocateurs* who try to incite violence to justify the most brutal oppression of our people. This violence isolates our people as "terrorists" and gives the RCMP or armed forces the opportunity to occupy our territory, undermine our right to self-determination, and oppress us. Even if we were not by nature non-violent, there would be no sane case to be made for our people, with our small populations, to advance violence as a solution to our struggle for self-determination.

Our strength today is that the world, as never before, is watching and that we can control the access to our lands and resources and otherwise cause economic uncertainty. And the world is increasingly ready to support the final wave of decolonization—the liberation of Indigenous peoples trapped within the Fourth World in countries like Canada, the United States, Australia, and New Zealand. The world is less and less impressed with the Canadian government's excuses and the untruths and half-truths that it reports to international bodies about its dealings with Indigenous peoples. In the fall of 2013, the UN sent its special rapporteur on the rights of Indigenous peoples, James Anaya, to Canada to review the status of Indigenous peoples within the country's borders. As he was leaving the country, Anaya observed that the gap in well-being between Indigenous peoples and Canadians was not narrowing, and that Canada was heading toward a crisis with its Indigenous peoples. The world sees the coming train wreck if the government does not begin to take our title and rights to our lands seriously.

To avoid the worst, we need our Canadian allies—including church, union, community, and environmental groups—to help us to educate the Canadian population about our rights as they are recognized internationally and about Canada's colonial position toward us.

At the same time, we know any nation-to-nation negotiations, once begun, will not be easy. The first obstacle in defining our new economic relationship with Canada will be the very heavy debt from the seizure and economic exploitation of our lands for almost 150 years since Confederation. This debt is enormous. I sometimes suspect that one of the main reasons the Canadian government refuses to acknowledge our Section 35 rights is that it would leave it open to paying us a percentage of the astronomical amount of wealth that has been taken out of our lands. In the *Delgamuukw* decision, the Supreme Court said that payment for past transgressions of our Aboriginal title was owed to us. But this debt—which has been accrued through generations of crushing poverty, illness, and despair—can strengthen our negotiating position.

We cannot continue to remain poor in our own territories while governments make all the decisions and corporations get rich off our land. We have to be recognized as decision makers regarding our territories and to be remunerated fairly for access to our lands and resources. Any fair arrangement has to recognize our Aboriginal title ownership of our territories today and into the future, and we have to be paid for access to our land and resources. As Grand Chief Ron Derrickson describes in his Afterword, we will need to speak about stumpage fees, payment for timber, mining, and oil and gas revenues, and portions of property tax schemes on our Aboriginal title lands, with the goal of finding common ground that both sides can live with. We will also need to set up new structures to protect our fragile ecosystems. Implementing Indigenous territorial authority and using Indigenous knowledge to ensure economically, culturally, and environmentally sustainable development will benefit all future generations. In light of the federal government's abdication of its responsibilities to the environment, Indigenous peoples can occupy this space. This will provide opportunities for our people and especially our youth to work in stewardship positions and to do work in line with Indigenous values. And there is an existing model in Russell Diabo's tripartite system that was put into effect in Barriere Lake by the community, the forestry companies, and the government stakeholders.

That will be the starting point. The negotiations will have to begin with the land itself and its needs before we impose new developments on it. This can best be done by giving the leading protection role to Indigenous peoples who have been taking care of these lands for thousands of years and who have the knowledge and commitment to them that outsiders lack. At a time when international institutions support Indigenous peoples serving as stewards of the land, our nations' role as protectors of the land should be immediately respected while we engage in the larger and more detailed negotiations over its shared economic and cultural uses. This could involve new regional environmental bodies that would see Indigenous peoples as decision makers engaging with recreational and industrial users of the land. With this structure in place, we can begin to define together our political and economic futures.

The real surprise for other Canadians, I suspect, will be that the path that we want to embark on is one that not only brings justice to Indigenous peoples but also builds a better, much more sustainable Canada.

# The End of Colonialism

ONE THING IS CERTAIN: the flood waters of colonialism are, at long last, receding. In 2005, Indigenous peoples watched the Aymara leader Evo Morales launch his campaign for the presidency of Bolivia under the *wiphala*, the ancient rainbow-coloured banner of the Incan peoples. When he promised to end five hundred years of colonialism in his country, his opponents accused him of calling for revolution. But Morales insisted his objectives were far more profound. Not a revolution, but a refounding of Bolivia as a country that is part of ancient Tawantinsuyu (land of the Inca).

For Indigenous peoples of the Americas, Evo Morales's victory was the dove returning to the ark with an olive twig in its beak. In 2007, the UN Declaration on the Rights of Indigenous Peoples was another sign that the question of the rights of Indigenous peoples was finally being addressed by the world, beginning with a recognition of our basic right to self-determination, which is guaranteed to all peoples by the International Covenants on Civil and Political and Economic, Social and Cultural Rights. As we have seen, even colonial courts in Canada and elsewhere have recognized the need of Indigenous peoples to give their prior informed consent to any development on our lands, and Canada's Supreme Court in the *Delgamuukw* decision recognized in principle our continued proprietorship over our territories. A more recent decision, the *Tsilhqot'in* decision on June 26, 2014, recognized Aboriginal title on the ground to almost two thousand square kilometres of Tsilhqot'in territory.

In paragraph 94 of the *Tsilhqot'in* decision, the Court could not have been clearer:

> With the declaration of title, the Tsilhqot'in have now established Aboriginal title to the portion of the lands designated by the trial judge. . . . This gives them the right to determine, subject to the inherent limits of group title held for future generations, the uses to which the land is put and to enjoy its economic fruits. As we have seen, this is not merely a right of first refusal with respect to Crown land management or usage plans. Rather, it is the right to proactively use and manage the land.

The *Tsilhqot'in* case is the legal and constitutional footing needed to bring into reality the story our Elders told us: Indigenous and non-Indigenous peoples should be travelling in two canoes on the river together, but each moving under their own power and in control of their own direction. The recognition of Aboriginal title on the ground is a fundamental decolonizing action. This case is the first in Canada where Indigenous peoples have repossessed their lost—or more accurately, stolen—inheritance. It is a monumental decision for the country and the provinces.

The *Tsilhqot'in* decision paves the way for this; it recognizes our Aboriginal title, and restates that it is collectively held by the people. To implement the decision on the ground will require implementing our own Indigenous governance, based on our Indigenous laws, not on processes funded and directed by the government.

But we know that the Canadian government has time and again proven itself lawless when it comes to Indigenous peoples. Despite losing more than 150 legal cases on Indigenous rights over the past fifteen years, it insists that it is in control of the Indian agenda and that Indigenous peoples have no rights. In fact, the Department of Indian Affairs' annual Corporate Risk Profiles describe its policy, without any sense of irony, as a "non-rights based policy" in contrast to the "rights-based" position of Indigenous peoples.

Dr. Shiri Pasternak used an Access to Information request to unearth these internal documents, and they show that while the Department speaks with great confidence in its public pronouncements, internally it admits that it is playing with fire in ignoring our rights. As the 2012 report puts it, "There is a tension between the rights-based agenda of

Aboriginal groups and the non-rights based policy approaches grounded in improving socio-economic outcomes." It predicts "an increase in demonstrations and public protests," and even hints at violence to come, with increased non-compliance of Indigenous people with federal and provincial regulations, a general public outcry against the government, and negative international attention.

In examining defensive measures, the government briefly looks at the Supreme Court's repeated exhortations that it act in line with the "honour of the Crown," but quickly dismisses this precept as unworkable. Instead, Canada's dishonourable governments pour money into the legal battles to the point where the Department of Indian Affairs is now the biggest consumer of legal services within the federal government. As we have seen, when conflict arises, their favourite tool is an injunction enforced by the RCMP or, if necessary, the Canadian army, to prevent us from exercising our rights against a system where they have seized 99.8 per cent of our land and shunted us off onto the remaining 0.2 per cent.

But what, finally, is now making the Harper government most worried is not the idea of protests, potential violence, and international reaction. It is the fear that, because of all these things, "economic development projects will be delayed."

That is where the risk lies for Ottawa, that the $650 billion in corporate investment vaunted by the prime minister will be disrupted, and some significant portion blocked by the government's refusal to address the cause of Indigenous rights. This explains the flurry of activity and "high-level" meetings with "resource bonds" and various systems of token compensation on the table.

None of these are acceptable substitutes for recognizing what the Supreme Court, the Canadian Constitution, and the world in the UN Declaration on the Rights of Indigenous Peoples have agreed is our right to our lands and our right as peoples to determine our own future.

This is why we must stop negotiating with governments that do not recognize our Aboriginal and treaty rights. We must stop negotiating with the governments to take over programs and services unless our Aboriginal and treaty rights are recognized and affirmed, so we can build an independent economic base for our people. We must stop negotiating under any policy that ends with our termination as peoples.

Indigenous peoples need to understand that the fundamental issue is our land and the natural wealth that it produces. Our biggest strength is in the economic uncertainty that our legal, constitutional, and political actions create for the status quo. Canada and the provinces have gotten used to the colonial privilege of having the final say on resource development in our Aboriginal and treaty territories. This must be changed.

We cannot have reconciliation until the extinguishment policy is off the table and our Aboriginal title and treaty rights are recognized, affirmed, and implemented by Canada and the provinces. Not only in the Constitution but also on the ground. We need to negotiate the dismantling of the colonial system, not bargain for cash deals that extinguish our rights and produce nothing except more debt and dependency. We need to stand up and fight colonialism in all its manifestations. We need to root out the racism and impoverishment that colonialism systematically creates for the vast majority of our peoples.

To achieve justice, Indigenous peoples need to connect our struggle from the local to the international level. We have a very strong position before the UN Human Rights Committee and other world bodies that are ready to support the cause of the world's 370 million Indigenous peoples in fighting to undo the damage done by usurpations of the peoples' land and liberty under the banner of colonialism. These injustices must be remedied today if we are to begin to address the exponentially higher rates of poverty, illness, crime, and human rights abuses that infect Indigenous peoples around the world.

As UN studies have concluded, recognition of our right to self-determination and our land rights are absolutely essential for the survival of our peoples. In the *Tsilhqot'in* decision, the Supreme Court explicitly recognized that our Aboriginal title gives us "the right to determine . . . the uses to which the land is put and to enjoy its economic fruits." We can now appear before the world as peoples with a recognized land base who are on the road to decolonization.

To Canadians who fear the changes that this will bring to this country, I can only say to them that there is no downside to justice. Just as there was no downside to abolishing slavery, to the winning of equal civil rights for blacks in Canada and the United States, to the emancipation of women. The moves away from the racism and misogyny in the past have only enriched the lives of all of us. The same will happen when racist doctrines still in force against Indigenous peoples are replaced by recognition of our rights.

We know that the Creator did not give the settlers the right to exclusively benefit from our natural wealth and resources. It is colonialism that gave settlers the power to economically exploit our lands, crush our cultures, and dominate our peoples. It is our responsibility to move Canada beyond this exploitation and help the global community move one step closer to peace and security for all peoples.

To be absolutely clear, we are not talking about stopgap programs and services that are created under federal and provincial legislation. And we are not talking about action that is purely for disrupting the establishment without any real plan of what kind of future we want to create. We are talking about fundamental change that recognizes our title to our territories and our right to self-determination.

This is where we are now heading. We invite all Canadians to join us to help move the final obstacles together. We can accomplish this as friends and partners as we have at times in the past. Or we can do it as adversaries, in anguish. Our path toward decolonization is clear. It is up to Canadians to choose theirs.

# AFTERWORD

## Grand Chief Ronald M. Derrickson

RTHUR HAS ASKED that I look ahead to outline the possibility of negotiations between our peoples and the government. I am pleased to do so because understanding the value of our land, as both our spiritual home and as what sustains us in our lives, is essential for our development as peoples.

In any negotiation there are things that you do not put on the table. For Indigenous nations, as for all nations, this includes surrendering our land. Instead, what Indigenous peoples in Canada can discuss is what kind of usage of our land we can live with and under what conditions. This, I know, will sound hard-headed to some Canadians, but it must be clear at the outset.

It was the lack of clarity on this issue that led us into the futility of the B.C. Treaty Process and of all of the country's current land claims negotiations. As they are structured today, they are not serious. As Arthur points out, the government has been dealing with us within the framework of a corporate risk management strategy at a time when most of our leaders have been providing them with virtually no risk. By entering into negotiations that have already put our Aboriginal title and rights on the table, our leaders have guaranteed that the result will also be one that we cannot live with.

I was faced with this issue when I was chief. After I came back into office in 1996, the band manager presented me with a contract for receiving government money to negotiate under the B.C. Treaty Process. I remember being astounded by this idea. Borrow money from your opponent to negotiate with them? That's a formula for endless, pointless discussion. In the end, you will have spent all your rewards at the negotiating table and walk away empty-handed. This suggestion was almost too stupid to believe. But it was what our hang-around-the-fort leadership and their five-hundred-dollar-a-day consultants were offering us at the time and, I'm afraid to say, are still offering us today.

At the same time, I recognize that bringing the government to the table for serious nation-to-nation negotiations will not be an easy task. In trying to develop a viable economy for our people as chief of the Westbank First Nation, I faced endless financial and political roadblocks that the governments put in our way and I was often insulted by the cynical undervaluing of our title and rights by a government that still takes a fundamentally racist attitude toward our people.

It is a racism based on guilt. Every time they see our faces, Canadians feel guilty. They know they took everything from us—our land, the minerals and fossil fuels, our forests that have been laid bare—and they gave nothing back. They know this and, deep down, they feel guilty about it.

But for us, this racism is something that we have to confront head-on. In fact, I even suggested to Arthur that he call his book *White Skin Is Not Better!* That is how central white racism has been in distorting our relationship with Canadian society. We as a people—who know very well that white skin is not better, and it certainly doesn't make you smarter—have to counter these harmful emotions with the love of our land and the love of our communities. That is what gives us our power and our strength.

Change will finally come from the determined actions of leaders like Arthur Manuel and groups like Idle No More that mobilize the hearts and minds of our people. Arthur offers an intellectual framework to this movement. As one of our most innovative leaders, he has brought our issues to the World Trade Organization, to Standard & Poor's, and to the United Nations. In the future, we will also have to let Europeans and other trading partners know that in buying Canadian commodities, they are buying stolen goods, because we have not been paid for our resources. Many companies in Europe have policies forbidding them from dealing with dishonest people, and we have to take advantage of these policies with direct international pressure.

These are areas that Arthur is exploring. That is his strength. But the power of the movement today is also in its breadth. I have seen this from within my own family. When my daughter, Kelly, a singer/songwriter, released a CD with a song dedicated to Idle No More that asked how we could look in the mirror while our people live in squalor, social media lit up with testimonies and support from people who said her words touched and motivated them. Arthur shows people what must be done, and artists like my daughter give people the desire to make a difference. The strength of the Idle No More movement is that everyone is called to make a contribution in their own way.

In my case, having spent a lifetime in business and in both public and private sector negotiations, it is in these areas that I would hope to make a contribution, areas where too often our people have been left behind. We have to take our future seriously, get rid of the opportunists in our ranks, and, when we deal with the government, be as tough with them as they have always been with us. Not with hat in hand, not as part of a polite and collegial Senior Officials Committee. But in serious negotiation with the forces that have oppressed us.

I should say, though, that I do not have any illusions about the struggle being an easy one. That has certainly not been my experience. As Arthur has mentioned in earlier chapters, as chief of the Westbank First Nation I personally faced a physical assassination attempt and then a character assassination attempt when I stood up to the racist and colonial-minded government. It is important that we show resolve and prepare ourselves with research and discipline before we sit down with the government.

This preparation is key. We have to know everything about for what and with whom we are negotiating, before we sit down at the table. We have to do the research and always look ahead. The value of our land is not only what we use it for today but also the uses that our children, grandchildren, and great-grandchildren will put it to. This fact has to be front and centre in all of our negotiations.

So what will be on the table in any true nation-to-nation negotiations between Canada and Indigenous nations? Everything except the surrender of the land. At the outset, we will likely not deal with the compensation due to us for the past usurpation and uses of our lands while we try to reach a deal that both sides can live with today and into the future. Once that is done, we will have the luxury of going back to look at the past and decide together what is to be done to address the economic injustice and the many shameful practices of Canada in their dealings with us.

Our revenue, finally, will come from the wealth of the land. Our nations will have to begin by doing the analysis that Standard & Poor's described to Arthur in his meetings with them. But at a first glance, we can say that forestry operations will require an Aboriginal as well as a provincial permit and that these Aboriginal permits will be issued only in an environmentally sustainable way. They will also, as with the provincial permits, come with stumpage fees that will be paid to Indigenous governments. These fees would only need to be a very small percentage of the Canadian industry revenues, which are close to $25 billion a year.

Similarly with the $36-billion-a-year mining industry. Companies will require Aboriginal as well as provincial mining permits, and our mining codes will put in very high environmental standards for operating on our land. These standards will reflect not only our Indigenous values but also an element of local control. I suspect if there was more regional control of environmental issues in Canada, the standards would rise everywhere—it is much easier to soil someone else's nest than your own.

Mining and oil and gas companies will be expected to pay royalties to our governments for the extraction of our mineral wealth. It is something we already see happening today. For example, the proposed open pit New Gold mine adjacent to Kamloops has offered the Kamloops and Skeetchestn bands $30 million in revenues over the life of the mine. It sounds like a lot of money when you are speaking of a payment to an individual, but this amount is to compensate the two communities over the expected twenty-three-year lifetime of the mine when the project is expected to mine 60,000 tonnes of ore per day to produce 110 million pounds of copper and 100,000 ounces of gold a year for a total of $26 billion in revenues.

Just 1 per cent of those revenues would be $260 million, which is almost ten times what the mine is offering today under the current system. With the requirement of an Indigenous permit, we would be able to negotiate these much more realistic amounts. Even 10 per cent is far from prohibitive for a resources company fee. Oil and gas revenues on Indigenous lands in Canada top $60 billion in a year. Serious negotiations on environmental concerns and royalty payments are long overdue with this industry, which is often uncontrolled in Stephen Harper's aspiring petro state.

These deals are doable. In fact, I have already negotiated better deals on Aboriginal rights in the private sector. In one recent example with three Métis settlements in Alberta, I negotiated a deal where the communities will hold a 45 per cent stake in a multimillion-dollar deal—potentially hundreds of millions of dollars—to turn waste timber into biomass. That is for three small communities. This is the type of deal we should be negotiating on the wealth of our own land. The money is there. We simply have to demand our fair share.

The other significant source of revenue from our lands is the same as for other governments: property tax. Our land has value and all of its non-Indigenous users should expect to pay some amount for its continued use. This is another area where the Indigenous fee will be likely significantly less than the provincial and municipal charges.

For Canadians, this charge would be largely offset by the fact that governments would no longer have to waste the billions of dollars a year they currently pay to keep their colonialist and largely self-serving Department of Indian Affairs afloat. As we build Indigenous economies, the Department would be eliminated, along with the racist Indian Act, as Indigenous governments are funded through their Indigenous economies just as provincial governments exist on their own-source revenues.

In fact, that provincial example is a useful one. As Arthur has shown, what we will see emerging with the Indigenous economy are Indigenous governments that exist under Section 35 of the Canadian Constitution, just as provincial governments draw their existence and their powers from Section 92. As these Indigenous governments emerge, they will negotiate what powers they need from both the provincial and federal governments to most efficiently exercise our peoples' Aboriginal title and rights and to protect and promote our languages and cultures. Of crucial importance to Canadians, the wealth generated by the new Indigenous economies will bring sustained economic benefits to regional economies throughout the country.

Considering that many of the revenues flowing to Indigenous economies will come from multinational companies that previously took these fees offshore as profits, it would be a net gain for the Canadian economy. So there are strong economic reasons for Canadians to support this plan.

The only reason for Canadians to refuse would be that they can't stand the idea of no longer having Indians under their thumb—simple, ugly racism. This is something Canadians themselves have to address when dealing with our people. But we should no longer feed into it by accepting anything less than what is our due as the First Peoples of this land.

As Arthur put it at the opening of this important book, "There is room on this land for all of us and there must also be, after centuries of struggle, room for justice for Indigenous peoples. That is all that we ask. And we will settle for nothing less."

My daughter Kelly echoes this call in her song "Warriors of Love," which ends with these words:

Wake up
Fight for it
The journey's just begun . . .

It is the message of our artists and the message new leaders like Arthur Manuel offer us. For Indigenous peoples today, it is the only journey worth taking.

# APPENDIX

## United Nations Declaration on the Rights of Indigenous Peoples

*The General Assembly,*

*Guided* by the purposes and principles of the Charter of the United Nations, and good faith in the fulfilment of the obligations assumed by States in accordance with the Charter,

*Affirming* that indigenous peoples are equal to all other peoples, while recognizing the right of all peoples to be different, to consider themselves different, and to be respected as such,

*Affirming also* that all peoples contribute to the diversity and richness of civilizations and cultures, which constitute the common heritage of humankind,

*Affirming further* that all doctrines, policies and practices based on or advocating superiority of peoples or individuals on the basis of national origin or racial, religious, ethnic or cultural differences are racist, scientifically false, legally invalid, morally condemnable and socially unjust,

*Reaffirming* that indigenous peoples, in the exercise of their rights, should be free from discrimination of any kind,

*Concerned* that indigenous peoples have suffered from historic injustices as a result of, inter alia, their colonization and dispossession of their lands, territories and resources, thus preventing them from exercising, in particular, their right to development in accordance with their own needs and interests,

*Recognizing* the urgent need to respect and promote the inherent rights of indigenous peoples which derive from their political, economic and social structures and from their cultures, spiritual traditions, histories and philosophies, especially their rights to their lands, territories and resources,

*Recognizing also* the urgent need to respect and promote the rights of indigenous peoples affirmed in treaties, agreements and other constructive arrangements with States,

*Welcoming* the fact that indigenous peoples are organizing themselves for political, economic, social and cultural enhancement and in order to bring to an end all forms of discrimination and oppression wherever they occur,

*Convinced* that control by indigenous peoples over developments affecting them and their lands, territories and resources will enable them to maintain and strengthen their institutions, cultures and traditions, and to promote their development in accordance with their aspirations and needs,

*Recognizing* that respect for indigenous knowledge, cultures and traditional practices contributes to sustainable and equitable development and proper management of the environment,

*Emphasizing* the contribution of the demilitarization of the lands and territories of indigenous peoples to peace, economic and social progress and development, understanding and friendly relations among nations and peoples of the world,

*Recognizing in particular* the right of indigenous families and communities to retain shared responsibility for the upbringing, training, education and well-being of their children, consistent with the rights of the child,

*Considering* that the rights affirmed in treaties, agreements and other constructive arrangements between States and indigenous peoples are, in some situations, matters of international concern, interest, responsibility and character,

*Considering also* that treaties, agreements and other constructive arrangements, and the relationship they represent, are the basis for a strengthened partnership between indigenous peoples and States,

*Acknowledging* that the Charter of the United Nations, the International Covenant on Economic, Social and Cultural Rights and the International Covenant on Civil and Political Rights, as well as the Vienna Declaration and Programme of Action, affirm the fundamental importance of the right to self-determination of all peoples, by virtue of which they freely determine their political status and freely pursue their economic, social and cultural development,

*Bearing in mind* that nothing in this Declaration may be used to deny any peoples their right to self-determination, exercised in conformity with international law,

*Convinced* that the recognition of the rights of indigenous peoples in this Declaration will enhance harmonious and cooperative relations between the State and indigenous peoples, based on principles of justice, democracy, respect for human rights, non-discrimination and good faith,

*Encouraging* States to comply with and effectively implement all their obligations as they apply to indigenous peoples under international instruments, in particular those related to human rights, in consultation and cooperation with the peoples concerned,

*Emphasizing* that the United Nations has an important and continuing role to play in promoting and protecting the rights of indigenous peoples,

*Believing* that this Declaration is a further important step forward for the recognition, promotion and protection of the rights and freedoms of indigenous peoples and in the development of relevant activities of the United Nations system in this field,

*Recognizing and reaffirming* that indigenous individuals are entitled without discrimination to all human rights recognized in international law, and that indigenous peoples possess collective rights which are indispensable for their existence, well-being and integral development as peoples,

*Recognizing* that the situation of indigenous peoples varies from region to region and from country to country and that the significance of national and regional particularities and various historical and cultural backgrounds should be taken into consideration,

*Solemnly proclaims* the following United Nations Declaration on the Rights of Indigenous Peoples as a standard of achievement to be pursued in a spirit of partnership and mutual respect:

*Article 1*

Indigenous peoples have the right to the full enjoyment, as a collective or as individuals, of all human rights and fundamental freedoms as recognized in the Charter of the United Nations, the Universal Declaration of Human Rights and international human rights law.

*Article 2*

Indigenous peoples and individuals are free and equal to all other peoples and individuals and have the right to be free from any kind of discrimination, in the exercise of their rights, in particular that based on their indigenous origin or identity.

*Article 3*

Indigenous peoples have the right to self-determination. By virtue of that right they freely determine their political status and freely pursue their economic, social and cultural development.

*Article 4*

Indigenous peoples, in exercising their right to self-determination, have the right to autonomy or self-government in matters relating to their internal and local affairs, as well as ways and means for financing their autonomous functions.

*Article 5*

Indigenous peoples have the right to maintain and strengthen their distinct political, legal, economic, social and cultural institutions, while retaining their right to participate fully, if they so choose, in the political, economic, social and cultural life of the State.

*Article 6*

Every indigenous individual has the right to a nationality.

*Article 7*

1. Indigenous individuals have the rights to life, physical and mental integrity, liberty and security of person.
2. Indigenous peoples have the collective right to live in freedom, peace and security as distinct peoples and shall not be subjected to any act of genocide or any other act of violence, including forcibly removing children of the group to another group.

*Article 8*

1. Indigenous peoples and individuals have the right not to be subjected to forced assimilation or destruction of their culture.
2. States shall provide effective mechanisms for prevention of, and redress for:

(*a*) Any action which has the aim or effect of depriving them of their integrity as distinct peoples, or of their cultural values or ethnic identities;

(*b*) Any action which has the aim or effect of dispossessing them of their lands, territories or resources;

(*c*) Any form of forced population transfer which has the aim or effect of violating or undermining any of their rights;

(*d*) Any form of forced assimilation or integration;

(*e*) Any form of propaganda designed to promote or incite racial or ethnic discrimination directed against them.

*Article 9*

Indigenous peoples and individuals have the right to belong to an indigenous community or nation, in accordance with the traditions and customs of the community or nation concerned. No discrimination of any kind may arise from the exercise of such a right.

*Article 10*

Indigenous peoples shall not be forcibly removed from their lands or territories. No relocation shall take place without the free, prior and informed consent of the indigenous peoples concerned and after agreement on just and fair compensation and, where possible, with the option of return.

*Article 11*

1. Indigenous peoples have the right to practise and revitalize their cultural traditions and customs. This includes the right to maintain, protect and develop the past, present and future manifestations of their cultures, such as archaeological and historical sites, artefacts, designs, ceremonies, technologies and visual and performing arts and literature.
2. States shall provide redress through effective mechanisms, which may include restitution, developed in conjunction with indigenous peoples, with respect to their cultural, intellectual, religious and spiritual property taken without their free, prior and informed consent or in violation of their laws, traditions and customs.

*Article 12*

1. Indigenous peoples have the right to manifest, practise, develop and teach their spiritual and religious traditions, customs and ceremonies; the right to maintain, protect, and have access in privacy to their religious and cultural sites; the right to the use and control of their ceremonial objects; and the right to the repatriation of their human remains.
2. States shall seek to enable the access and/or repatriation of ceremonial objects and human remains in their possession through fair, transparent and effective mechanisms developed in conjunction with indigenous peoples concerned.

*Article 13*

1. Indigenous peoples have the right to revitalize, use, develop and transmit to future generations their histories, languages, oral traditions, philosophies, writing systems and literatures, and to

designate and retain their own names for communities, places and persons.

2. States shall take effective measures to ensure that this right is protected and also to ensure that indigenous peoples can understand and be understood in political, legal and administrative proceedings, where necessary through the provision of interpretation or by other appropriate means.

## Article 14

1. Indigenous peoples have the right to establish and control their educational systems and institutions providing education in their own languages, in a manner appropriate to their cultural methods of teaching and learning.

2. Indigenous individuals, particularly children, have the right to all levels and forms of education of the State without discrimination.

3. States shall, in conjunction with indigenous peoples, take effective measures, in order for indigenous individuals, particularly children, including those living outside their communities, to have access, when possible, to an education in their own culture and provided in their own language.

## Article 15

1. Indigenous peoples have the right to the dignity and diversity of their cultures, traditions, histories and aspirations which shall be appropriately reflected in education and public information.

2. States shall take effective measures, in consultation and co-operation with the indigenous peoples concerned, to combat prejudice and eliminate discrimination and to promote tolerance, understanding and good relations among indigenous peoples and all other segments of society.

## Article 16

1. Indigenous peoples have the right to establish their own media in their own languages and to have access to all forms of non-indigenous media without discrimination.

2. States shall take effective measures to ensure that State-owned media duly reflect indigenous cultural diversity. States, without prejudice to ensuring full freedom of expression, should encourage privately owned media to adequately reflect indigenous cultural diversity.

*Article 17*

1. Indigenous individuals and peoples have the right to enjoy fully all rights established under applicable international and domestic labour law.
2. States shall in consultation and cooperation with indigenous peoples take specific measures to protect indigenous children from economic exploitation and from performing any work that is likely to be hazardous or to interfere with the child's education, or to be harmful to the child's health or physical, mental, spiritual, moral or social development, taking into account their special vulnerability and the importance of education for their empowerment.
3. Indigenous individuals have the right not to be subjected to any discriminatory conditions of labour and, inter alia, employment or salary.

*Article 18*

Indigenous peoples have the right to participate in decision-making in matters which would affect their rights, through representatives chosen by themselves in accordance with their own procedures, as well as to maintain and develop their own indigenous decision-making institutions.

*Article 19*

States shall consult and cooperate in good faith with the indigenous peoples concerned through their own representative institutions in order to obtain their free, prior and informed consent before adopting and implementing legislative or administrative measures that may affect them.

*Article 20*

1. Indigenous peoples have the right to maintain and develop their political, economic and social systems or institutions, to

be secure in the enjoyment of their own means of subsistence and development, and to engage freely in all their traditional and other economic activities.

2. Indigenous peoples deprived of their means of subsistence and development are entitled to just and fair redress.

*Article 21*

1. Indigenous peoples have the right, without discrimination, to the improvement of their economic and social conditions, including, inter alia, in the areas of education, employment, vocational training and retraining, housing, sanitation, health and social security.

2. States shall take effective measures and, where appropriate, special measures to ensure continuing improvement of their economic and social conditions. Particular attention shall be paid to the rights and special needs of indigenous elders, women, youth, children and persons with disabilities.

*Article 22*

1. Particular attention shall be paid to the rights and special needs of indigenous elders, women, youth, children and persons with disabilities in the implementation of this Declaration.

2. States shall take measures, in conjunction with indigenous peoples, to ensure that indigenous women and children enjoy the full protection and guarantees against all forms of violence and discrimination.

*Article 23*

Indigenous peoples have the right to determine and develop priorities and strategies for exercising their right to development. In particular, indigenous peoples have the right to be actively involved in developing and determining health, housing and other economic and social programmes affecting them and, as far as possible, to administer such programmes through their own institutions.

*Article 24*

1. Indigenous peoples have the right to their traditional medicines and to maintain their health practices, including the conservation

of their vital medicinal plants, animals and minerals. Indigenous individuals also have the right to access, without any discrimination, to all social and health services.

2. Indigenous individuals have an equal right to the enjoyment of the highest attainable standard of physical and mental health. States shall take the necessary steps with a view to achieving progressively the full realization of this right.

*Article 25*

Indigenous peoples have the right to maintain and strengthen their distinctive spiritual relationship with their traditionally owned or otherwise occupied and used lands, territories, waters and coastal seas and other resources and to uphold their responsibilities to future generations in this regard.

*Article 26*

1. Indigenous peoples have the right to the lands, territories and resources which they have traditionally owned, occupied or otherwise used or acquired.
2. Indigenous peoples have the right to own, use, develop and control the lands, territories and resources that they possess by reason of traditional ownership or other traditional occupation or use, as well as those which they have otherwise acquired.
3. States shall give legal recognition and protection to these lands, territories and resources. Such recognition shall be conducted with due respect to the customs, traditions and land tenure systems of the indigenous peoples concerned.

*Article 27*

States shall establish and implement, in conjunction with indigenous peoples concerned, a fair, independent, impartial, open and transparent process, giving due recognition to indigenous peoples' laws, traditions, customs and land tenure systems, to recognize and adjudicate the rights of indigenous peoples pertaining to their lands, territories and resources, including those which were traditionally owned or otherwise occupied or used. Indigenous peoples shall have the right to participate in this process.

*Article 28*

1.  Indigenous peoples have the right to redress, by means that can include restitution or, when this is not possible, just, fair and equitable compensation, for the lands, territories and resources which they have traditionally owned or otherwise occupied or used, and which have been confiscated, taken, occupied, used or damaged without their free, prior and informed consent.

2.  Unless otherwise freely agreed upon by the peoples concerned, compensation shall take the form of lands, territories and resources equal in quality, size and legal status or of monetary compensation or other appropriate redress.

*Article 29*

1.  Indigenous peoples have the right to the conservation and protection of the environment and the productive capacity of their lands or territories and resources. States shall establish and implement assistance programmes for indigenous peoples for such conservation and protection, without discrimination.

2.  States shall take effective measures to ensure that no storage or disposal of hazardous materials shall take place in the lands or territories of indigenous peoples without their free, prior and informed consent.

3.  States shall also take effective measures to ensure, as needed, that programmes for monitoring, maintaining and restoring the health of indigenous peoples, as developed and implemented by the peoples affected by such materials, are duly implemented.

*Article 30*

1.  Military activities shall not take place in the lands or territories of indigenous peoples, unless justified by a relevant public interest or otherwise freely agreed with or requested by the indigenous peoples concerned.

2.  States shall undertake effective consultations with the indigenous peoples concerned, through appropriate procedures and in particular through their representative institutions, prior to using their lands or territories for military activities.

*Article 31*

1. Indigenous peoples have the right to maintain, control, protect and develop their cultural heritage, traditional knowledge and traditional cultural expressions, as well as the manifestations of their sciences, technologies and cultures, including human and genetic resources, seeds, medicines, knowledge of the properties of fauna and flora, oral traditions, literatures, designs, sports and traditional games and visual and performing arts. They also have the right to maintain, control, protect and develop their intellectual property over such cultural heritage, traditional knowledge, and traditional cultural expressions.
2. In conjunction with indigenous peoples, States shall take effective measures to recognize and protect the exercise of these rights.

*Article 32*

1. Indigenous peoples have the right to determine and develop priorities and strategies for the development or use of their lands or territories and other resources.
2. States shall consult and cooperate in good faith with the indigenous peoples concerned through their own representative institutions in order to obtain their free and informed consent prior to the approval of any project affecting their lands or territories and other resources, particularly in connection with the development, utilization or exploitation of mineral, water or other resources.
3. States shall provide effective mechanisms for just and fair redress for any such activities, and appropriate measures shall be taken to mitigate adverse environmental, economic, social, cultural or spiritual impact.

*Article 33*

1. Indigenous peoples have the right to determine their own identity or membership in accordance with their customs and traditions. This does not impair the right of indigenous individuals to obtain citizenship of the States in which they live.
2. Indigenous peoples have the right to determine the structures

and to select the membership of their institutions in accordance with their own procedures.

## Article 34

Indigenous peoples have the right to promote, develop and maintain their institutional structures and their distinctive customs, spirituality, traditions, procedures, practices and, in the cases where they exist, juridical systems or customs, in accordance with international human rights standards.

## Article 35

Indigenous peoples have the right to determine the responsibilities of individuals to their communities.

## Article 36

1. Indigenous peoples, in particular those divided by international borders, have the right to maintain and develop contacts, relations and cooperation, including activities for spiritual, cultural, political, economic and social purposes, with their own members as well as other peoples across borders.
2. States, in consultation and cooperation with indigenous peoples, shall take effective measures to facilitate the exercise and ensure the implementation of this right.

## Article 37

1. Indigenous peoples have the right to the recognition, observance and enforcement of treaties, agreements and other constructive arrangements concluded with States or their successors and to have States honour and respect such treaties, agreements and other constructive arrangements.
2. Nothing in this Declaration may be interpreted as diminishing or eliminating the rights of indigenous peoples contained in treaties, agreements and other constructive arrangements.

## Article 38

States, in consultation and cooperation with indigenous peoples, shall take the appropriate measures, including legislative measures, to achieve the ends of this Declaration.

*Article 39*

Indigenous peoples have the right to have access to financial and technical assistance from States and through international cooperation, for the enjoyment of the rights contained in this Declaration.

*Article 40*

Indigenous peoples have the right to access to and prompt decision through just and fair procedures for the resolution of conflicts and disputes with States or other parties, as well as to effective remedies for all infringements of their individual and collective rights. Such a decision shall give due consideration to the customs, traditions, rules and legal systems of the indigenous peoples concerned and international human rights.

*Article 41*

The organs and specialized agencies of the United Nations system and other intergovernmental organizations shall contribute to the full realization of the provisions of this Declaration through the mobilization, inter alia, of financial cooperation and technical assistance. Ways and means of ensuring participation of indigenous peoples on issues affecting them shall be established.

*Article 42*

The United Nations, its bodies, including the Permanent Forum on Indigenous Issues, and specialized agencies, including at the country level, and States shall promote respect for and full application of the provisions of this Declaration and follow up the effectiveness of this Declaration.

*Article 43*

The rights recognized herein constitute the minimum standards for the survival, dignity and well-being of the indigenous peoples of the world.

*Article 44*

All the rights and freedoms recognized herein are equally guaranteed to male and female indigenous individuals.

*Article 45*

Nothing in this Declaration may be construed as diminishing or extinguishing the rights indigenous peoples have now or may acquire in the future.

*Article 46*

1. Nothing in this Declaration may be interpreted as implying for any State, people, group or person any right to engage in any activity or to perform any act contrary to the Charter of the United Nations or construed as authorizing or encouraging any action which would dismember or impair, totally or in part, the territorial integrity or political unity of sovereign and independent States.

2. In the exercise of the rights enunciated in the present Declaration, human rights and fundamental freedoms of all shall be respected. The exercise of the rights set forth in this Declaration shall be subject only to such limitations as are determined by law and in accordance with international human rights obligations. Any such limitations shall be non-discriminatory and strictly necessary solely for the purpose of securing due recognition and respect for the rights and freedoms of others and for meeting the just and most compelling requirements of a democratic society.

3. The provisions set forth in this Declaration shall be interpreted in accordance with the principles of justice, democracy, respect for human rights, equality, non-discrimination, good governance and good faith.

*Adopted, 107th plenary meeting, 13 September 2007*

# NOTES

1  United Nations Permanent Forum on Indigenous Issues, "Preliminary Study of the Impact on Indigenous Peoples of the International Legal Construct Known as the Doctrine of Discovery," New York, April 19–30, 2010.

2  Eric Hanson, "UN Declaration on the Rights of Indigenous Peoples," First Nations Studies Program at the University of British Columbia, indigenousfoundations.arts.ubc.ca.

3  "The Memorial to Sir Wilfrid Laurier," Shuswap Nation Tribal Council, shuswapnation.org.

4  Shuswap Nation Archives.

5  Ibid.

6  Brian Titley, *A Narrow Vision: Duncan Campbell Scott and the Administration of Indian Affairs in Canada* (Toronto: University of Toronto Press, 1986), 50.

7  "Statement of the Government of Canada on Indian Policy" (The White Paper, 1969), presented to the First Session of the Twenty-Eighth Parliament by the Honourable Jean Chrétien, Minister of Indian Affairs and Northern Development.

8  Prime Minister Trudeau, Remarks on Indian Aboriginal and Treaty Rights, Vancouver, British Columbia, August 8, 1969.

9  Harold Cardinal, *The Unjust Society* (Vancouver: Douglas & McIntyre, 1999).

10  House of Commons Debates, July 11, 1969, 6310.

11  Harold Cardinal interview, 1991.

12  Indian Chiefs of Alberta, "Foundational Document: Citizens Plus" (June 1970), 230. Subsequent quotes drawn from pp. 189, 190, 197.

13  *Indian News*, June 1970, 7.

14  Harold Cardinal interview, 1991.

15  The James Bay and Northern Quebec Agreement (JBNQA), electronic version obtained from gcc.ca.

16  Sean McCutcheon, *Electric Rivers: The Story of the James Bay Project* (Montreal: Black Rose Books, 1991), 43.

17  "George Manuel's Response to Recent Federal Position Regarding James Bay," press release, January 1974.

18  Union of B.C. Indian Chiefs, "Aboriginal Title and Rights Position Paper," 1978.

19  "Constitution Report of the UBCIC," October 1981, cited in speaking notes of Louise Mandell, QC, UBCIC Chiefs Council, November 22, 2011.

20  Cited in Union of B.C. Indian Chiefs, "The Substance of Great Britain's Obligations to the Indian Nations," presented at the Fourth Russell Tribunal, Rotterdam, Netherlands, November 1980.

21  George Manuel's address to the Union of B.C. Indian Chiefs' 13th Annual Assembly, October 1981.

22  Constitution Express poster (April 11, 1981), Union of B.C. Indian Chiefs Archive.

23  Union of B.C. Indian Chiefs, "Constitutional Express," ubcic.bc.ca.

24  Cited in Melvin H. Smith, Q.C., "Some Perspectives on the Origin and Meaning of Section 35 of the *Constitution Act, 1982*," Public Policy Sources, 41 (Vancouver: The Fraser Institute, 2000).

25  Government of Canada, Draft Cabinet Memorandum (The Nielsen Report), April 12, 1985.

26  Cited in Mary C. Hurley, *Settling Comprehensive Land Claims* (Library of Parliament Research Publications, Social Affairs Division, September 21, 2009).

27  United Nations Human Rights Committee, "Consideration of Reports Submitted by States Parties under Article 40 of the Covenant, Fifth Periodic Report, Canada [27 October 2004]," International Covenant on Civil and Political Rights, General, CCPR/C/CAN/2004/5, November 18, 2004.

28  "Canada's First Nations: More Pow Than Wow: Global Talks about Land Rights," *The Economist*, August 25, 2012.

29  "Interview with a Defender: Wolverine Speaks to John Shafer," *Source of Resistance* 3 (Summer 1997), ssis.nativeweb.org.

30  "U.S. Judge Critical of Canada's Aboriginal Policy," *Windspeaker* 18.9 (2001), 17.

31  Cited in *Journal of Aboriginal Economic Development* 2.2 (2002), 112.

32  *Report of the Royal Commission on Aboriginal Peoples: Volume 1, Looking Forward Looking Back* (Government of Canada, 1991), Sec. 1.16.

33  *Report of the Royal Commission on Aboriginal Peoples: Summary of Recommendations, Volumes 1–5*, chapter 3 Governance, recommendations 7 and 8.

34  Published on turtleisland.org, June 17, 2003.

35  "Concluding Observations of the Human Rights Committee: Canada, 07/04/99," CCPR/C/79/Add.105.Sec.C, Principal Areas of Concern and Recommendations, para. 8.

36  KAIROS letter to the Hon. Geoff Plant, November 13, 2001.

37  The official, tortuously long title of the submission was: "Comments Regarding US and Canadian Tribal Interests Submitted by the Indigenous Network on Economies and Trade on the Proposed Policies Regarding the Conduct of Changed

Circumstances Reviews under the Countervailing Duty Order on Softwood Lumber from Canada" (C 122 839); available online at enforcement.trade.gov.

38  Al Price, Advisor, Intergovernmental Affairs, B.C. Region DIAND, letter to Chief Dan Wilson, May 2, 2002.

39  Naomi Klein, "The Olympics Land Grab," *The Guardian*, July 16, 2003.

40  High Court of Australia, *Mabo v. Queensland* (No. 2) ("Mabo case") [1992] HCA 23; (1992) 175 CLR 1 (June 3, 1992).

41  Bruce Elliott Johansen, *The Encyclopedia of Native American Legal Tradition* (Greenwood Publishing Group, 1998), 84.

42  George Manuel and Michael Posluns, *The Fourth World: An Indian Reality* (Toronto: Collier-Macmillan Canada, 1974).

43  Quotations regarding the WCIP founding meeting taken from Douglas Sanders, "The Formation of the World Council of Indigenous Peoples," April 1980.

44  Ibid.

45  United Nations Permanent Forum on Indigenous Issues, 11th Session, New York, May 7–18, 2012, item 3, Discussion on the special theme for the year.

46  *Report of the World Commission on Environment and Development: Our Common Future* (Brundtland Report) (United Nations, 1987), para. 46.

47  Statement by Maurice F. Strong, Secretary-General of the United Nations Conference on Environment and Development, Rio de Janeiro, June 3–14, 1992.

48  Grace Visconti, "Jessica Clogg WCEL Explains Bill C-45, First Nations Rights, and FIPA," *Digital Journal* (March 5, 2013).

49  No. 30 Bulletin of the Canadian Indigenous Biodiversity Network Summer 2002, UNEP/CBD/COP/6/L.25, para. 16–18, April 2002.

50  Claudia Sobrevila, *The Role of Indigenous Peoples in Biodiversity Conservation: The Natural but Often Forgotten Partners* (The International Bank for Reconstruction and Development / The World Bank, May 2008).

51  Cited in "Shadow Report in Response to Canada's 19th and 20th Periodic Report to the United Nations Committee on the Elimination of Racial Discrimination (CERD)," January 30, 2012, 10.

52  The Report of the British Columbia Claims Task Force, June 28, 1991, fns.bc.ca.

53  Justine Hunter, "Head of BC Treaty Commission Suggests Shutting It Down," *The Globe and Mail*, October 12, 2011.

54  "On 20th Anniversary of Treaty Negotiations in BC; First Nations Summit Leaders Call for Renewed Commitment from Governments," press release, September 21, 2012.

55  Bill Gallagher, *Resource Rulers: Fortune and Folly on Canada's Road to Resources* (On Demand Publishing, LLC–Create Space, 2012).

56  Tim Groves and Martin Luckacs, "Assembly of First Nations, RCMP Co-operated on Response to Mass Protests in 2007," *Toronto Star*, February 15, 2013.

57  Defenders of the Land, "Who We Are," defendersoftheland.org.

58  Ibid., "Declaration of Non-Indigenous Support for Defenders of the Land."

59  "Idle No More Solidarity Spring: A Call to Action from Idle No More and Defenders of the Land," March 13, 2013.

# INDEX